Gothic Kings
of Britain

GOTHIC KINGS OF BRITAIN

The Lives of 31 Medieval Rulers, 1016–1399

Philip J. Potter

McFarland & Company, Inc., Publishers
Jefferson, North Carolina, and London

LIBRARY OF CONGRESS CATALOGUING-IN-PUBLICATION DATA

Potter, Philip J., 1943–
Gothic kings of Britain : the lives of 31 medieval rulers, 1016–1399 / Philip J. Potter.
        p.   cm.
Includes bibliographical references and index.

ISBN 978-0-7864-4038-2
softcover : 50# alkaline paper ∞

1. Great Britain—Kings and rulers—Biography.
2. Great Britain—History—Medieval period, 1066–1485.
3. Scotland—Kings and rulers—Biography.
4. Scotland—History—1057–1603.
5. Monarchy—England—History.
6. Monarchy—Scotland—History.
        I. Title.
DA177.P67   2009   941.009'9—dc22   2008044459

British Library cataloguing data are available

©2009 Philip J. Potter. All rights reserved

No part of this book may be reproduced or transmitted in any form or by any means, electronic or mechanical, including photocopying or recording, or by any information storage and retrieval system, without permission in writing from the publisher.

On the cover: Image of King Stephen (in the Quire Screen of York Minster, York, England), reproduced by permission of the Dean and Chapter of York; background part of an old gate ©2008 Shutterstock.

Manufactured in the United States of America

McFarland & Company, Inc., Publishers
Box 611, Jefferson, North Carolina 28640
www.mcfarlandpub.com

To Joyce: The flower of love and life

Table of Contents

Preface	1

PART ONE: GOTHIC KINGS OF ENGLAND

Genealogical Charts	5
Pre-Norman Invasion, Late House of Anglo-Denmark, 1016–1066	8
CNUT, 995–1016–1035	9
HAROLD I, 1017–1035–1040	14
HARTHACNUT, 1018–1040–1042	17
EDWARD III, 1005–1042–1066	19
HAROLD II, 1022–1066–1066	26
House of Normandy, 1066–1154	35
WILLIAM I, 1027/28–1066–1087	35
WILLIAM II RUFUS, 1060–1087–1100	43
HENRY I, 1068–1100–1135	48
STEPHEN, 1096 1135–1154	54
House of Plantagenet, 1154–1399	61
HENRY II, 1133–1154–1189	61
RICHARD I, 1157–1189–1199	68
JOHN, 1167–1199–1216	75
HENRY III, 1207–1216–1272	82
EDWARD I, 1239–1272–1307	87
EDWARD II, 1284–1307–1327	94
EDWARD III, 1312–1327–1377	101
RICHARD II, 1367–1377–1399–1400	108

PART TWO: GOTHIC KINGS OF SCOTLAND

Genealogical Charts	117
House of Canmore, 1058–1290	119
MALCOLM III, 1031–1058–1093	119
DONALD III, 1033–1093–1097–1099	124
DUNCAN II, 1060–1094–1094	126
EDGAR I, 1074–1097–1107	128
ALEXANDER I, 1077–1107–1124	130
DAVID I, 1085–1124–1153	133
MALCOLM IV, 1141–1153–1165	141
WILLIAM I, 1143–1165–1214	144
ALEXANDER II, 1198–1214–1249	150
ALEXANDER III, 1241–1249–1286	155
MARGARET I, 1283–1286–1290	160
House of Bruce, 1292–1371	161
JOHN BALLIOL, 1250–1292–1296–1313	161
ROBERT I, 1274–1306–1329	164
DAVID II, 1324–1329–1371	174
Appendix: Contemporary Gothic Rulers of Europe	181
Bibliography	185
Index	187

Preface

Gothic Kings of Britain is a biographical history describing the institution of monarchy as the central governing authority in the kingdoms of England and Scotland. The narrative recounts the dramatic and chaotic span of the four hundred years between 1000 and 1400, a period during which the great European monarchies were in their formative stages. This book discusses the lives of seventeen English and fourteen Scottish monarchs and through them the history of their realms. The Gothic centuries are rich in interest, with an amazing array of rulers who are chronicled in the context of their age, evoking their personalities, achievements and failures.

The Gothic history of England begins with the last great Viking conquest of Swein I and his son, Cnut, and ends with the forced abdication of Richard II in 1399. As the British Isles slowly emerged from the Dark Ages, there was a procession of strong, effective—along with weak, benign—kings whose rule was the driving force behind the emergence of a national identity. During this period England was governed by three separate dynasties that each, in varying degrees, advanced the procession towards a united realm controlled by an absolute central authority in the person of the king. The era is rich in well-known personalities, such as William I the Conqueror and Richard I the Lion Heart. However, it also contains leaders unjustly neglected by history, including Stephen and Henry III. The sovereigns created the beginnings of a nationalist spirit and the growth of English civilization and culture. The Gothic English monarchs fought in the Crusades, enforced their feudal rights throughout the kingdom, sponsored the growth of representative government through the parliament and created a military power that later dominated European affairs.

By the mid–eleventh century the kingdom of Scotland had emerged as the recognized central authority on the northern British mainland. It was governed by the House of Canmore, founded by Malcolm III, who had usurped the kingship from the MacAlpin family by force of arms. The Scottish Gothic age was a history dominated by foreign invasions and ongoing power struggles between the institution of the monarchy and the local warlords. During this era Scotland was ruled by two dynasties, both of which defended their borders against attacks by Norway and England and relentlessly pursued the unification of their realm by military might and diplomacy. Robert I Bruce, who defeated the English in the Wars of Independence and asserted his control over the recalcitrant Scottish magnates, is the best known Scottish king. However, there are many largely unknown sovereigns whose kingships forged a Scottish identity and unique civilization, ushering in a golden age; among these are David I and Alexander III. Among the Scottish Kings there was also one queen—

Margaret I—though she succeeded to the throne while a young child and spent her four years as queen in Norway in her father's court. Margaret I was the last of her house to hold the title of monarch, and, tragically, died en route to the land over which she was to reign.

The English and Scottish rulers are grouped by house (family) and arranged chronologically. An overview of each house is followed by a discussion of the various rulers. An appendix lists the rules of various European powers contemporaneous with the English and Scottish monarchs who are the subject of the book.

Dates as given in the table of contents, genealogies and with each ruler's entry correspond to the birth, beginning of rule and death of the individual. In the case when a king was forced to abdicate, four dates are given, being birth, beginning of rule, date of abdication and death.

The Gothic age has largely been ignored by institutions of education as well as the casual reader of history and is generally a forgotten time. However, it set the stage for the development of the absolutist states of Europe and the study of its history is the foundation for a greater understanding of how the great nations of Europe evolved. The purpose of this book is to relate, through the lives of the monarchs, the historical progression of England and Scotland during the formative period that was the Gothic era.

PART ONE

GOTHIC KINGS OF ENGLAND

Genealogical Charts

Chart 1
Late House of Denmark, 1016–1042

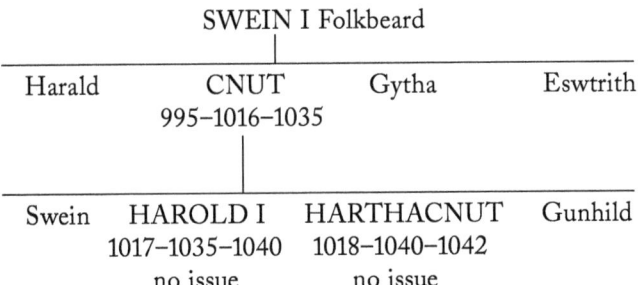

Kings of England are in ALL CAPITAL letters.

Chart 2
Late Anglo-Saxon House, 1042–1066

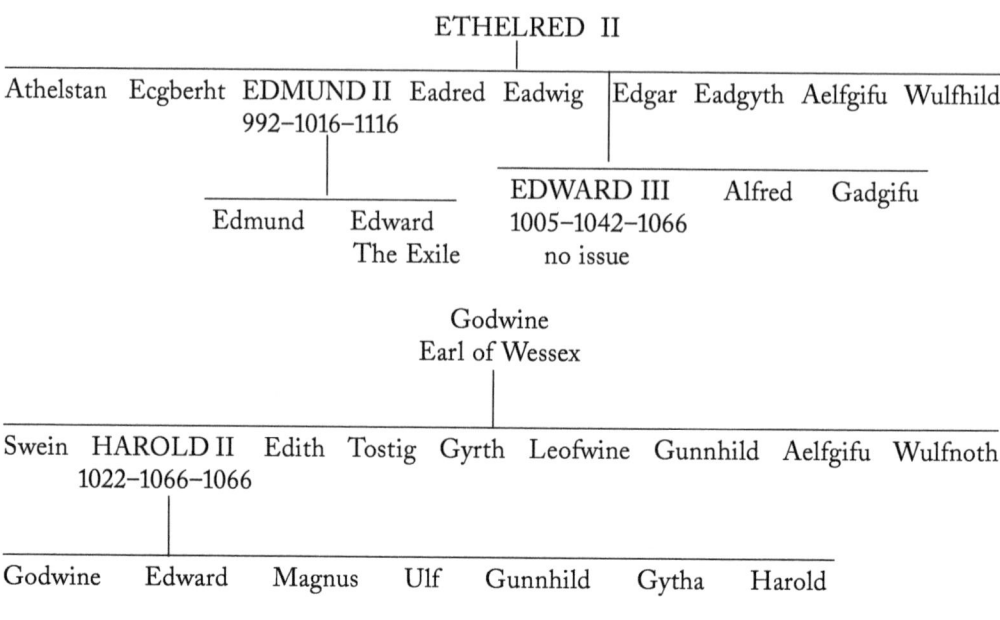

Chart 3
House of Normandy, 1066–1154

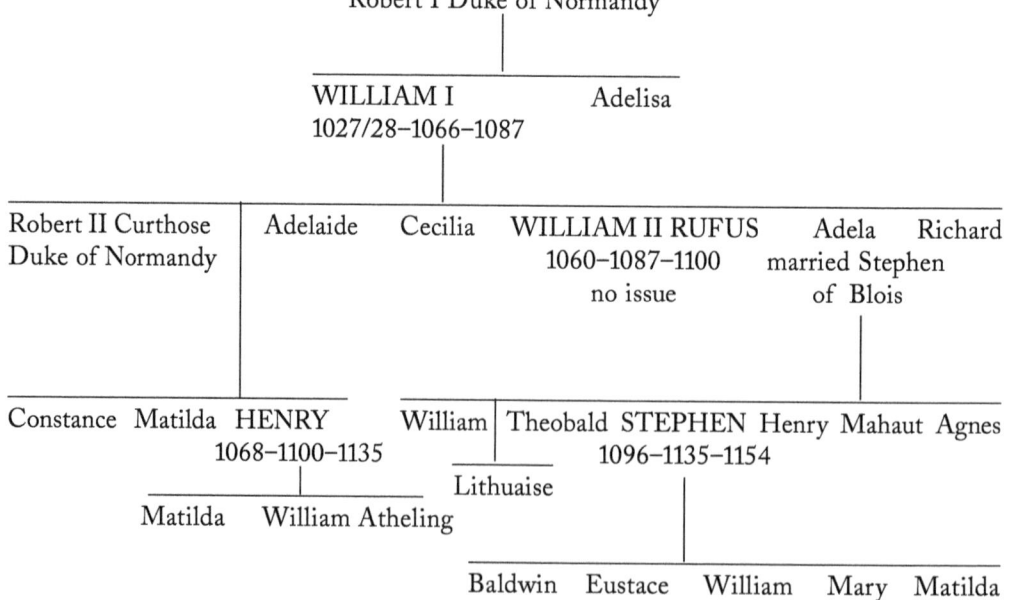

Genealogical Charts

Chart 4
House of Plantagenet
1154–1399

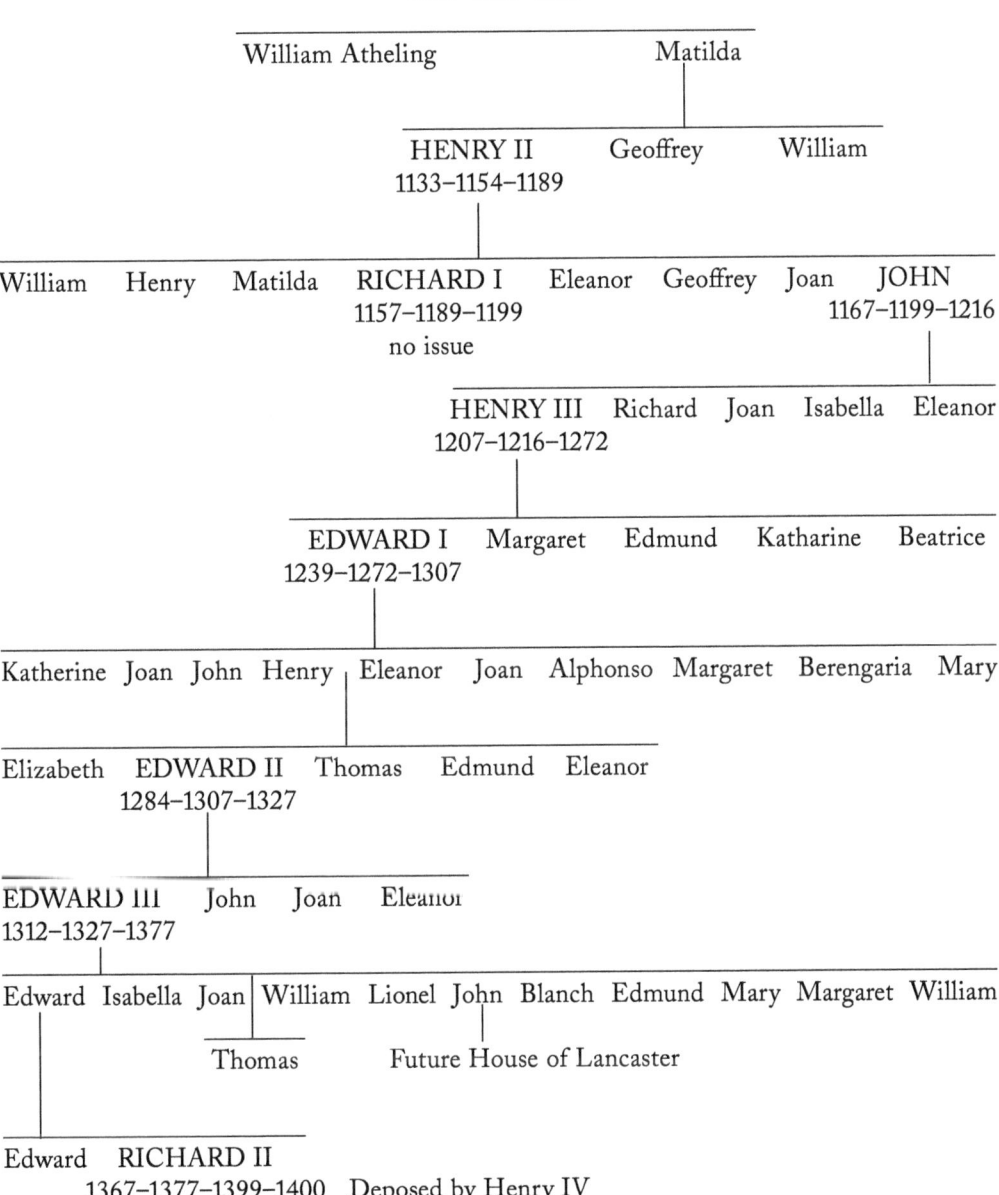

Pre-Norman Invasion, Late House of Anglo-Denmark, 1016–1066

The dissolution of the Roman Empire's occupation of the British Isles during the fifth century was followed by the invasion of England by the Angles and Saxons from Germany, which slowly evolved into seven independent kingdoms. However, by the early ninth century, by force of arms Egbert of Wessex had achieved supremacy over a united England. As his descendents consolidated their power, the Anglo-Saxon regime became increasingly threatened by Viking raiders who first began to appear along the coast in their longboats, mounting small sporadic marauding incursions. Gradually the size of the pillaging parties increased as their assaults were made farther inland against the larger cities, while permanent Norse settlements began to appear. In 865 the Danish Great Army landed in East Anglia, advancing to the north to seize the kingdom of Northumbria. Following the suppression of the region, the Danes began to move south into the Midlands, occupying the realm of the Mercians. Only the southernmost fiefdom of Wessex escaped conquest when Alfred the Great defeated the Vikings at the battle of Edington in 878. Over the next century the Wessex warlords drove the Scandinavians out of England and reclaimed sovereignty. Nevertheless, the Norse again returned in large numbers, during the reign of Ethelred II in 979. However, under the Danish king, Swein I Folkbeard, the Northmen's attacks intensified and by 1014 they had re-imposed their domination. With the Norse triumph, the Saxon monarch, along with the royal family was forced into exile in Normandy. At the death of Swein I England was ruled by his son Cnut, who married Emma, the widow of the deposed Ethelred II, to legitimize his kingship over the former Anglo-Saxon realm. England continued to be under the authority of the Northmen until the death of the last Danish king, Harthacnut, in 1042 when the English high magnates and bishops elected Cnut's stepson Edward as the next sovereign. Edward III the Confessor reinstated the former Anglo-Saxon dynasty, reigning for twenty-three years. In 1066 he died without a direct heir and the crown was usurped by Harold II, who held the monarchy until his defeat and death at the battle of Hastings in October.

Cnut, 995–1016–1035

In 1013, the Danes renewed their sporadic war of conquest against England when Swein I Folkbeard and his nineteen-year-old son Cnut invaded the kingdom with a formidable army, forcing the Saxon king Ethelred II to flee into exile. Cnut was the second son of Swein I and Gunhild of Poland and was born in Denmark around 995. Soon after the young prince's birth, Eric of Sweden drove his father and the royal family out of their northern realm and, with his mother, Cnut was banished to Poland. While Swein I sought allies in Norway and England for his restoration, Cnut was taken to be raised in the Viking tradition in Pomerania at the court of the Scandinavian warlord Thorkell. In the Norse household of his guardian, he was taught the basics of reading and writing in the local language, later receiving instruction in Latin. Cnut was a natural leader and was trained in the battle skills of a Viking warrior, learning the use of the spear, sword and axe. He prepared for warfare by stalking wild boar and deer in the thick forest and hunting with hawks. As the son of a mariner king, his practical education included swimming, navigation and sailing. The warrior-prince began to participate in the Danish pillaging forays against England, gaining a reputation as a determined and ruthless raider in his first battle against the city of Norwich.

While Cnut grew into a formidable Viking warlord, Swein I increasingly began to mount plundering attacks against England. In 1003 he arrived on the east coast with a large raiding force to pillage and sack the towns and countryside over the next three years before agreeing to withdraw to Scandinavia for the payment of a large indemnity. Three years later he sent his army to again ravage the Anglo-Saxon kingdom of Ethelred II, advancing deep into central England before finally abandoning the campaign in 1012 after receiving a large tribute in silver. However, the Danish assaults had so devastated the realm that the central government of the king largely lost control while the local lords began to establish their autonomous power. When Swein I returned with Cnut and a formidable invasion army, landing near Sandwich in 1013, Ethelred II was unable to withstand the onslaught, fleeing late in the year to Normandy in exile.

In 1013 Swein I negotiated the marriage of Cnut to Aelfgifu, the daughter of the earl of Northampton, in a political agreement to bind the new monarchy to the northern warlords. The union was in the form of a contract between the two families and was not sanctioned by the Church. This style of marriage was common in eleventh-century England and any resulting children were considered legitimate. Cnut had two sons with Aelgifu: Harold, who succeeded his father to the English throne; and the older, Swein, who became the nominal king of Norway with his mother acting as regent.

With the defeat and banishment of the Saxon regime, Swein I was declared overlord and during the winter began to consolidate his power. While Cnut commanded the Viking fleet at Gainsborough in Lincolnshire, his father suddenly died on February 3, 1014, after a reign of only two months. Following the death of Swein I, the Scandinavian warlords elected Cnut as his successor. As the new ruler was imposing his suzerainty from his northern stronghold in Lincolnshire, the English high council of prelates and earls known as the Witan invited Ethelred II to again assume the monarchy. The deposed sovereign crossed the Channel in the spring of 1014, joining his allies in the south to advance against the Danes in East Anglia. The speed and resolve of Ethelred II's campaign caught Cnut unprepared, compelling him to abandon England, sailing to Denmark to join his elder brother, King Harald II, who had earlier been granted the northern kingdom by Swein I.

The Danish court welcomed Cnut and, with the aid of Harald II, he began to recruit a large fleet and military force for his English restoration. While he remained in exile, negotiating with Scandinavian warlords for their military aid, Ethelred II became increasingly ill and his rule ineffective. As the Saxon king's allies and vassals continued to desert the regime, his son Edmund began to contend for the monarchy. With the loyalties of many regional earls divided in September 1015, Cnut landed near Sandwich on the Kent coast to regain his inheritance by force of arms with a host of over ten thousand soldiers. His army included levies from Denmark commanded by Harald II and Norwegians under Eric of Lade, along with a contingent of Polish infantry from his mother's family. The Danes advanced west into Wessex, which soon submitted to Cnut's overlordship. Following the conquest of the south, the earl of Mercia, Eadric, declared his fealty to the Danes, joining their campaign. Without the personal leadership of the Saxon sovereign, who remained secluded in London, his troops lacked the resolve to fight as the Anglo-Danes marched north, subduing Northumbria in early 1016. By the spring much of the kingdom had declared for Cnut but the death of Ethelred II resulted in a new spirit of English resistance.

On April 23, 1016 the Anglo-Saxon king died and was succeeded by his son, Edmund II. Unlike his father, Edmund II was a natural leader, skilled soldier and energetic military captain. Under his active command, a new army was recruited in the south and the war carried into Wessex where the local Danish garrisons were defeated while Cnut with his main forces began siege operations against London. After the conquest of Wessex the Saxons advanced against the Northmen in the London area. Through the summer the two armies fought several bloody but inconclusive encounters as Edmund II attempted to relieve the blockade. The Danes were finally compelled to abandon their investment due to the lack of provisions and the relentless attacks of the Saxons. As Cnut withdrew to re-supply his militia, the English closely pursued his line of march. On October 18 the troops of Edmund II intercepted the Danes at Ashingdon in Essex; however, in the resulting battle, the Anglo-Saxons were decisively overwhelmed and forced to retreat south.

Despite his defeat Edmund II refused to submit, withdrawing into Wessex to raise a new army. With the end of the campaigning season and his troop strength depleted by the recent encounters, paired with the stubborn resolve of the English to continue the war, Cnut offered to negotiate a peaceful settlement. The two rivals met on an island in the Severe River, agreeing to partition the kingdom with the suzerainty of Edmund II acknowledged south of the Thames River while Cnut was to rule over Mercia and Northumbria with London as his capital. However, the division of England was short-lived and, with the unexpected death of Edmund II on November 30 the Wessex earldom soon surrendered to the Anglo-Danish overlord to once again unite the realm. In December Cnut was anointed by the archbishop of Canterbury in London as king of England to publicly associate his reign with the Church.

After his succession to the crown, in early 1017 Cnut began the process of consolidating his rule and establishing a government. To create his inner council he drew on his seasoned military commanders, who were also well trained and experienced in statesmanship, appointing his former guardian, Thorkell, and the captain of the Norwegian contingent, Eric of Lade, as chief advisors. The kingdom was partitioned into four occupation districts to better facilitate its administration. Thorkell was granted authority over East Anglia, Northumbria was given to Eric, Mercia to its former Saxon earl Eadric, and the throne retained Wessex. In late 1017, to further unify and secure his reign, Cnut began to eliminate powerful and influential Saxons who posed a threat against his crown. Many prominent English nobles were executed on the king's orders, including the earl of Mercia, who had begun to plot against the regime. The surviving royal Anglo-Saxon family was banished to prevent a conspiracy from rallying around the young sons of the deposed sovereign, Ethelred

II. Cnut also began negotiations with Richard II of Normandy for marriage to the duke's sister, the English dowager queen Emma. The union with the former wife of Ethelred II and the mother of their two sons, Edward and Alfred, would serve to neutralize their claims to the monarchy while associating his usurped kingship to the previous dynasty. A contract of marriage was signed with the duke stipulating that the issue of Cnut and Emma would succeed as king of England. Unlike his first marriage agreement with Aelgifu, the second was performed and sanctioned by the Church with Emma anointed as queen. The political union resulted in the births of two children, with the only son, Harthacnut, rising to the overlordship of both Denmark and England. By the end of the year the danger of internal rebellion had been largely eliminated and Cnut held a firm hand on his realm.

By 1018, with his monarchy secured, Cnut returned the majority of his fleet and army to Denmark after imposing a large tax on his realm to pay the mercenary forces. He retained a small number of ships as a coastal defense against marauding pirates and as a first line of defense against invasion. To further strengthen his relationship with the English, the Witan was summoned to the Wessex city of Oxford where Cnut agreed to reinstate the law code of the former Saxon king Edgar. The restoration of the previous laws was popular among both the northern and southern earldoms and religious institutions. The statute was widely accepted and familiar throughout the kingdom serving to bind the new regime to the nobility, Church and shires. At the Oxford meeting of the high prelates and magnates, the Anglo-Danish sovereign's initiatives solidified his rule, gaining the support and friendship of both the Saxons and Danes. He remained in Wessex touring the earldom and by the force of his presence and personality asserted his authority over the former heartland of Ethelred II and Edmund II. To further unite his government with the English, he introduced new reforms to promote economic expansion in the agricultural and trade sectors and the system of coinage was put on a uniform and standardized basis. His programs slowly resulted in an increase in prosperity and a more stable kingship.

Soon after his conquest of England Cnut was compelled to appoint Danish magnates to govern along his western boundaries with Wales in defense of his sovereignty. During his reign relations with the Welsh continued to be hostile, with numerous plundering attacks between both realms. Despite the ongoing raiding activities Cnut succeeded in forcing the acknowledgement of his overlordship from southern Wales but the local warlords frequently broke their pledges of loyalty, renewing their ravaging assaults. The Welsh princes largely retained their local autonomy, with the English crown exerting little authority or power.

In 1018 King Harald II of Denmark died and, with Cnut's rule over England secure, he began military and administrative preparations to sail to the northern kingdom to impose his suzerainty. After assuring the loyalty of the nobles and appointing the earl of East Anglia, Thorkell, as regent, he departed in late 1019 with a force of armed retainers. At the death of Harald II political factions had been forged to fill the void of a recognized central authority, which now opposed Cnut's presence and attempted seizure of the monarchy. While the Danes were resisting the usurpation campaign of Cnut, the realm was thrown into further disorder as their coastline came under increasing attacks from marauding pirates. After his arrival Cnut had become allied with his local supporters, spending the winter months asserting his supremacy over the Danish warlords and aggressively pursuing and defeating the Viking raiders. By the spring of 1020, through the payments of bribes and by military might, he was acknowledged as his brother's successor. With the elimination of the Danish resistance Cnut appointed his brother-in-law, Ulf, as governor to administer his government before departing to England.

Arriving in England Cnut assumed the kingdom from Thorkell and summoned his great earls and prelates to Cirencester in Gloucestershire to reassert his authority. At the Witan he received the pledges of loyalty from his magnates while banishing the earl of Wessex for his acts of disobedience during his absence in an exhibition of royal power. With his kingship confirmed Cnut continued to tour his realm, administering his laws and justice. In October the king was in Essex to personally dedicate the church, which he had ordered built at the site of his triumph over Edmund II in 1016. The act of patronage to the Church served to enhance his friendship and bond to the important and influential ecclesiastic institution.

Cnut had appointed his former guardian, Thorkell, as the earl of East Anglia shortly after his victory over Edmund II in 1016. The earl was a powerful and ambitious warrior with a large private army and navy. In the eastern region Thorkell continued to expand his supremacy, becoming an increasing danger to the throne. As his local power increased in November 1021, he was banished from England to prevent a rival political faction from rallying around him. The successful removal of the formidable warlord was a demonstration to the remaining earls that Cnut would not tolerate a challenge against his reign and possessed the military might to enforce his will. While Cnut's decisive actions had again secured his crown, during early 1023 he was forced to muster his fleet near the Isle of Wight to protect the coastline against the threat of seaborne raids from the exiled Thorkell in another display of his resolve to protect his sovereignty. The Anglo-Danish ships patrolled the southern waterways; however, no attacks occurred and Cnut's authority remained unchallenged.

While Cnut had taken the precautions to defend his shorelines, Thorkell had abandoned his English ambitions, sailing across the North Sea to establish a presence in Denmark. In 1023 the king traveled to his northern kingdom to safeguard the regime against a revival of the exiled earl's usurpation initiative by forging a reconciliation with him. However, with Thorkell's expulsion from England, he had lost his base of power and wealth, now posing little danger and with his many skills in government and diplomacy was appointed as regent for the Danish realm after pledging his loyalty. With the regency administration in place and his kingship secured, Cnut departed for England before the onset of winter.

In his southern kingdom Cnut assumed control of his government, continuing to enforce his laws and will against the Church, shires and magnates. He was constantly traveling throughout the realm, ensuring the peace with his presence and the might of his military. While the Anglo-Danish overlord remained in England, Thorkell died and was replaced by the former regent Ulf, who began to conspire with the new king of Norway, Olaf II, and Anund Jacob of Sweden.

As the overlord of both England and Denmark, Cnut possessed considerable wealth and military might, posing a threat to the continued autonomy of Olaf II of Norway and Anund Jacob of Sweden. To protect their kingdoms against attack from the Anglo-Danish throne, the two Scandinavian kings agreed to unite their fleets and troops for their mutual defense. With the death of Thorkell, the courts of Sweden and Norway began to plot with Ulf to gain control over Denmark to secure their southern flanks and weaken the power of Cnut. Seeking to gain the kingship for himself, the regent joined the alliance against his liege lord. In 1026 Cnut was informed of the mounting danger against his northern fiefdom and assembled his fleet and army sailing to southern Sweden to contend the allies. In the ensuing sea battle at Holy River after a bloody struggle with many casualties, the Norwegians and Swedes were vanquished and Olaf II was forced to flee with a decimated navy and army. The Holy River victory safeguarded Cnut's rule over Denmark while allowing him reclaim suzerainty over parts of southern Sweden that had been previously under the authority of his father.

The triumph at Holy River had destroyed the Swedish-Norwegian initiative to conquer Denmark while shattering their coalition. With the threat against his kingdom eliminated, Cnut was free to make a pilgrimage to Rome in a visible display of his Christian piety and to seek the patronage of the Holy See. The voyage to Italy was also planned to coincide with the papal anointment of Conrad II as German emperor, allowing Cnut to associate his regime with the most powerful ruler in Europe and acquire his friendship for the protection of his southern Danish border. Departing from England, he first visited religious shrines and churches in France before sailing south to Rome. Cnut arrived in March 1027 and was warmly welcomed by Conrad II and Pope John XIX. He attended the coronation with the most eminent princes of Europe, which was a ceremony of great magnificence with a rich mixture of pomp and spirituality. Following the celebrations the Anglo-Danish king met privately with the pope, who granted numerous ecclesiastic privileges and concessions to the English Church. He also negotiated a commercial agreement with Conrad II for a substantial reduction in the tariffs charged against his merchants passing through German territories and secured the pledge of military support for the defense of southern Denmark. After ending his deliberations with the papacy and the German emperor, Cnut departed for England by sea.

While Cnut remained in Italy, the magnates of Norway rose in rebellion against the oppressive policies of Olaf II. To further his pursuit of Scandinavian domination, Cnut dispatched orders from Rome to his Anglo-Danish court for silver and gold to be sent to support the uprising. After his arrival in England he began to prepare and assemble his military forces for an invasion of the northern fiefdom. In 1028 the royal fleet sailed to Denmark, where the local navy and militia joined the expedition. Before initiating the campaign, the crown negotiated an alliance with the Norwegian dissidents led by Hakon to buttress its war effort. The combined effects from the liberal use of English bribes and the internal assaults from the rebels destroyed the military might and resolve of the Norwegian throne's defenses and when Cnut's troops landed Olaf II was compelled to withdraw after only a token resistance. The Norwegian Church and warlords pledged their homage to Cnut to secure his conquest. With the kingdom under his domain, the Scandinavian overlord established his government, appointing Hakon as regent before returning to England the following year. However, in 1030 Hakon was drowned at sea, emboldening Olaf II to invade his forfeited realm in an attempt to reestablish his authority. At the arrival of the deposed monarch, the Norwegians maintained their loyalty to Cnut, attacking and killing their former ruler. A new administrative council was created with Cnut's first wife, Aelfgifu, acting as royal viceroy for their eldest son, Swein.

From his English kingdom Cnut continued to rule his Scandinavian empire, maintaining the peace while fostering justice and good government. The king established his capital at Winchester in Wessex where he began to increasingly rely on the military and political skills of the local earl, Godwine. In 1016 in the aftermath of the death of Edmund II, the earl had quickly pledged his fealty to the Anglo-Danish regime and had been rewarded for his loyalty and substantial abilities. Godwine frequently joined his militia with the crown's army, supporting the wars of Cnut while growing into the preeminent warlord in Wessex. He was appointed to the inner council, becoming his sovereign's chief advisor and, with Cnut's numerous absences from England, he acquired the powers of a royal viceroy.

While Cnut had asserted his sovereignty over England and the northern kingdoms, in Scotland Malcolm II had united his realm and had begun to expand south into the English demesne. In 1031 Cnut traveled to the court of his Scottish neighbor to negotiate an alliance of friendship and an end to the seizures of his lands. Meeting with Malcolm II's governing council, the Anglo-Danish king demanded the return of his usurped lordship of Bernica and parts of Northumbria. With an overwhelming show of English military might assembled against it, the Scottish regime was forced to abandon authority over the disputed territories allowing Cnut to claim the eastern march and secure his border lands.

During Cnut's visit to Rome in 1027, friendly relations had been established with Conrad II of Germany. Contacts continued between the two realms and it became the foreign policy of the Anglo-Danish court to maintain their close association to protect the Danish southern border. To further bind their kingdoms in friendship, negotiations were begun for the marriage of the king's daughter, Gunhild, to the emperor's son, Henry, which were finalized in 1035. In a show of good will Conrad II ceded the March of Schleswig to the Scandinavian overlord to further buttress Cnut's southern Danish defenses against foreign invasion.

Cnut's marriage in 1016 to Queen Emma, the sister of the Norman duke Richard II, had been the foundation of his policy for preserving peace with the duchy. However, Richard II died in 1026, causing increasingly strained relations between the two courts. The new Norman duke, Robert I, began to aggressively promote the inheritance rights of his two wards, Edward and Alfred, the sons of Emma and Ethelred II. A large Norman invasion fleet was assembled in 1033 in support of their claim to England, but war developed between Robert I and Alan III of Brittany, preventing the ships from being used in the cross–Channel campaign. Relations continued to be hostile until 1035 when the duke died on his return from a pilgrimage to Jerusalem, resulting in local rebellion at the succession of his young son, William. With Normandy now distracted internally Cnut's English kingship remained unchallenged.

During the later contentious years of the Norman crisis, the Anglo-Danish king began to show signs of being seriously ill. In late 1035 he began to prepare for the partition of his empire by bestowing Norway to his eldest son, Swein, while the second son, Harold, was granted England and the only male issue from the second marriage to Queen Emma, Harthacnut, was bequeathed Denmark. During his reign Cnut had been a generous benefactor to the Church with gifts of lands, money and holy relics and with death now approaching he made special donations to secure the remission of his sins. Cnut died on November 12, 1035, at Shaftesbury at age forty and a reign of nineteen years. He was buried in the cathedral at Winchester.

HAROLD I, 1017–1035–1040

Harold was the second son of King Cnut and Aelfgifu, the daughter of the earl of Northampton, and was born in 1017. He spent his early years with his older brother, Swein, in the Scandinavian- dominated household of his father, maturing into a formidable warrior while being exposed to Viking institutions, culture and law. As overlord of an extensive northern empire encompassing Norway, Denmark, England and parts of Sweden, Cnut began to prepare for the future partition of his lands at his death by increasingly providing military and diplomatic training for his sons and associating them with his government. In late 1035 he divided his realm by bequeathing Norway to Swein and Denmark to Harthacnut, the only son from his second wife Emma of Normandy, while suzerainty over England was granted to Harold. However, as part of his marriage agreement with the Norman court, Cnut had pledged to cede the Anglo-Danish kingdom to the issue of his union with Emma. As the king continued to rule his vast demesne with Queen Emma from England, Swein was sent to assume his overlordship in Norway while Harold and Harthacnut remained in the royal court. After Cnut's death in November 1035 Harthacnut immediately crossed the North Sea to defend his Danish inheritance, leaving the dowager queen to secure his English claim under the Norman marriage contract against the challenges of Harold.

While his half-brother was detained in Denmark with internal rebellion, Harold formed a political alliance with the prevailing Norse northern Mercian and Northumbrian earldoms to assert his right to the throne. He had a large following among the Danish-dominated warlords and clerics and was recognized as king north of the Thames River. As his campaign for the monarchy intensified, in Winchester Emma forged a counter-party with Godwine of Wessex and the southern lords to defend the interest of her absent son. With the threat of civil war emerging, both factions agreed to mediate a resolution, summoning the kingdom's high council or Witan to Oxford. Despite the opposition of Godwine, in the negotiated compromise Harold I was acknowledged as monarch for the lands above the Thames with London as his capital while Harthacnut was ratified as overlord for the south with his mother acting as regent from Winchester.

The largely Anglo-Saxon southern barons strongly favored a monarchy under Harthacnut and only reluctantly agreed to the Oxford accord. However, despite their urgent appeals to the Danish king for his personal assumption of power, he stayed in the north, occupied with an invasion from Norway as Emma ruled in his name from her court in Winchester. While he remained away from his realm, the local lords began to desert his regime, pledging their loyalty to Harold I. With Harthacnut distracted in Denmark, the northern English king ordered a contingent of his household troops to attack Winchester and seize the treasury of his father in defiance of the southern coalition to further weaken the standing of his half-brother. After Harold I's bold success his supporters now declared him sovereign over all of England. Despite being accepted by the magnates, the archbishop of Canterbury and chief prelates refused to perform the ceremony of coronation and he remained unacknowledged by the Church.

While Harold I was consolidating his regime, with Harthacnut's continued absence in Denmark Emma began to plot with the sons from her first marriage, Alfred and Edward, for their overthrow of the crown. As the only surviving issues of the traditional Anglo-Saxon dynasty, the two brothers possessed a hereditary claim to England and had a large following among the southern nobility. In 1036 Edward began to negotiate with the English warlords and prelates to gain their support for his seizure of the throne. He assembled a small Norman fleet and army, crossing the Channel to raise a revolt among the southern earldoms. Landing at Southampton he advanced to Winchester, joining his forces with Emma. However, the Anglo-Saxon magnates failed to rally to Edward's banner when his Norman retainers rebelled against his authority, pillaging the towns and farms. As a result of their brutality, the local barons abandoned Edward's campaign and attacked his troops, compelling him to abandon his attempted usurpation and withdraw to Rouen. With the failure of Edward to unite the southern lords, the rule of Harold I remained unchallenged throughout the kingdom.

Despite the failed campaign of Edward, his brother, Alfred, became determined to mount a second attempt to reestablish the Anglo-Saxon dynasty. He left Rouen, traveling to the county of Boulogne to conspire with Count Eustace for his support to seize the crown of England. He collected a small military force and sailed to southern England, landing on the coast of Kent. The rebel leader now advanced toward Canterbury where he was joined by the earl of Wessex, Godwine, who pledged his support. However, the Wessex earl had secretly abandoned his Anglo-Saxon allies, forming an alliance with the king, and took Alfred to Guildford where the invading army was seized by a contingent of royal troops sent by Harold I. Under orders from the court Alfred's soldiers were killed while he was taken to Ely and brutally blinded and murdered.

With the assassination of Alfred and the defection of Godwine to the monarchy of Harold I, all support for Harthacnut among the southern earls disappeared and in early 1037 Emma was forced to abandon all further attempts to place her son on the throne from England. The dowager queen fled to Flanders where a court in exile was established and she continued to conspire with Harthacnut in Denmark and her allies in England for the overthrow of Harold I. After Emma's departure Harold I was acknowledged as king throughout the realm by the Witan and consecrated by the Church while Harthacnut's claim to England was declared forfeited due to his prolonged absence.

By late 1037, with his authority over England secured and the challenges of both Harthacnut and Emma's Saxon sons thwarted, Harold I began to direct his foreign policy toward expansion into Wales and Scotland. Edwin, brother of the earl of Mercia, was ordered to invade and force the subjugation of northern Wales, but in the ensuing battle at Rhyd-y-Groes the local prince Gruffydd triumphed over the Saxon army. The Welsh troops outmaneuvered the English and nearly destroyed their entire invasion force, killing Edwin and many prominent warlords. The defeat was so overwhelming that Harold I was compelled to withdraw from the border region and end all future operations to seize full suzerainty over Wales. With the victory Gruffydd was free of all fealty to England and governed as an autonomous ruler. Harold I's attempts to aggrandize his domain into Scotland were similarly defeated, resulting in a weakening of his personal prestige and support among the Anglo-Danish lords and clerics.

While Harold I's wars against Scotland and Wales had damaged his supremacy and stature, to regain the friendship and backing of the Church he initiated a program of royal patronage directed at the clergy. He publicly exhibited his piety and kept royal chaplains in his personal service. The king became a sponsor of numerous abbeys and chapels, made popular appointments to the vacant bishoprics and granted gifts of lands and money to the churchmen. When without his knowledge the revenues of the Canterbury archbishopric were seized by his retainers, he ordered an immediate restitution. In 1039 Harold I's standing in the kingdom was temporarily revived when the attempted capture of the Northumbrian city of Durham by the army of Duncan I of Scotland was defeated by the crown's vassals, who rallied to defend his monarchy. However, despite the success at Durham, over the coming months his kingship became increasingly threatened by internal rebellion. While the Anglo-Danish court actively sought the approval of the Church, in an attempt to win the favor of the magnates and towns Harold I maintained the size of the royal fleet at only sixteen vessels, thereby keeping the tax levies low, and introduced a policy of patronage to gain the support of the nobility. Nevertheless the high lords and bishops resented his ineffective rule and opulent and frivolous lifestyle of frequent hunting parties and banquets, causing Harold I's esteem and popularity to steadily decline.

In late 1039, as the reign of Harold I moved increasingly toward civil war, in Denmark Harthacnut finally negotiated a settlement with Magnus I of Norway and was free to assert his right to the English crown. However, before he could launch his invasion fleet, Harold I died of unknown causes on March 17, 1040, at Oxford. He was twenty-two years old at the time of his death and had ruled England for four years. Harold I was buried at Westminster Abbey but when Harthacnut became king he ordered the body of his half-brother to be exhumed and thrown into a marsh along the Thames River.

HARTHACNUT, 1018–1040–1042

With the death of Harold I in March 1040, the northern Danes and southern Anglo-Saxons united around Harthacnut, conferring the crown of England to him. Harthacnut was born in England during the year 1018 and was the only son of Cnut and his second wife, Emma, the English dowager queen of Ethelred II and sister of Richard II of Normandy. His early years were spent at his father's households in England and Denmark, where he became exposed to both Anglo-Saxon and Norse institutions, culture and society. The prince developed a large following in Wessex through his mother, who was held in high esteem among the largely Anglo-Saxon earls and prelates through her close association to the deposed dynasty. As part of the marriage treaty with the court of Normandy, the Anglo-Danish king had agreed to name the male issue from his union with Emma as his successor to the English throne. As the only son of the marriage with Emma it was widely acknowledged that Harthacnut would inherit England. However, in November 1035, shortly before he died, Cnut named him as his heir to Denmark and his second son from his first marriage, Harold, as ruler for England. At the death of the monarch, Harthacnut was in the English kingdom and appointed his mother as regent for the Anglo-Danish realm to protect his rights under the marriage contract while he sailed to Denmark to assert his inheritance.

After his arrival in Denmark Hathacnut established his court and assumed the government of his father. However, the new king was able to establish only a small loyal political faction as many of the prominent Danes resented being ruled by an alien Anglo-Saxon and in protest rose in revolt. As he was imposing his monarchy through force of arms and diplomacy, the overlord of Norway, Magnus I, seeking to exploit the internal conflict, invaded Denmark in an attempt to seize the kingdom. The energy and might of the internal rebellion and Norwegian attack forced Harthacnut to remain in his northern realm and rely on Emma to enforce his English rights.

While her son was confined to events in Denmark, Emma formed a formidable political faction with the largely Anglo-Saxon–dominated southern lordships. She attracted the preeminent English warlord, Earl Godwine of Wessex, to her coalition and through his influence and prestige most of the magnates from south of the Thames River also pledged their support to the monarchy of Harthacnut. With Godwine acting as her chief advisor, the queen established her government at Winchester and began to rule in the name of her absent son.

While Emma was solidifying Harthacnut's kingship over much of lower England, the northern lords rallied to Harold. With the kingdom increasingly moving toward civil war, the great earls and prelates agreed to resolve the conflict by summoning the Witan to Oxford. At the meeting of the high council a compromise was arranged, resulting in Hathacnut's acceptance as king for the earldoms below the Thames River while his half-brother was recognized as ruler of the north. With the prolonged absence of her son, Emma was appointed as regent for his realm, governing with full authority.

As the war with Norway continued to drag on, Harthacnut was forced to remain in Denmark while Emma attempted to impose his suzerainty over lower England. However, without the personal presence of their monarch, support for his rule began to decline among the warlords and clerics. His standing was further damaged when the treasury of Cnut, which was under the safekeeping of the regent in Winchester, was seized by the household troops of his half-brother, resulting in Harold I's affirmation as the overlord of a united England. By 1037 Harthacnut's backing had collapsed and the dowager queen was compelled to flee to Flanders as Harold I was recognized as king throughout the realm.

In exile Emma established her court in Bruges and continued to conspire with her allies for her son's restoration. Harthacnut remained isolated from English affairs, defending his Danish throne against Magnus I while his mother kept his cause alive. In 1039 the Danish king forced the Norwegians into negotiations, finally resulting in the withdrawal of the invading army and an end to their ongoing power struggle. With his rule over the northern realm now secure, he raised a fleet and soldiers for the overthrow of Harold I. Harthacnut assembled his invasion ships and troops, sailing to Flanders joining his forces with Emma's private navy. However, in March 1040, as the Danish ruler made his final preparations, he was informed of the death of Harold I and his succession to the Anglo-Danish crown.

With the death of their sovereign the English Witan authorized a commission of bishops and magnates to travel to Bruges and officially confer the monarchy to Harthacnut as all factions of both Anglo-Saxons and Danes supported his ascension. By mid-June negotiations had been completed and the king crossed the Channel with his sixty-vessel fleet to be warmly greeted by the population in Sandwich. From the south coast the royal party advanced to London, receiving a triumphant reception, followed a few days later by the official coronation ceremony. With Harthacnut's sovereignty widely recognized his first policy initiative was directed against the warlords and prelates who had been instrumental in challenging his succession at the death of Cnut. On his orders the earl of Northumbria was murdered while the bishop of Worcester was abjured of his bishopric. The vengeance of the throne was also directed at Earl Godwine. However, he was able to use his considerable wealth to win reinstatement with the gift of a magnificently appointed sailing vessel and his pledge of fealty to the crown. Harthacnut also turned his revenge against his dead half-brother, ordering his body to be exhumed from Westminster Abbey and thrown into the marshes along the Thames River.

Initially the Anglo-Danish king enjoyed widespread favor among the English; however, as he replaced the Anglo-Saxon lords in his ruling council and court with his Danish friends and favorites, his popularity began to languish. The Danes treated the local magnates and clerics cruelly and with disdain, causing support for the crown to increasingly erode. Nevertheless, it was an increase in the tax rate to finance his large Danish fleet and army that was the cause for revolt.

The prior monarchies had reduced the size of their realm's fleet and the taxes necessary to fund the vessels and sailors as the danger of foreign invasion had subsided. However, Harthacnut was still in need of a strong navy and army to protect Denmark against attacks from Norway and increasingly drew upon the English for the necessary revenues. The new levy on the Anglo-Danish kingdom now increased four times the usual rate to an amount necessary to support sixty ships in lieu of the previous sixteen. The imposed duty created a heavy burden and was met with widespread avoidance and resentment. As the resistance grew, the king ordered his household troops to forcefully collect the assessments, resulting in numerous insurrections. In the city of Worcester the population rose in open rebellion against the tax, killing two of the crown's soldiers. In response to the assaults Harthacnut assembled his earls, commanding them to ravage Worcestershire and burn Worcester. The brutal foray against the shire and the harsh imposition of the ship levy created far-reaching discontent throughout the royal domain, as the regime became increasingly unpopular and threatened by internal revolt.

With his sovereignty falling into disfavor, in 1041 Harthacnut summoned his half-brother Edward from exile in Normandy. Edward was the only surviving son of the former Anglo-Saxon ruler Ethelred II and Queen Emma and remained popular among the southern earldoms. He was closely associated with the throne's court and inner council to win the good will of the kingdom. Still without a direct heir the king appointed his half-brother as successor to further his affiliation with the failing administration. Despite these attempts to win favor, Harthacnut continued to be held in little regard. However, his reign was to be short as he unexpectedly died while at a wedding feast on June 8, 1042. He was buried in Winchester Cathedral after having ruled England for just two years and was twenty-four years old at his death. Harthacnut died without a direct descendent, ending the Anglo-Danish dynasty with his kingship.

Edward III, 1005–1042–1066

At the death of Harthacnut in June 1042, his half-brother Edward was readily acknowledged as his successor to reestablish the traditional Anglo-Saxon dynasty, beginning a reign of over twenty-three years of peace and prosperity following two unpopular monarchies. Edward was born in 1005 in Oxfordshire, England, and was the eldest son of the English monarch Ethelred II and his second wife, Emma of Normandy. The young prince spent his early years in the Saxon household of the king along with his six half-brothers from his father's first marriage and his younger brother, Alfred. Monks from the Church provided his limited academic education and he was taught the basics of reading, writing and studied religious doctrine. Although Edward had not been highly educated, as sovereign he did associate with learned scholars and actively recruited them to his court. The primary focus of his training was as a feudal warlord and he became skilled in the sword, battle-axe, and spear and the use of the Saxon shield.

In 1013 Swein I Folkbeard of Denmark invaded England with a formidable army, forcing Ethelred II and Emma, along with her three children, to flee to sanctuary in Normandy. However, following the triumph, the Danish overlord died two months later and the deposed Ethelred II began negotiations with his English allies and friends for his restoration, sending Edward with his emissaries as the pledge of good faith and resolve. After vowing to govern with the consultation of the Witan, in the spring of 1014 Ethelred II arrived in England to unite with his eldest surviving son from his first marriage, Edmund, quickly re-conquering much of the kingdom. While he was consolidating his assumption of power, Swein I's son, Cnut, landed in England from Denmark, renewing the war against the Anglo-Saxons. During the conflict against Cnut, the eleven-year-old Edward was a member of the crown's militia, distinguishing himself in battle with his skills as a warrior-prince. As the struggle against the Danes continued the Saxon king grew ill while Edmund increasingly took command of the war effort and troops. With the death of Ethelred II in April 1016 Edmund assumed the throne.

Edmund II quickly resumed the conflict against the Danes, with Edward again serving with the household troops. The English prince also became a member of his half-brother's inner council, gaining exposure in government and diplomacy. As Edward continued his association with the English court, in October Cnut defeated the Anglo-Saxons at Ashingdon, gaining suzerainty over the demesne north of the Thames River, forcing Edmund II to withdraw into Wessex. Despite the decisive Danish victory the English king refused to abandon the struggle, recruiting a new army to renew his attack. The Saxon fighting resolve convinced Cnut to initiate negotiations for the partition of the kingdom. Meeting on an island in the Severn River, the Danish overlord was recognized as the ruler of the north with Edmund II acknowledged in Wessex. However, shortly after assuming control of his realm, the Saxon monarch died, allowing Cnut to force the submission of Wessex.

Without the military might of his half-brother, Edward was compelled to flee into exile in Normandy.

The death of Edmund II eliminated the last pillar of Anglo-Saxon authority in England, destroying the possibility of any future succession from the ancient English royal dynasty. However, Queen Emma was determined to have her son assume the monarchy and through him retain her influence over governmental affairs. In 1016 she negotiated a treaty of marriage with Cnut, stipulating that their male children would inherit the English crown. The agreement severely compromised Edward's right to the throne and after his mother departed to England he came under the protection of his uncle, Duke Richard II of Normandy. The Saxon prince's formal education was renewed and he received military training as a Norman knight. In 1018 Emma gave birth to a son, Harthacnut, securing the Anglo-Danish dynasty and further diminishing Edward's claim to the kingship. The political realities forced him to remain in exile in Normandy at the ducal court and in the lands of his mother's relatives. Through his long years in western France, Edward developed a preference for the local culture, customs and institutions, which were later imported to England during his reign. As the Anglo-Saxon émigré stayed isolated from the English government, the sudden death of Cnut in November 1035 caused a dramatic change in the possibilities for his assumption to power.

Despite the wishes of Queen Emma and the treaty of marriage, before his death the Anglo-Danish king granted his northern realm, Denmark, to Harthacnut instead of England, which was bequeathed to Harold, the second son from his first marriage. Following Cnut's death Harthacnut soon left his mother's court to enforce his inheritance over the Danish kingdom while Emma established an alliance of southern earldoms to defend his claim to the English sovereignty in opposition to his half-brother. As civil war increasingly threatened, the warring factions agreed to resolve the succession through the intervention of the high council of prelates and earls. At the Oxford Witan, Harold was recognized as overlord of the northern fiefdoms while Harthacnut received the region below the Thames River. However, Harold I continually pressed his aggrandizement initiative against his half-brother's lands and, with Harthacnut's prolonged delay in Denmark due to internal rebellion, Emma encouraged her two exiled Saxon sons to defend the southern kingdom.

In response to the dowager queen's pleas, in 1036 Edward crossed the English Channel with a small Norman army, landing on the south coast to unite with his mother in Winchester. He had earlier negotiated an alliance with the local warlords and bishops for their support. However, despite their pledges of military aid, when Edward's Norman troops began to uncontrollably sack and pillage the local towns and farms, he was attacked by the southern militias and compelled to flee into exile, abandoning his quest for the crown.

Following Edward's failed invasion he returned to the Norman court while Emma's second son, Alfred, mounted a new campaign to seize the southern earldoms. He negotiated a treaty with the count of Boulogne for a small French fleet and army and sailed to England, landing in Kent. From the coast Alfred advanced toward Canterbury where he was intercepted by Earl Godwine of Wessex. The earl had earlier been an ally of Emma and pledged to join his retainers in the rebellion against Harold I. However, Godwine had secretly deserted the southern coalition, surrendering Alfred and his troops to Harold I, who had the invaders brutally murdered, leaving Edward as sole direct heir to the Anglo-Saxon crown.

At the defection of the powerful Wessex earl along with his allies and vassals, support for the restoration of Emma's sons among the southern lordships dissolved as Harold I was now acknowledged as the king of an united realm. The dowager queen was forced to abandon England, crossing the Channel to Flanders where a court in exile was established. She remained in contact with Harthacnut in Denmark and Edward in Normandy, plotting for their recovery of the English regime.

Over the next three years, Edward remained isolated from English affairs in Normandy and the surrounding French countships while Harthacnut pressed his campaign against the Danish revolt and defended his kingdom against the Norwegian invasion of Magnus I. Finally in late 1039 the rebels had been pacified and a settlement negotiated with the Norwegians, allowing Harthacnut to now direct his military might against Harold I. He assembled a fleet and troops, sailing to Bruges to unite with the invasion forces of his mother. However, as the final preparations for the attempted conquest of England were made, in March 1040 Harold I unexpectedly died and Harthacnut was readily acknowledged as the new king.

In the early summer of 1040 Harthacnut sailed to England, where he was greeted with a great ceremony of welcome and anointed by the Church as sovereign. While his half-brother was imposing his authority and consolidating his English rule, Edward stayed in Normandy, taking no part in the establishment of the new administration. However, the king quickly became unpopular throughout his realm by initiating oppressive acts of vengeance against the former allies of Harold I, favoring his Danish friends with court appointments and imposing a large tax increase to finance his formidable Danish fleet. The English strongly resented paying for a foreign navy rebelling against the levies' forced collection. In an attempt to win support, Harthacnut summoned Edward to participate in his government. In 1041 the Anglo-Saxon exile crossed the Channel to England, joining the regime of his half-brother and becoming closely associated with the inner ruling council. During the following year, Edward continued to share in the kingship but on June 8, 1042, Harthacnut unexpectedly died, leaving his half-brother as the successor to the crown.

At the time of his death Harthacnut had never married and had left no direct heir. While he had earlier named his half-brother as successor, in eleventh-century England there was no formally established procedure for the selection of a new monarch, forcing Edward to forge a series of alliances to secure his birthright. As the only surviving member of the historical Anglo-Saxon dynasty in England, he attracted Earl Godwine of Wessex, the city of London and prominent southern bishops and magnates to his political faction. Despite his expanding coalition he was not immediately recognized as the heir by the northern earldoms and it was through the influence and intervention of the Wessex earl that Mercia and Northumbria were won to his cause. Edward III was proclaimed king in London in June and anointed at Winchester on April 3, 1043, by the archbishops of York and Canterbury.

Despite the many obstacles placed in his path to kingship, Edward III had finally ascended to the throne at age thirty-seven. Now he had to solidify and unify his control over the Anglo-Saxon south dominated by Godwine and the Danish northern earldoms of Mercia and Northumbria. Upon assuming the government he made few changes to the existing prevalent Danish administration, which served to appease the earls of Northumbria and Mercia. To reward and retain the friendship of the Wessex warlord, two of his sons were made earls to enhance the Godwinson family's already extensive lands and power. The three great magnates of Wessex, Mercia and Northumbria became Edward III's chief counselors and it was their advice that prompted him to distance his reign from his domineering mother to rule independently. He also served notice to the Church that appointments to bishoprics and abbacies remained the prerogatives of his crown, filling three vacancies unopposed with his appointees. The new abbots and bishops were the sovereign's men, who owed their positions and loyalties to the Saxon regime. Edward III retained the established practice of personally presiding over ecclesiastic councils, ensuring his will was enforced. While his initiatives had imposed his monarchy over the great barons and Church to further unite the nobility and shires to his suzerainty, in 1044 Edward III assumed personal command of his fleet to defend his southern coast against an anticipated Norwegian invasion. While no attack occurred, he had visibly and decisively exhibited his willingness to fight for his realm to further elevate his stature among the prelates and lords. Similar musterings of the navy were repeated in the following years with Edward III again taking total charge. By the end of 1048 Edward III's policies of royal patronage, combined with the assertion of his rights and accommodation with the earls, had consolidated his supremacy as he was fully acknowledged as monarch. Nevertheless Godwine, supported by his formidable alliances, immense wealth and demesne, was an obstacle to the unrestricted authority of Edward III.

In early 1045 Edward III was married to Edith of Wessex, the eldest daughter of Earl Godwine. Following the official wedding ceremony she was anointed as queen by the Church. The political arrangement with the Godwinsons had been negotiated by the earl to further enhance his standing with the royal court and by the king to associate his rule with a powerful and influential Anglo-Saxon family. Also at the time of his marriage Edward III was nearly forty years old and needed to quickly eliminate the political instability of being without a direct heir. However, their union proved to be childless creating a future succession crisis. Edith had been well educated in a highly respected convent and was described by contemporaries as possessing great beauty, grace and a pious nature. During the early years of the marriage Edward III and Edith were ill suited to each other, with her husband exhibiting little affection. Nevertheless she was a queen of intelligence and energy, assuming an active presence at court and aggressively pursuing the advancement of her father and brothers. Late in the reign the queen played an increasing role in the governing of the kingdom and Edward III relied heavily on her advice and counsel.

In 1049 Edward III redirected his foreign policy against the expansion of Flanders and Denmark into the fiefdoms bordering the North Sea, joining an alliance with the German emperor. In support of the war against the Flemish league the English throne assembled the fleet at Sandwich to protect the shoreline against seaborne raiders. While the ships were on station, Swein, the previously outlawed son of Godwine, returned, seeking the king's pardon for his crimes and reinstatement to his lands and military commands. Under pressure from the Wessex earl, his son was restored, joining the navy on the Kent coast. Despite his reconciliation he soon became involved in a dispute over his previously forfeited fiefdom, murdering the captain of the naval forces. Swein was again compelled to abandon the kingdom, seeking sanctuary in Flanders. While his son remained in exile Godwine and his allies petitioned Edward III to absolve Swein of the crime, promising his pilgrimage to Jerusalem for the remission of his sin. To gain authority over the earl and distance himself from reliance on his political power, the rogue was allowed to return.

In 1051 Edward III made a series of ecclesiastic appointments, filling important vacant dioceses. Earl Godwine had advanced his appointee to the archbishopric of Canterbury to gain control over the Church's central governing body but the king had disregarded his advice, naming Bishop Robert of London. Following his consecration the archbishop personally attacked the Wessex magnate in an attempt to disgrace him and gain prominence over the ruling council. Robert claimed that the earl had previously seized Church properties, forcibly demanding their return. As the Canterbury prelate escalated his assaults, Godwine increasingly lost the crown's favor and personal influence over Edward III. To further dilute the Wessex warlord's power, Edward III granted estates and high offices to his Norman and French relatives and friends in an attempt to create a loyal political faction. While the earl's position at court deteriorated, the riot in the city of Dover was the spark that ignited his open confrontation with the regime.

As Edward III continued to politically maneuver against the dangerous Godwine, in September 1051 Eustace of Boulogne arrived in England to meet with the Saxon regime to negotiate an alliance and renew their bonds of friendship. On the homeward journey he traveled to Dover, demanding lodging for the night for his retainers. When the city refused to provide any housing, Eustace ordered his troops to attack the offenders. The French foray was stubbornly resisted, causing the deaths of several of the count's soldiers. Eustace was forced to abandon the city, withdrawing to Edward III's court to personally complain about the affront. The sovereign agreed to satisfy the injustice, ordering Godwine to sack the city. Dover was within the lands of the great earl and he refused to assault his own fiefdom, withdrawing to muster his private army to defend his demesne.

In mid–September Edward III summoned his militia to Gloucester while the Wessex lord and his allies advanced, preparing to give battle. As the two armies faced off Edward III began talks with Godwine to find a peaceful resolution ordering him to appear before the great council. As the negotiations dragged on, the crown's military might continued to grow with the arrival of the earls of Northumbria and Mercia while support for the Wessex magnate began to crumble as many of his vassals deserted to the king. With his forces now greatly depleted and confronted with a vastly superior army, Godwine abandoned England, crossing the Channel into exile in Flanders. After his flight he was declared an outlaw with his earldoms forfeited to the throne. The purge of the Wessex warlord removed the last obstacle to Edward III's total independent rule, as he was master of the earls and prelates.

While Edward III's supremacy remained unchallenged in England, in Flanders Godwine used his considerable wealth to recruit an army and ships for his restoration by force of arms. In the summer of 1052 his fleet sailed from Bruges to southern England, where he was joined by many of his loyal vassals to begin a campaign of pillage against the coastal cities. The king reacted to the outlaw's attacks by mustering his navy and sending it south to protect his domain. Sailing down the shoreline of Kent the flotilla intercepted and compelled the earl to abandon his raids and withdraw to Flanders. In August Godwine again crossed the Channel to plunder the region around the Isle of Wight. He was later reunited with his second son Harold, who brought a small number of vessels from Ireland to reinforce his father's war effort. Together the Godwinsons traveled up the Channel in September, gathering additional ships and soldiers before landing near London to join with their army. As the exiles were advancing up the coast Edward III again mobilized his militias preparing to defend his realm. By mid–September both military forces were positioned to give battle when negotiations were initiated by envoys from the Church. Unlike the 1051 confrontation the crown did not possess the full support of the Northumbrian and Mercian earls and from a weakened position was compelled to accept the demands of Godwine. Under the ensuing resolution the earldoms of the rebels were restored, the French appointees exiled while the Godwinson family pledged its loyalty to the throne. The settlement restored the monarchy's relationship with Godwine to the pre-revolt period, with the earl again resuming his high posts at court and the inner ruling council.

While Godwine had managed to regain his high offices and considerable demesne, the confrontation against the crown had seriously weakened his health. In late 1052 the earl, who had been at the center of political power and intrigue for over thirty years, suffered a stroke, dying in April of the following year, leaving a large vacuum in the governmental structure of the kingdom. His earldom of Wessex was granted to his second son Harold, who also assumed his father's place as the preeminent warlord in the realm. With the death of the great earl, at least temporarily Edward III once again became unchallenged in his overlordship of England.

With his kingdom free of internal rebellion Edward III directed his council's policy toward securing his northern border by placing a vassal-sovereign on the Scottish throne. In 1040 the monarchy of Scotland was usurped by Macbeth, who killed King Duncan I and forced his family into exile. The deposed overlord's eldest son, Malcolm Canmore, was banished to England spending time at Edward III's court and with his uncle, Earl Siward of Northumbria. Over the following years, as the rule of the government became more tyrannical, the Scottish magnates began to increasingly appear in England, offering to support the outlawed prince in his overthrow of the regime. Malcolm repeatedly petitioned the Saxon crown for military assistance to claim his birthright and finally in the summer of 1054 Edward III granted him the right to raise an army of Scottish dissidents while ordering Siward to unite his personal militia with the invading forces. In July Macbeth was defeated, but the victory was not decisive and the war continued until the Anglo-Scottish troops killed the king in July 1057 and his son Lulach I in March of the following year allowing Malcolm to finally claim the sovereignty. With the assumption of power by the Canmore family, Edward III gained a friend and ally along his northern frontier counties.

Soon after Siward led the Anglo-Scottish invasion against Macbeth, in 1055 the earl died, leaving only an infant son as his successor. To fill the power void in the turbulent north, Edward III granted the fiefdom to Tostig, the younger brother of Harold Godwinson. The lord of East Anglia, who also had aspirations for the earldom, openly opposed the appointment and was exiled by the crown for his acts of treason. Aelfgar soon formed an alliance with the Welsh prince, Gruffydd ap Llewelyn of Gwynedd, seeking to regain his forfeited estates by force of arms. The allies attacked and ravaged the English border city of Hereford, compelling Edward III to send Harold to restore the order. The Wessex warlord advanced into Wales with a powerful army, forcing Aelfgar and his ally to agree to peace talks. A treaty was negotiated, with the deposed earl agreeing to pledge his fealty to the Saxon king for the return of his former demesne while the Welsh were ceded lordships along the frontier.

The king's intervention had reestablished order along his western border but relations remained contentious. In 1056 the bishop of Hereford renewed the conflict against Gruffydd in an attempt to regain the territories granted to the Welsh in the previous year. As he marched his militia into the contested region his army was outmaneuvered and vanquished. Edward III was forced to again command his chief advisor, Harold, to contend the Gwynedd prince and reassert his authority in the marchlands. As the Wessex earl advanced with a formidable levy into the disputed border lands, the Welsh withdrew, refusing to challenge the English, offering to negotiate a resolution. In the ensuing settlement Gruffydd was acknowledged as prince of Wales for his pledge of fealty to Edward III. The Saxon king's decisive and quick response to the escalating border war secured the peace in his western lordships with an overwhelming show of military power, avoiding a direct confrontation.

In 1054 Edward III was almost fifty years old and still without a direct heir. With little prospects for his ten-year marriage to Edith ever generating a successor, the ruling council sent the bishop of Worcester, Ealdred, to Germany to negotiate the return of the king's half-nephew, Edward the Exile. He was the last remaining descendent of the Saxon line and was banished from England in 1016 at the usurpation of the crown by Cnut, traveling to sanctuary in Hungary. Edward had stayed in the Magyar court, later marrying the daughter of the German emperor. The bishop attempted to open his deliberations from Cologne but Hungary and Germany were at war and with the interruption of communications little progress was made.

Two years after the failed mission of Ealdred, with relations between Hungary and Germany improved, the English throne renewed the effort to re-open talks with the Magyar court, dispatching Harold of Wessex to Regensburg. From the German city the earl successfully negotiated the return of Edward the Exile, escorting him and his family to England in early 1057. However, soon after his arrival, the king's half-nephew died, leaving a young son, Edgar, as heir. Edgar became a ward of the royal household and was widely considered as the sovereign's most likely successor, temporarily resolving the inheritance issue.

The English crown's treaty with Gruffydd of Wales in 1056 had resulted in a brief period of peace to the western lordships. However, in late 1057 the earl of Mercia died and was succeeded by his ambitious and aggressive son, Aelfgar. Upon assuming the earldom, to buttress his defenses against the threat of invasion from the Godwinson family who controlled the surrounding regions, he reformed his coalition with the Welsh prince and was quickly outlawed for his acts of treason. To force his reinstatement the Mercian earl with his ally terrorized and ravaged the English frontier with little opposition. As the allies continued to plunder, they united with a powerful Norwegian raiding army to inflict a devastating attack against the throne's border towns and countryside. Under increasing pressure from his high council, Edward III was compelled to negotiate a treaty, agreeing to restore Aelfgar to his demesne while granting marchlands to Gruffydd and paying a large indemnity to the Norwegians. Rather than risk war with the Welsh and Aelfgar and possibly draw the kingdom of Norway into the conflict, the king chose to pursue a safe peaceful resolution, restoring order to his western region.

Following the reinstatement of Aelfgar to his earldom, a period of peace and prosperity resulted for England. Edward III was able to devote time to his favorite sport of hawking and the rebuilding of Westminster Abbey in London. While the king continued to enjoy hunting, in late 1062, the sudden death of Aelfgar and the renewal of plundering raids by Gruffydd along the Welsh marchlands shattered the political stability. Under a directive from the crown in December, Harold was ordered to launch a lightning attack with a small force of cavalry to attempt the assassination of the Welsh prince. Despite the speed and secrecy of the raid at the approach of the English knights, Gruffydd managed to board a ship and escape. While the mission failed to eliminate the recalcitrant warlord, Edward III became determined to impose his full authority over Wales.

During the spring of 1063 preparations were made at the royal court for a double pronged campaign against Gruffydd ap Llewelyn. The earl of Wessex was given command of the western sea-borne assault force while his brother Tostig was ordered to invade and pillage the northern Welsh princedom of Gwyndd. The objective of the war was to destroy the fighting resolve of the Welsh by their relentless pursuit and destruction of food supplies and shelters. By the summer Gruffydd had been defeated and forced to flee to the mountains as all of Wales was subjugated and occupied. The Welsh nobles were compelled to submit to Edward III and accept the partition of their kingdom with Bleddyn named to rule Gwyndd and Maredudd appointed as prince of the southern fiefdom of Deheubarth. With the triumph the king was overlord of all the British Isles.

After the negotiated settlement with Godwine in 1052, acting through the three preeminent earls of Wessex, Mercia and Northumbria, Edward III's policies had maintained the domestic peace. He successfully manipulated one earl against the other to control their ambitions and actions and, through the warlords, their vassals. However, in 1065, the earldom of Northumbria rose in rebellion against Tostig. He had been in power since 1055 but his reign had increasingly become more tyrannical and beset with heavy taxes. The rogue leaders formed an alliance with Morcar, the brother of Edgar of Mercia, appointing him as their new overlord. The insurgent army marched south into Mercia where Earl Edgar joined his troops in the revolt. The region north of the Thames River was now under the supremacy of the rebels, threatening to split the kingdom. Edward III responded to the mounting danger of civil war by summoning the high council of magnates and prelates to Oxford, where Harold of Wessex was appointed to meet and begin negotiations with the dissident faction.

In October Harold advanced north to Northampton to personally present the king's proposal of reconciliation. In the resulting deliberations the Northumbrians and their Mercian allies refused to accept Tostig as their earl. At the inflexibility of the rebels, the Wessex earl was forced to return to Oxford, advising Edward III to accept the dissidents' demands of a full pardon along with the crown's appointment of Morcar as overlord and the exile of Tostig. With the full support of its advisors, the Saxon monarchy reluctantly agreed to the terms. As was the hallmark of his reign, Edward III again utilized peaceful negotiations and accommodations in lieu of brute force to resolve the danger of internal revolt.

The threat of civil war and the ensuing negotiations had caused a severe strain on the health of the sixty-five-year-old king. In November 1065, as Edward III's strength continued to weaken, he suffered a stroke. He was able to sufficiently recover to attend the Christmas celebrations but was too ill to appear at the consecration of his new abbey at Westminster. Over the following week Edward III became increasingly weak dying on January 5, 1066, after a reign of twenty-three years. With the Saxon successor Edgar still a minor, shortly before his death the sovereign appointed Harold Godwinson as his heir.

Soon after the death of Edward III there were reports of numerous miracles attributed to the mercy and godliness of the king during his life where the sick and infirmed were cured of their illnesses. He became increasingly renowned for his many acts of piety to the poor and gifts to the Church. This was followed by additional accounts of new healings at Edward III's tomb and prophetic visions of future events. The stories became so widespread and well known that a popular cult began to form around the former Saxon sovereign. By 1120 a movement was begun by the prelates of Westminster Abbey to have Edward III recognized as a saint. Through successive abbots the campaign was pressed with the Holy See and finally in 1160, under papal instructions, a formal petition for sainthood was sent to Rome. In February 1161 Pope Alexander III approved the request recognizing Saint Edward III the Confessor.

HAROLD II, 1022–1066–1066

In January 1066 Edward III the Confessor died without a direct heir and, as the first peer of the realm and deputy to the Saxon throne, Harold Godwinson seized the monarchy of England, usurping the hereditary claim of the king's great-nephew, Edgar. Harold was born in 1022 and was the second son of the earl of Wessex, Godwine, and Gytha, the cousin of Swein I Folkbeard of Denmark. Through his loyal support to the Anglo-Danish monarchies, Godwine had risen to power, stature and wealth. While the Wessex earl was establishing his dominance over English political and administrative affairs, Harold spent his early years on the lands of his father, growing into a tall, robust, muscular and formidable warrior skilled in equestrianship and feudal weapons. He was an avid hunter, especially enjoying the sport of hawking. During the reign of Harthacnut, the young Wessex lord began to increasingly participate in the government of the kingdom, enhancing his earlier military and diplomatic training received at the court of his father. He was a generous benefactor to the Church with numerous grants of estates and as king sponsored the construction of new chapels and abbeys. Harold was also a zealous collector of holy relics, which were given as gifts to his favorite churches and prelates.

Through their close blood relations with Scandinavia, the Anglo-Danish sovereigns had largely remained at peace with their northern Norse neighbors. However, in 1044 Magnus I of Norway initiated a bellicose foreign policy against England and began to prepare for a military campaign of conquest. To buttress the defenses of his eastern shoreline, Edward III ceded the earldom of East Anglia to Harold. In support of the Saxon throne the new earl was ordered to lead the East Anglian navy to Sandwich to thwart the anticipated invasion of Magnus I. However, the Norwegians failed to attack, allowing Harold to fully assume authority over his demesne, serving as the crown's local representative, enforcing the king's will and justice while commanding the royal levies. Along with the administration of his fiefdom he also became a prominent member of the regime's governing inner council. As the earl of East Anglia, Harold received a large income from his estates and was able to win the loyalty of the region's warlords through generous patronage with gifts of land and money. Following his grant of East Anglia the earl continued to aggressively add to his property holdings, attracting a large political faction while becoming the wealthiest and most powerful magnate in eastern England.

To solidify his authority over East Anglia, in 1044 Harold was married to Edith, the daughter of a prominent local family. The earl had few personal allies or friends in his new acquisition and the union brought him lands and stature among the Anglian warlords. The marriage was in the Danish manner and was not recognized by the Church. However, this was a common practice and widely accepted in the eleventh century, with the children considered legitimate. Edith was described by contemporaries as a woman of beauty and grace, possessing great wealth and prestige. Despite being an arranged marriage, Harold and Edith developed a close personal and loving relationship. Nevertheless, again for political reasons, in early 1066 he repudiated his wife to marry Alditha, the sister of the earls of Mercia and Northumbria. After his succession to the kingship, the two northern earldoms had initially wavered in their support for Harold II and the marriage alliance served to bind the regional lords to the new monarchy.

In 1046 Swein Godwinson, the elder brother of Harold, was exiled from England for the abduction of the abbess of Leominster. Harold's loyal and faithful service to the Saxon crown was rewarded with the grant of half of his brother's demesne. However, in 1049, under pressure from earl Godwine and the increasing threat of attacks from Flemish sea raiders in support of their count's war effort against England, Swein was reinstated, joining Harold's fleet to protect the coastline. Nevertheless, despite his reconciliation the deposed earl soon murdered the captain of the naval forces in a dispute over his previously seized fiefdom. Swein was declared an outlaw and compelled to flee to the continent for safety. Harold had steadily refused to support his brother's cause, which served to advance his personal relationship with Edward III and his court. In exile Swein continued to intrigue through his father and the family's retainers with the English ruling council to gain his pardon and was reinstated for his pledge of a pilgrimage to Jerusalem for the remission of his crimes. His forfeited earldom remained the domain of Harold, who increased his lands and stature at Swein's expense.

Soon after Earl Godwine had negotiated the reparation of his eldest son, he became involved in an ongoing dispute with the new archbishop of Canterbury, Robert Champart. Robert had been appointed to the vacant archbishopric of Canterbury by Edward III despite the opposition of the Wessex warlord. Soon after his consecration he initiated a conspiracy to discredit Godwine and replace him as the king's principal advisor. To further his cause the archbishop demanded the return of ecclesiastic lands, which he claimed had been seized by the earl. Under the influence of the chief prelate Edward III, who was desirous of reducing Godwine's considerable power and wealth, increasingly supported the initiatives of Robert. As the earl of Wessex continued to lose favor with the Saxon throne a confrontation in Dover led to the Godwinsons' exile.

In 1051 Count Eustace of Boulogne met with the English king in London to negotiate an alliance against Flanders and renew their bonds of friendship. After settling the terms of their treaty, the Boulogne count traveled to Dover on his way home. In the city he demanded lodging from the residents for his retainers and, when this was refused, attacked the residents. In the ensuing encounter several of his soldiers were killed and he personally complained to Edward III. To satisfy the grievance, the Saxon throne commanded Earl Godwine to sack the city and plunder the surrounding countryside. The region was the fiefdom of the earl and he refused to launch a harrying strike against his vassals, rallying his sons — including Harold — to his banner, demanding restitution for the damages. In September Godwine raised a large military force threatening civil war to enforce his cause. Edward III responded to the danger by ordering the Wessex earl and his sons to appear before the high council of prelates and nobles to answer charges of treason while mobilizing a formidable army to counter the mounting insurrection. The earl refused the summons and along with his family was banished by the Witan. In October, facing arrest by the royal militia, the Godwinsons abandoned their demesnes, with Harold traveling to sanctuary in Leinster at the court of the local Irish king.

While Harold had escaped to Ireland his father had sailed to Flanders. From their safe havens the Godwinsons used their considerable wealth to assemble ships and troops for the restoration of their fiefdoms by force of arms. During the summer of 1052 Harold began to raid the southwest English shore, collecting military stores and new recruits while the earl of Wessex plundered the region around the Isle of Wight. The East Anglian earl soon joined his navy with Godwine's forces and together they continued their attacks against the crown. In September their combined fleet sailed up the Channel, recruiting additional soldiers from their allies along the Sussex and Kent coast, landing near London to unite with their armed retainers from East Anglia and Wessex. As the Godwinsons were preparing for war, Edward III mustered his levies, advancing to defend his sovereignty. However, Godwine along with Harold offered to negotiate a resolution with the Witan. The king's army, unlike in the previous confrontation with Godwine in 1051, was without the military might of the earls of Northumbria and Mercia, readily accepting the overture. In the ensuing settlement the earldoms of the exiled lords were returned, Archbishop Robert was outlawed and the rebels renewed their pledges of fealty. The revolt against the throne had seriously deteriorated the health of Godwine and shortly after the reconciliation he suffered a stroke. He was able to partially recover, but his strength increasingly weakened and the earl died in the spring of 1053. With the deaths of the Wessex warlord and his oldest son, Swein, during his pilgrimage to Jerusalem, as the recognized leader of the Godwinson family, Harold was granted all the lands of his father by Edward III, rendering him the wealthiest and most powerful earl in the kingdom.

As the new Wessex earl was asserting his authority over his fiefdoms, in 1055 the magnate of Northumbria died, leaving only an infant son as his heir. In the absence of a strong forceful successor to protect his northern borders, Edward III named Tostig, the younger brother of Harold, as the new earl. However, Aelfgar, who had replaced Harold as lord of East

Anglia, disputed the choice and was outlawed by the royal court for his acts of defiance. Seeking to regain his seized lands, he fled to Ireland, raising a small military force of mercenary ships and infantry. Lacking an adequate army to directly confront the Saxon crown, the exiled earl negotiated a treaty of alliance with the Welsh prince, Gruffydd ap Llewelyn of Gwynedd. As part of their accord Aelfgar, agreed to unite his troops with Gruffydd and together first invade and conquer the southern Welsh princedom of Deheubarth where the Gwynedd warlord had been contending for the overlordship. Augmented by the Irish mercenaries of Aelfgar the allies quickly defeated and occupied the south. Following the victory the coalition attacked across the border into Herefordshire in support of the deposed earl's cause for restoration. The city of Hereford was sacked and the local militia of the throne defeated. The regional baron, Ralph, was unable to contain the incursion and restore the monarchy's supremacy as Harold was now summoned to command the campaign of subjugation.

Assuming control of the campaign, Harold advanced his formidable army into Herefordshire, forcing the Welsh-Aelfgar alliance to abandon their conquest and withdraw into southern Wales. From their safe haven the allies refused to challenge the powerful host, offering to negotiate a settlement. Having reasserted the crown's sovereignty over the seized lands, the Wessex earl accepted the proposal. In the ensuing treaty Aelfgar was reinstated to his Anglican earldom, the Welsh were granted borderlands and both rebel warlords pledged peace and fealty to Edward III while Tostig was confirmed as earl of Northumbria. The incursion against Wales was Harold's first independent success and its quick and decisive result gained him the favor of the king.

While the earl of Wessex's campaign of 1055 had reinstated order along the western territories, the death of the bishop of Hereford again led to open confrontation with Wales. At the intervention of Harold, the king appointed Leofgar as the prelate for Hereford. Unlike the former cleric the new primate was more militant and began to actively contend the Welsh in their newly acquired lands. In June 1056 the warrior-bishop led the Hereford militia against Gruffydd and, in the resulting battle at Glasbury, Leofgar was killed and his troops defeated. With war again threatening along the frontier Harold, with Earl Leofric of Mercia, was directed by the royal court to advance the crown's army into Herefordshire and restore the peace. At the approach of the formidable English military force the Welsh prince again offered to negotiate a resolution. Under the ensuing settlement the Saxon throne agreed to recognize Gruffydd's overlordship for the whole of Wales while he pledged his fealty as Edward III's vassal.

With order restored to the border region, Harold returned to the administration of his earldoms and his duties with the royal court. While he continued to expand his personal demesne and enlarge his following of warlords and prelates, he was soon summoned to the Saxon council to perform a vital diplomatic mission. Edward III still had no direct heir and the next in line to the crown, Edward the Exile, had been outlawed to Hungary in 1016. The Wessex earl was directed to depart to the Magyar court and arrange the repatriation of the exile and his family to secure the succession. In November 1056 Harold crossed the Channel and in December began deliberations from Regensburg with the Hungarian king, Andrew I. While waiting for a response to his proposal, the English magnate visited Rome for Easter celebrations as the guest of Pope Victor II, participating in the religious ceremonies and visiting churches and holy sites while collecting relics as gifts for his clerics. Following the Easter observances he traveled back to Germany, concluding his negotiations by arranging the release of Edward and personally escorting him and his three children to England.

Arriving at the royal court in late 1057 after a successful diplomatic mission, Harold's stature and influence over Edward III and his ruling council were now greatly enhanced, solidifying him as the preeminent earl of the realm. Soon after his return the lord of Herefordshire, Ralph, died, creating a serious void in the security along the English-Welsh border region. As the most powerful warlord in England, Harold was ceded the Welsh marchlands, adding to his already extensive holdings. However, in late September the earl of Mercia, Leofric, died and his son, Aelfgar of East Anglia, was appointed by the Saxon crown as his successor. With Harold's recent grant of the frontier lands and Tostig's possession of Northumbria, the new Mercian earl became surrounded by the Godwinson family and, feeling threatened again, forged an alliance with the prince of Wales in defense of his fiefdom. His actions were considered an act of treason and in 1058 Aelfgar was exiled for the second time. He escaped to the court of Gruffydd and together they plundered western England to force his reinstatement. As the allies continued their raiding they united with a marauding Norwegian fleet whose leader, Magnus, son of King Harald III Hardrada, agreed to attack Northumbria. The great devastation from the triple alliance's campaign and pressure from Harold and the high magnates for a reconciliation to avoid civil war compelled Edward III to agree to a settlement, resulting in the restoration of Aelfgar to his earldom and additional border concessions for Wales. The negotiated resolution brought peace to the western march but the powerful Aelfgar-Gruffydd league still remained a serious ongoing threat to both Harold and the Saxon throne.

The reinstatement of Aelfgar to Mercia resulted in a period of peace for England, allowing Harold to fully impose his suzerainty over his new acquisitions along the border. He continued to administer his estates and act as the throne's local representative in the south. However, the relative calm was broken in late 1062 with the sudden death of Aelfgar. The Mercian earl and his Welsh ally had remained a constant peril to the security of the king's and Harold's domains and, with the elimination of a possible counterattack from Mercia, they now became resolved to end the threat from Gruffydd. In late December Edward III ordered the head of the Godwinson family to assemble a small cavalry force for a quick strike into Wales to assassinate Gruffydd. At the approach of the raiders, the Welsh prince managed to escape by ship but his town and palace were pillaged and burned and the fleet destroyed, removing any future danger of a seaborne sally from his navy. While the raid against Wales had failed to achieve its objective, when Gruffydd renewed his forays into Mercia, Edward III and his chief advisor became determined to remove the menace against the kingdom.

In early 1063 Harold was given command of a large army and prepared a two-pronged campaign of subjugation against the Welsh with his brother Tostig leading the northern incursion and the Wessex earl advancing from the west. While Tostig launched his attack into Gwynedd to ravage the towns and countryside, Harold took a fleet of seaborne infantry to devastate the central princedoms. With the destruction so great and his soldiers repeatedly defeated, Gruffydd was forced to flee to the mountains as his bases of support were lost under the relentless assaults of Harold. Under English occupation the Welsh pledged fealty to Edward III and renounced their prince, later murdering him. The Welsh nobles were compelled to accept the harsh terms dictated in August by Harold agreeing to accept the partition of Wales with Bleddyn controlling Gwynedd and Maredudd ruling the fiefdom of Deheubarth as vassals of the English while committing to restore the previously transferred English border lordships and cede parts of eastern Wales to the Saxon crown. Harold returned to court in triumph as the most powerful earl in the realm and an enhanced authority as a military captain, having destroyed the unity of Wales and reasserted English sovereignty. From his position of preeminence in the royal council, Harold increasingly assumed the burdens of the kingdom's government as Edward III's first minister and advisor.

In the spring of 1064 Edward III sent Harold to Normandy on a diplomatic mission to the court of Duke William. During the Channel crossing, his ship was caught by a gale and blown to Ponthieu, bordering on the coast of Normandy. He was quickly seized by the local count, Guy, and held for ransom. To secure support for his ongoing quest for the English crown, the Norman duke negotiated the release of Harold. Count Guy personally escorted his prisoner to William at Eu and the earl was taken to Rouen where he was warmly welcomed and entertained.

The Norman duke had been expanding his sphere of supremacy over western France by force of arms and had been engaged in a sporadic war against Conan II of Brittany. During the Wessex lord's stay in Rouen, the Normans launched a raid into Brittany, inviting Harold to participate. The duke's army, along with the Saxon earl and his retainers, crossed the border in support of a local rebel who was revolting against his Breton overlord. The Norman troops attacked Conan II at Dol, relieving his siege against the rogue warlord's castle and compelling the Bretons to retreat. After the victorious campaign, where Harold had distinguished himself, the invading forces were withdrawn.

Returning to Rouen, the Wessex earl remained with the Norman court where he increasingly realized that he was being held at the will of the duke. William revealed his reason for arranging Harold's release, demanding an oath on holy relics for the earl's support in his pursuit of the English throne. Fearing that he would become the prisoner of William, the Saxon warlord pledged his fealty, agreeing to defend the duke's rights to the monarchy of England. After rendering his vow, Harold was released, sailing to his homeland and reporting the results of his voyage to Edward III and the ruling council.

Following his return Harold resumed his duties with the Saxon court and the administration of his earldoms. However, in 1065 he was forced to intervene in Northumbria, which had risen in revolt against the unpopular rule of his brother, Tostig. The younger Godwinson earl had governed the fiefdom successfully for ten years; however, he increasingly became autocratic, replacing the Northumbrian magnates in his government with his alien friends and vassals while expanding the tax levy. As their influence over the earldom declined and their tax burden increased, the Northumbrians rebelled in October, attacking the capital at York and declaring Tostig an outlaw while appointing Morcar, the brother of the Mercian overlord, as their new earl.

After their successful uprising the rogue lords advanced south toward London to present their grievances to Edward III. The king sent Harold as his personal representative to negotiate a resolution and restore order. The earl met the northern insurgents at Northampton where he initially supported the restoration of his brother. However, it became clear from the defiance of the Northumbrians that Tostig's reinstatement was not possible and this recommendation was reported to the royal council at Oxford. In order to avoid civil war the Wessex earl advised the sovereign to accept the demands of the Northumbrians and reluctantly he agreed. The Saxon court officially appointed Morcar as the new earl and deposed Tostig while pardoning the rebels. However, Tostig refused to abandon his estates and was exiled, fleeing to Flanders to avoid arrest.

Following the revolt in Northumbria the health of Edward III steadily declined and, as the premier warlord of the kingdom, Harold increasingly assumed the control of the government. The king had no direct heir and his closest relative, Edgar, son of Edward the Exile, was still a minor and unable to effectively assert his authority over the ruling council. In the absence of a strong successor from Edward III's lineage to govern the turbulent realm, the Wessex lord began to plan for his assumption to the throne. To secure the crown peacefully he needed the support of the four major earls. Two of the magnates, Gyrth of

East Anglia and Leofwine of East Midlands, were brothers of Harold and they readily defended his claim. Harold had maintained friendly relations with the two remaining nobles, Edwin of Mercia and his brother, Morcar of Northumbria. He had sponsored Morcar as earl in the northern fiefdom, winning his favor and approval. The two warlords agreed to aid Harold's campaign for his pledge to enforce the banishment of his brother, Tostig. Their agreement was ratified with the marriage of Harold to Alditha, the sister of Morcar and Edwin.

While Harold was negotiating the backing of the great earls, he also gained the approval of the archbishops and chief primates, who were anxious to protect their royal patronage. To further solidify the Wessex earl's position, as Edward III approached death, he appointed Harold as his heir. Having won the Church and magnates, along with their many vassals, to his cause, when the king died on January 5, 1066, there was little opposition to Harold's succession to the crown of England.

The new monarch was consecrated by the Church prelates on January 6, 1066, in Westminster Abbey. Having secured the kingship he now needed to consolidate his throne. Taking charge of the government, Harold II ruled with a firm hand, enforcing his laws while retaining the policies and practices of Edward III. He had had a long period of close association with the ruling council of Edward III and had increasingly taken control of the realm, making his transition to total power with little protest. The administration continued largely as before with few new appointees, as most of the former king's personnel were retained.

Harold II's succession to the English monarchy was not without international opposition. In Normandy, when Duke William learned of Godwinson's usurpation of the crown, he began to prepare his military forces for an invasion to assert his hereditary rights. While the Normans assembled their host, the Saxon king's brother Tostig began raiding the Kent coast in opposition to the regime and later negotiated an alliance with Harald III Hardrada of Norway for their seizure of England. To protect the kingdom against foreign attack, the realm was placed on a war footing. A fleet was assembled near the Isle of Wight to guard the coast while the army was positioned at strategic locations to prevent a landing by foreign troops.

Harold II's succession had been generally accepted throughout the realm; however, the warlords of Northumbria did not fully recognize his right to rule. To solidify his monarchy, in the early spring the king visited York, meeting with the local malcontents to reassure them that Morcar would remain as their overlord and that the earl had pledged fealty to his throne. Through the initiative the northern lords were won to Harold II's cause and his authority was acknowledged throughout England.

Soon after his return to London from Northumbria, the king's exiled brother Tostig, who had assembled a fleet and troops in Flanders and from his former lands, began to raid the towns and shires along the south coast, advancing toward Sandwich to exhort the return of his lands by force of arms. The regime responded to the attacks by marching its army into Kent to defend the royal demesne. The crown's militia launched an assault against Tostig, forcing him to abandon his southern campaign and flee north where he plundered Lincolnshire. The earls Edwin and Morcar held responsibility for the defenses of the region and they marched their combined forces against Tostig, defeating him and compelling his retreat to the court of Malcolm III in Scotland where he remained for most of the summer.

In the summer of 1066 Tostig began negotiations with the Norwegian king Harald III Hardrada for his aid in recovering his forfeited lands. Harald III had a hereditary claim to the English crown through Harthacnut and its usurpation would be a rich addition to Norway. Under the influence of the Godwinson exile, Harald III agreed to invade England and began the task of mobilizing a sizable navy and army. In early September he sailed to Scotland, uniting his ships with Tostig's smaller flotilla and together they advanced down the North Sea, landing south of York. The allied troops were marched north, where on September 20 they encountered the waiting forces of Edwin and Morcar at Gate Fulford. In the ensuing bloody battle in defense of Yorkshire, the English militia was defeated and vanquished with heavy losses. With the victory the allies were able to claim control over the northern region of England.

Prior to the battle at Gate Fulford Harold II had received the news of the Norwegian fleet's landing and was hastily reassembling his army, which had been disbanded at the end of summer. In mid–September he advanced with his household troops from London, collecting the shire levies and the personal militia of his brother, Gyrth of East Anglia, on his journey north. By a series of rapid marches he arrived in Yorkshire on September 25 where the local residents informed him of the Norse location at Stamford Bridge. In the hope of catching the invaders unprepared after their Gate Fulford triumph, the English forces were immediately moved forward to engage Hardrada and Tostig. The Norse were completely surprised at the appearance of Harold II and were quickly driven across the bridge where the English encountered the main host, commanded by Harald III of Norway. The battle was long and bloody and was won late in the day with the slayings of both Tostig and Hardrada. The remnants of the Northmen fled from the field, aggressively pursued by the Saxons. The military forces of Tostig and the Norwegians were completely destroyed, giving Harold II his greatest victory over a respected and renowned warrior and seemingly securing his crown.

While the king was defending his sovereignty against the attack of Harald III of Norway and Tostig, in Normandy Duke William waited for a change in the northern winds to launch his assembled invasion fleet against England. Finally on September 27 the direction of the breeze shifted and the Normans sailed across the Channel, landing unopposed the next day on the south coast at Pevensey while Harold II was still in Yorkshire. The absence of all English opposition allowed William the time to construct a fortified camp at Hastings and begin the pillaging of the surrounding towns and farms to provoke battle from Harold II while scouts were positioned to protect against a surprise assault.

The Saxon king received news of the duke's threat in late September and immediately reformed his battered troops, marching south to again defend his monarchy. As he advanced toward London, reinforcements were added from the shire militias to replace the losses at Stamford Bridge. Arriving in London in early October, Harold II paused to rest and reorganize his army while collecting additional soldiers. With his forces prepared he moved into the Sussex lordship, first encountering the Norman outposts near Hastings on October 13.

At Hastings the English host was largely composed of foot soldiers with little cavalry, while the Norman army consisted of both light and heavy infantry, archers and a formidable cavalry. Both forces carried similar weapons; spears, swords and battle-axes. On the morning of October 14, 1066, the English assumed a strong defensive position, protected by their wall of shields on a ridgeline, taunting their enemy with shouts of, "Out, Out, Out," as William initiated the battle. The Normans first attacked with a barrage of arrows from their largely mercenary archers, followed by an infantry assault, which was beaten back with heavy losses. After the withdrawal of the first wave the cavalry charged the fortified ridgeline but they were also repulsed. The battle lasted through the entire day with repeated Norman sorties of pikemen and knights and was finally decided late in the afternoon with the death of Harold II, who was fatally struck by an arrow. At the slayings of their king and his brothers, Gyrth and Leofwine, the Saxon army began to lose its fighting spirit and took flight as the Norman men-at-arms finally broke through their ranks.

Following the battle at Hastings the body of Harold II was buried on orders from the Norman duke in an unmarked grave close to the coastline to prevent him from becoming a martyred rallying point for future Saxon resistance. Harold II of Wessex was forty-four years old at his death and had ruled England for less than ten months.

House of Normandy, 1066–1154

The House of Normandy was founded by Duke William, who had become by 1065 the dominant warlord in western France. In September 1066 he crossed the English Channel, defeating the Saxon army of the usurper King Harold II at the battle of Hastings to seize the crown of England. Through the ruthless imposition of his kingship by the end of his twenty-one-year reign, William I had established a loyal Anglo-Norman power base among the barons, shires and Church and his authority was unchallenged. His lineage ruled England for eighty-eight years through four separate monarchs. The royal house began the conquest of the British Isles by seizing control of eastern Wales and securing the overlordship of Scotland. In France the Normans regained suzerainty over Normandy, successfully defended their borders against the repeated encroachments of the Capet regime and began the expansion of their continental lands. The dynasty attained its summit under Henry I, who reformed the English judicial and financial systems to initiate an era of prosperity, stability and peace. However, the nineteen-year reign of Stephen resulted in the loss of the French fiefdoms and produced a prolonged violent and bloody civil war as two warring Norman factions contended for the throne, which was only resolved by the death of the king and the assumption of the monarchy by Henry Plantagenet.

WILLIAM I, 1027/28–1066–1087

The duchy of Normandy had long maintained close contacts with the kings of England binding their alliances through numerous marriages. In early 1066 when the English crown became vacant with the death of Edward III the Confessor, the reigning duke of Normandy had a lawful claim to the monarchy through his Saxon grandmother. To enforce his right of inheritance William crossed the English Channel at the head of an invasion army, deposing the usurper Harold II to seize the throne. William of Normandy was born late in 1027 or early in the following year at the ducal castle of Falaise in western France. He was the illegitimate son of the Norman Duke Robert I and Herleva, the daughter of a local wealthy tanner. Soon after his birth William, with his mother, left Falaise to reside in the capital of Rouen in the household of his father. Duke Robert I had assumed the duchy of Normandy shortly before the birth of his son and his rule was marked with internal rebellion and alien incursions against his borderlands from the lords of Flanders and Brittany. To retain his authority Robert I was compelled to make grants of lands, titles and offices in his government to secure the power necessary to thwart the threat. He fostered friendly relations with the courts of England and France while continuing his predecessors' policy of giving sanctuary to the fugitive Saxon heirs, Alfred and the future Edward III the Confessor. His family's affiliations with the English regime greatly influenced the future course of the reign of William.

In 1035 Robert I assembled his magnates and high prelates to announce his pilgrimage to Jerusalem. To protect William's inheritance the duke compelled his vassals to acknowledge his son as heir designate and swear an oath of fealty. Before his departure the Norman overlord appointed a regency council to govern in the successor's name and act as guardians. However, he never returned to his homeland, dying in the city of Nicaea in present-day Turkey. When the news of Robert I's death reached Normandy the eight-year-old William was freely acknowledged as the new duke.

While William had readily succeeded to his father's throne, numerous political factions broke their pledges of loyalty and began to conspire to gain control of his governing council. To protect the duke from assassination or kidnapping, he was initially removed from Rouen to the stronghold at Vaudreuil. There were several attempts to seize him, resulting in the murders of his guardians and several family members. With a fragmented and weak ruling administration the fiefdom was plunged into anarchy as numerous warring magnates disregarded ducal authority by engaging in private wars and plunder. As the danger mounted the duke was frequently moved from castle to castle for his protection. During these turbulent times he was under the custody of various relatives who provided for his care, education and military training. Tutors were appointed for his academic instruction; however, William's studies were severely limited by the ongoing violence. During his stormy youth the prince grew into a charismatic overlord of piety and dignity, possessing great physical strength and martial talents. While his formal education had been largely ignored he became skilled in horsemanship and in the use of the broadsword and archery and was knighted by King Henry I of France on the battlefield. William was a natural leader with an imposing military presence who energetically defended his feudal rights.

As the ongoing lawlessness of the Norman magnates escalated unchecked, in 1042 William began to exert his personal rule. Upon assuming full ducal power his first independent initiative was to proclaim the *"Truce of God"* over the warring lords of his fiefdom. The Catholic Church had instituted the doctrine to end the acts of violence directed against ecclesiastic properties, churchmen and the poor during designated holy periods. The duke summoned his barons and prelates to Caen where the assembled council recognized the *Truce* and under penalty of excommunication agreed to respect its covenants. The reconciliation resulted in a brief interval of peace that was broken in 1047 by the rebellion of William's cousin, Count Guy of Burgundy.

The Burgundian count was a direct descendent of the reigning Norman House, possessing a valid claim of succession against the duchy. Guy had acquired wealthy estates and had attracted a large following among the local nobles, knights and towns. He began to intrigue against the duke, promising the warlords of western Normandy local autonomy in exchange for their military alliance in the overthrow of William. To thwart the ambitions of his cousin, with much of his duchy in open revolt, the Norman duke was compelled to personally appear before his ally and overlord, Henry I of France, to ask for his intervention. After meeting with the king at his court in Poissy, the French army marched into Normandy, joining forces with the duke, who had earlier advanced to confront Guy's troops, near Val-es-Dunes. In the ensuing battle the allies quickly overwhelmed the rogue barons in a series of determined and spirited cavalry charges. The victory saved the duchy from usurpation, securing William's reign to initiate a period of peace where his vassals and prelates now respected his authority and obeyed his laws.

The duke's success at Val-es-Dunes allowed him the opportunity to consolidate his supremacy and by late 1049 the throne was secure, enabling him to respond to the request for military support from his French overlord. The formidable count of Anjou, Geoffrey the Hammer, had risen in rebellion against Henry I, seizing two castles on the Normandy-Maine border that were claimed by William. To buttress the war effort of the French king and in defense of his rights, the duke marched his forces against the stronghold at Domfront, placing it under siege. While the investment wore on, the main Norman army advanced against the second fortification of Alencon. As the duke approached the outer defenses the soldiers placed animal hides over the walls, ridiculing his illegitimate birth with repeated jeers of "Hides for the tanner's son." The enraged William mercilessly assaulted the outpost, seizing the defenders. He ordered their feet and hands to be amputated and thrown over the ramparts of the castle, demanding the garrison's immediate surrender. Fearing similar treatment the fortified town quickly submitted and was pardoned for its revolt. As the news of the savage acts reached Domfront, the residents quickly agreed to terms. The fortresses were garrisoned with loyal troops, becoming a strong Norman defensive barrier against future attacks by Geoffrey of Anjou.

In 1051 William was married to Matilda, the daughter of Baldwin V of Flanders, in a political agreement that secured an ally along his northern borderlands. The union with the powerful count brought prestige to the Norman court and signified the duke had attained a place of superiority among the western princedoms. However, the Roman Church refused to sanction the marriage, claiming there existed a close blood relationship, placing the duchy under an interdiction to force its dissolution. It was several years before papal approval could be finally negotiated. Matilda was described as a princess of intelligence and grace who became renowned for her many acts of piety. They enjoyed a generally happy relationship, with the duke remaining faithful to his wife. The succession of the House of Normandy was secured in 1053 with the birth of Robert. William I and Matilda had a total of nine children, two of whom became kings of England.

After fulfilling his feudal obligations to the French crown and buttressing his border area, the Norman warlord was confronted with a series of internal revolts by a coalition of his vassals. With the full power of the duchy's formidable army behind him, William assembled his troops, marching against the rebels. Confronted with an overwhelming show of force, the rogue lords surrendered their castles and were exiled for their acts of defiance. However, to end the rebellion of his uncle, Count William of Araques, the duke was compelled to mount an attack to forcibly seize his lands. The campaign against Araques took on feudatory implications when the dissident count's castle was invested, forcing him to appeal to Henry I for relief. The French court had previously rendered powerless Geoffrey of Anjou and increasingly began to fear the rising military might of the Normans. To reduce the threat the Capet king turned against his former ally, sending an army to raise the siege. With the approach of the royal levies the duke mobilized his retainers, launching an assault to repel the French. Following the withdrawal of the Capet soldiers, the blockade was continued until the count finally agreed to surrender and submit. Henry I had been checked in his initial attempt to subdue his vassal, however, he remained determined to enforce his will. William had gained additional prestige by successfully defending his ducal authority against his recalcitrant magnates.

In 1054 the French monarch became reconciled with Geoffrey of Anjou and together with numerous rebel Norman barons they renewed the war against Normandy, advancing against the duke's capital. William assembled his loyal knights and household troops, successfully blocking the invaders, compelling the allies to abandon their incursion. Three years later Henry I again launched a campaign into Normandy, pillaging the countryside and burning towns to force William into battle. However, facing superior military might, the duke was only willing to engage in small skirmishes until he outmaneuvered the French army as it crossed the Dives River at Varaville. When the Capet crown's levies became separated on two riverbanks, the Normans mounted their lightning cavalry charge, destroying the rearguard. Henry I and Geoffrey the Hammer withdrew their shattered forces from the occupied lands, dissolving their alliance. The victory at Varaville ended the rivalry between France and Normandy, secured the duke's borders against future attacks and compelled the rogue warlords to submit to William's overlordship. After the triumph an uneasy peace ensued between the two realms until the death of Henry I in 1060. He was succeeded by his minor son, Philip I, which required the establishment of a regency government to rule until the king reached the age of majority. The new administration was headed by William's friend and father-in-law, Baldwin V of Flanders, and under his direction a permanent reconciliation was negotiated between both courts, resulting in the normalization of relations.

By 1060 William had thwarted the rebellious ambitions of his recalcitrant vassals and had secured their unquestioned loyalty to unite his realm. The kingdom of France was under the control of Baldwin V of Flanders, the duke's friend and ally, which guaranteed his eastern and northern borders. Only the duchy of Brittany and the county of Maine in the south were a potential danger to the security of Normandy. In 1059 Geoffrey of Anjou, who had previously occupied Maine by overthrowing Count Herbert, died and the deposed lord appealed to the Normans for military aid to regain his seized birthright. A treaty was forged between the two courts, with William agreeing to intervene in Herbert's favor for his oath of fealty for Maine. However, before the campaign could be initiated, the count died and William claimed his lordship. In March 1062 he invaded Maine but the local population offered a strong resistance, giving their allegiance to the neighboring count of Vexin, Walter. As the Normans advanced the Vexin warlord withdrew his army to the capital of Le Mans while William systematically ravaged the countryside and seized numerous castles. With the countship occupied and Le Mans under siege, Walter was forced to submit, securing the conquest. With the occupation of Maine, only Brittany remained outside the sphere of William's domination. In 1065 the opportunity to impose his power came when he attacked the duchy in response to a series of pillaging raids by the duke of Brittany, Conan II. In an overwhelming show of Norman military might, Conan II was defeated and compelled to pledge his fealty. The triumph solidified the duke's supremacy over the western French barons, guaranteeing security for his duchy and making him the preeminent overlord.

The minority years of William's reign had resulted in the near total dissolution of his duchy's administrative structure. After securing his dominance over Normandy and safeguarding his borders, he reorganized his government based on the feudal model, where all authority and power was in his hands. Viscounts were appointed by the reigning council to collect local taxes and enforce the laws. A chancery was utilized as a civil service to administer the duchy while a central legal court settled all judicial matters. The Norman Church remained under the ducal prerogative as the warlord successfully defied papal custom by naming his own bishops and resolving all ecclesiastic issues. William built a strong relationship with his prelates and was a generous benefactor and protector of his Church. He traveled extensively throughout the realm, imposing his suzerainty and presiding over his justice. By 1066 a highly effective centralized system of government had been established and the fiefdom was well ruled.

The dukes of Normandy had a long history of fostering friendship with the crowns of England and had arranged numerous marriages between the two courts. In 1016 the Normans gave sanctuary to the deposed Saxon king, Ethelred II, who had been overthrown by the Danish overlord Swein I and his son Cnut. Ethelred II and his queen Emma, who was William's great-aunt, remained in the ducal household and their two sons, Alfred and Edward, grew up under the care and protection of the dukes. To give legitimacy to the Danish usurpation of the English throne after the death of Swein I, his heir Cnut married the widowed Emma. In 1042 Cnut's successor, Harthacnut, died without a direct heir and the Witan, an assembly of earls and high bishops, elected Queen Emma's son, Edward, as the new sovereign. William continued to maintain friendly relations with his cousin, later making an official visit to the English court. In 1051 Edward III still had no successor to his kingdom and promised the duke recognition as the next king.

While William was securing his ducal overlordship, in England Edward III had come under the influence of the Godwinson family with the appointment of Harold as earl of Wessex and his brother, Tostig, as baron of Northumbria. Harold's stature was further enhanced when he became the king's chief advisor and commander of the royal army. In 1064 the Saxon court sent the Wessex lord to Normandy on a diplomatic mission. His ship was blown off course to the Flemish coast, where he was captured and held for ransom by Count Guy of Ponthieu. To secure an ally in his quest for the English throne, William agreed to negotiate Harold's release. The Saxon earl became the duke's vassal, swearing an oath to support his claim to the kingship.

On January 5, 1066, Edward III the Confessor died and Harold defied his pledges to William, seizing the English throne. One day later the Witan recognized him as sovereign and he was formally anointed by the archbishop of Canterbury. When the Norman duke was informed that Harold II was king of England, he became enraged and determined to enforce his perceived right to the crown through military might. A council of war was summoned and preparations for the campaign were begun. A fleet of over six hundred vessels was constructed and an army of seven thousand was assembled, which included not only Normans but Flemish and Breton archers and crossbowmen, while knights were recruited from France. While arrangements continued envoys were dispatched to Rome to acquire Pope Alexander II's blessing for the invasion. Harold II had replaced the Holy See's appointed archbishop of Canterbury with his vassal and the papacy was anxious to regain ecclesiastic sovereignty over the English Church, readily agreeing to sanction a holy crusade. The decree had the effect of legitimizing the expedition as God's enterprise.

The Norman fleet sailed on September 27, landing unopposed on the Sussex coast at Pevensey Bay the next morning. After a fortified camp was established the army began the systematic ravaging of the local countryside to force the new Saxon king into battle. However, Harold II was not in the south but had rapidly advanced to York to counter the invasion of his rebellious brother, Tostig, and his Viking ally, Harald III Hardrada of Norway. In a bloody and brutal battle at Stamford Bridge, he defeated the Northmen, where several days later he learned of the duke's pillaging raids. To defend the realm, the English troops quickly marched to London, where preparations were made and additional forces mobilized for the encounter against William. On the morning of October 14 Harold II held the high ground, occupying a ridgeline at Hastings. The Saxon soldiers deployed into a defensive wall of shields, challenging the invaders to assault their position. The Normans formed into attack formation with the archers occupying the front rank, followed by the foot soldiers in the center and the men-at-arms under the direct command of the duke and his half-brother, Bishop Odo of Bayeux, in the rear. William's infantry and cavalry made repeated charges but the battle was only won late in the day when the English sovereign was killed and his demoralized militiamen fled the field.

After the Hastings triumph the Norman army advanced unopposed through the southeastern counties, terrorizing the local population and burning their towns and farms. The campaign turned to the west and, by December, William's relentless harrying tactics had destroyed the resolve of the Saxons, compelling the archbishop of Canterbury to offer the surrender of London. On Christmas Day 1066 in Westminster Abbey, William of Normandy was crowned king of England by the primate of York. The traditional Saxon ceremony of enthronement was employed to legitimize the successor as the rightful heir of Edward III the Confessor.

William I remained in his new realm until March 1067, consolidating his rule and receiving the fealty of numerous English barons and bishops. He systematically looted the towns and churches, sending vast amounts of treasure to his duchy and allies. Before sailing to Normandy to contend the encroachments of the French, the king appointed his half-brother Odo and William Osberen as lieutenant generals to continue the conquest of the still defiant western and northern earls and prelates.

After spending nearly a year in Normandy personally imposing his supremacy over western France, in early 1068 William I crossed the Channel to England to take command of the subjugation campaign. During his absence the Saxon rebels had united with the Welsh to continue their opposition against the Norman occupation. William I directed his Anglo-Norman army into the border lordships, overwhelming the local resistance. After the submission of the warlords a castle was built at Warwick while towns were fortified and garrisoned with loyal troops to enforce Norman sovereignty and laws. With the conquest of the western counties William I marched north to York and, by a show of military might, the region was subordinated to his will. A series of fortifications was constructed and Norman lords were appointed to administer the district. Late in the year the king departed for Rouen, believing the Saxons had fully acknowledged his reign.

Soon after William I's arrival in Normandy the northern English barons rose in revolt under the banner of Edgar, a distant nephew of Edward III. The Norman regime's ruthless campaigns of subjugation, its forced redistribution of Saxon lands to reward faithful retainers and the building of numerous castles had given cause to their uprisings. Many of the crown's garrisons were overrun and their defenders killed. In early 1069 the king was compelled to return to England to initiate a fire-and-blood intervention campaign against the recalcitrant northern lordships. The city of York was sacked and the region occupied with Norman soldiers, once again securing the throne's dominance.

While the northern barons and bishops had been twice thwarted in their attempts to depose the crown's occupation, they remained defiant in their opposition and began deliberations with the Danish king, Swein II, for his usurpation of the monarchy. The Danes had a long-standing presence in the York demesne and their military intervention was widely popular among the local population. Swein II agreed to intervene, sending a fleet of nearly 250 ships in the autumn of 1069 under the command of his brother, Osbern. The Vikings raided the eastern English coast before landing on the Northumbrian shore, where they were joined by a formidable Saxon army led by Edgar. The Anglo-Danish forces advanced against York, quickly destroying the counterattack of the local garrison, seizing the city as other areas of England rebelled against Norman overlordship. In response to the uprisings William I marched to the Midlands while his warlords and prelates quickly suppressed the insurgencies in the western and southern lordships. The main Norman army under William I's personal command defeated the Saxons at Stafford, resecuring his supremacy over the territory.

Only the Northumbrian district maintained its autonomy and the throne's troops were soon launched against the region of Yorkshire.

As the Normans approached York the Danish abandoned their ally, seeking the safety of their ships. William I began the total systematic harrying of the northern towns and countryside as farms and houses were burned, crops and animals destroyed and many thousands of residents murdered. So severe was the devastation that a widespread famine followed, which killed over ten percent of the total population. The monarch continued his campaign of pillage into the winter months of 1070, relentlessly pursuing the rebels throughout the Northumbrian wilderness, forcing their submission one at a time. To enforce the royal will a chain of castles was built and strongly garrisoned by the crown's vassals. By the spring of 1070 England had once again been subjugated to the sovereignty of William I.

While the Norman king was suppressing the Yorkshire revolt, the Vikings had remained on their ships, unchallenged by the throne. In the spring of 1070 Swein II personally brought reinforcements to his brother's army. The Norse warriors joined a band of brigand Saxons on the remote Isle of Ely to instigate a campaign of plunder against the Norman occupiers. To end the rebellion the royal court negotiated a treaty with the Danes and for an indemnity they agreed to abandon England. The remnants of the rebels were attacked in the summer of 1071 in their stronghold and destroyed, eliminating the last serious pocket of resistance.

With his supremacy acknowledged by his English vassals, in 1072 William I mounted a punitive campaign into Scotland to punish King Malcolm III for his numerous pillaging raids against Northumbria. The Scots rendered little resistance, offering to negotiate a reconciliation. The ensuing Treaty of Abernethy recognized Scottish rights over the northern counties and Malcolm III pledged his fealty for the lordships.

After securing his sovereignty over England William I began the process of establishing a governmental system based on Norman feudalism. The lands of the Saxon warlords, who had resisted him, were confiscated, with a share retained by the crown and the remainder granted to his retainers and allies as rewards for faithful service. By the end of William I's reign in 1087 there were very few Anglo-Saxon lords or bishops who still maintained possession of their estates. To protect against further rebellion a network of strong castles was constructed throughout the realm and garrisoned with loyal troops. The tax system was revised and an annual levy based on land value was initiated. The existing English courts continued to be utilized but were augmented with Norman regional and special courts. To administer the throne's justice the offices of sheriff were enhanced and were headed by powerful nobles. The king's rule brought Norman laws, institutions and culture, creating the foundations for a highly effective central administration, producing a period of stability, national unity and prosperity.

While restructuring his government William I's reform measures were extended to the English Church. The existing ecclesiastic structure was reorganized, new monasteries and churches erected and the Saxon abbots and prelates replaced with Normans. The king's friend and ally, Lanfranc, was appointed to the archbishopric of Canterbury where he energetically continued the transformation of the Church. Lanfranc defended his sovereign's privileges to appoint his own abbots and bishops, successfully defying papal opposition. The archbishop was an able and loyal administrator and William I named him as regent during his many absences on the continent. Like all aspects of English society the control of the Church remained the prerogative of the crown.

As William I remained in England, occupied with his suppression of the Saxons, by 1071 his once supremacy over the western French fiefdoms had largely come unraveled and, for the balance of his reign, the duchy of Normandy was subjected to revolt and foreign invasions. The county of Anjou was ruled by the hostile Fulk IV, who turned more bellicose, threatening to seize Maine. In 1073 William I was forced to travel to Normandy and lead his army against Maine, which had risen in rebellion at the encouragement and support of Fulk IV. The towns and countryside were brutally ravaged, compelling the citizen government of Le Mans to readily accept the suzerainty of the Norman duke.

While William I had reimposed his authority over neighboring Maine by force of arms, relations with France continued to deteriorate as Philip I increasingly maneuvered to enforce his feudal rights over Normandy. To contain the territorial ambitions of the Norman king in 1072 the French regime negotiated a military alliance with the new count of Flanders, Robert I of Frisia. As the conflict turned more hostile with Philip I's seizure of the strategic county of Vexin, a sporadic war ensued between the two rival realms, with William I successfully repelling the allies' incursions into his duchy while restricting the conflict to only the border region.

Before his departure to England in 1066 William I had recognized his eldest son, Robert Curthose, as the heir to Normandy. Reaching the age of majority, he was described as ambitious and impatient, demanding his birthright to the duchy. The monarch's refusal to acknowledge his son as duke drove him into open rebellion against the ducal throne. He became allied with Philip I of France, who gave him financial support and encouragement. The rogue lord attracted a large following of disenchanted Norman and French nobles and from his sanctuaries in France he pillaged his father's demesne. William I was forced to lead a punitive attack against Robert to impose his overlordship, engaging the rebels near the French-Norman border. The incursion failed to resolve their struggle and they were only temporarily reconciled at the intervention of Queen Matilda. The conflict was renewed in 1080, resulting in the permanent departure of Curthose from the royal court.

While William I stayed in France to defend his Norman realm, several of his vassals in England united to revolt against their overlord, demanding a greater share in the spoils of the conquest and occupation. The rebels negotiated an alliance with Denmark, conspiring to overthrow the king's government. The plot was revealed to the crown's regent, Lanfranc, archbishop of Canterbury, who quickly marched against the dissidents, defeating them before their Viking allies could reach England. When the Northmen arrived in the kingdom they found little local support and could only raid the coast before sailing to Denmark. William I's authority over England was unchallenged for the remainder of his reign with the exception of the brief 1082 uprising of his half-brother Odo, bishop of Bayeux. The bishop openly defied the throne by raising an independent army threatening to usurp the ruling council. However, he was quickly arrested before any insurgency movement could gain momentum as the kingdom continued to be firmly under William I's supremacy.

As William I continued to be occupied in Normandy with the ongoing wars against his eastern ducal borders, in Flanders Count Robert began negotiations with Cnut IV of Denmark for their joint invasion of England. To defend against the expected attack, the Norman king departed to his kingdom to begin raising an army and hiring foreign mercenaries. A national survey was ordered to find the revenue necessary to fund the expected war, to offset the large expenditures for the construction of the defenses in England and the ongoing wars in Normandy. The compiling of a census was also needed to provide an accurate record of land ownership after years of property transfers under Norman kingship. During 1086 royal agents were sent to assign a value to each manor and farm by collecting its size, number of tenants, livestock and crops to determine a tax amount, which became known as the *Doomsday Book*. However, while the census was being conducted Cnut IV died and, with the threat of an attack thwarted, William I was able to again cross the Channel to Normandy to personally contend the escalating encroachments against his eastern demesne by France.

During the duke's absence in England, Philip I of France had financially supported and encouraged the nobles in the county of Vexin to plunder the Norman border settlements and farms. After reestablishing his court in Rouen in July 1087 the king personally led a retaliatory raid against the repeated incursions of the Vexin warlords by sacking their capital at Mantes. During the course of the attack William I, who had grown excessively obese in his later years, sustained a serious injury, which ruptured his intestine. As the condition grew increasingly worse he was moved to the ducal castle at Rouen. With death near William I acknowledged his eldest son, Robert Curthose, as the heir to Normandy while the second issue, William Rufus, was granted the kingdom of England and the youngest son, Henry, was given five thousand pounds of silver and some minor English estates and castles. On September 9, 1087, William I died at age fifty-nine and after a reign in England of nearly twenty-one years. He was buried at the abbey of Saint Stephen in Caen.

WILLIAM II RUFUS, 1060–1087–1100

At the death of William I in September 1087 his demesne was divided among his two eldest surviving sons. The oldest, Robert Curthose, was granted the duchy of Normandy while the second and favorite, William Rufus, received the kingdom of England. William was born in 1060 in Normandy and was the third of the four male issues of William I and Queen Matilda. Clerical tutors were provided for his education and the Norman prince was instructed in religion and learned to speak some Latin, though he was not taught to read or write. He began his military training for knighthood around the age of seven and as he entered adolescence had become a skilled horseman and mounted warrior. As part of his martial instruction he spent long hours hunting in the dense forest of Normandy, learning to handle the spear, sword and battle-axe. The lord became part of his father's household cavalry and was trained in military tactics, becoming a capable and energetic leader. William was described physically as medium in height with a stocky build and a red beard with yellowish long hair. Unlike his older brother, Robert, the Norman warlord remained loyal to his father, joining him on the many campaigns in England and against the incursions into Normandy of the French king, Philip I. In 1077 William Rufus was knighted by the English sovereign and continued his service with the Norman army as a landless mercenary soldier.

In July 1087 William I was seriously injured during a punitive raid against the city of Mantes in the French county of Vexin. As his health steadily deteriorated he provided for the partition of his empire by appointing Robert Curthose to the duchy of Normandy and granting William the kingdom of England. The Norman prince was ordered to immediately depart to his new realm to prevent the outbreak of rebellion and to firmly impose his supremacy. William left his father's deathbed on September 8 with a small party of loyal allies and advisors.

After arriving in England Rufus quickly made his way to meet with the archbishop of Canterbury, Lanfranc, to receive his allegiance and recognition as the heir. No precedent existed for the selection of a new Norman monarch and the active support of Lanfranc was key to his succession. The archbishop accepted the decision of William I and on September 26 anointed William II as king at Westminster Abbey. With his formal and ecclesiastic investiture to the throne, the English lords and clerics now freely acknowledged their new suzerain. After receiving the homage of his vassals and bishops, he began the process of consolidating his government. He appointed many of his father's advisors and prelates to his royal council and maintained the existing system of administration. The treasury was retained at Winchester while the supreme political authority rested with the royal court in the person of William II. The office of chamberlain remained as the primary counselor to the crown. After his coronation William II traveled through his realm, securing his rule and establishing friendly relations with the Church. By the time of the Christmas celebrations in London he believed his monarchy had been firmly accepted by his Anglo-Norman and Saxon lords, clerics and shires.

The bishop of Bayeaux, Odo, had been imprisoned by his half-brother, William I, on charges of treason during the final years of his reign. In December 1087 his nephew reinstated the bishop and restored his lands and titles. Soon after his release Odo again began to plot against the English kingdom, forming an alliance with his older nephew, Duke Robert II of Normandy. A faction of Anglo-Norman barons also joined the rebellion, hoping to replace the dominating rule of William II with the easily controlled duke. In April 1088 the rogue warlords attacked the throne's castle garrisons in Sussex and Kent, capturing many of the cities while Curthose began to assemble an invasion force in support. With many of his Anglo-Norman magnates and prelates, along with their retainers, in revolt, William II was compelled to rely on the English militiamen and his still loyal Norman lords. To ensure their fealty he pledged to return many of the former Saxon privileges and to provide agreeable government. While the regional royal soldiers easily subdued the uprisings in their areas, the crown's army counterattacked the rebels' central strongholds at Rochester and Pevensey. The castles were placed under siege while Odo waited in vain for the relief troops of Robert II. As the investments wore on the duke abandoned his allies and by July, with disease spreading throughout the garrisons and food supplies depleted, the defenders surrendered. The leaders of the insurrection were exiled while the lesser nobles and clerics were pardoned for their oaths of homage.

After reimposing his reign William II ignored his pledges to the English militia and began to aggressively tax their lands and the estates of the nobles. He initiated an assault against the Church, raiding its properties and, at the deaths of the local governing prelates, placing their bishoprics and monasteries under crown control. Through its ruthless execution of the tax system, the throne generated huge sums of money, filling its treasury, successfully defying the will of the See of Rome.

William II and his older brother, Robert II Curthose, had remained rivals and largely on unfriendly terms since childhood. With his royal coffers full the king began to prepare for his revenge against the duke's involvement in the aborted 1088 invasion attempt. In the summer of 1090 he entered into negotiations with numerous friendly Norman warlords, who were bribed with English silver into supporting his campaign. His cross–Channel allies began to fortify their castles and prepare for war against their duke. As the rebels mounted their attack they initially captured numerous strongholds and towns, forcing Robert II in November to forge an alliance with his youngest brother, Henry. The ducal coalition launched a counter-assault against Rufus's forces at Rouen, defeating his vassals to secure the duke's sovereignty, thwarting the ambitions of the English.

While William II spent the Christmas season at Winchester, in Normandy Duke Robert II was occupied by war in his eastern demesne as the French again renewed their attacks to impose their overlordship. With the fiefdom in turmoil and still retaining the loyalty of the northern Norman barons the English crown began to prepare for a second and larger invasion. In February the king landed in his brother's lands, quickly seizing and garrisoning numerous castles and towns. With an overwhelming army of Normans, Saxons and mercenary soldiers allied against him, the duke was compelled to seek terms. Under the resulting peace treaty he granted the seaports of Fecamp and Cherbourg along with the county of Eu to William II Rufus, while the English sovereign pledged to aid his brother in the recovery of the eastern counties that had been lost to the French. Both rivals agreed to name the other as heir and to seize the properties of their younger brother, Henry, count of Cotentin, who had earlier purchased the Norman lordship in 1088 from the duke to finance his planned invasion of England. The two brothers launched their united armies against the count at Mont Saint Michel, placing the fortified abbey under siege. In April 1091 the garrison surrendered and Henry was forced to abandon his estates.

As part of the reconciliation between William II Rufus and Robert II, the Saxon heir to the English crown, Edgar, who had earlier been granted sanctuary in Normandy, was to be exiled from the duchy. The Pretender was forced to sail to Scotland, where he joined the army of Malcolm III of Canmore in his campaign of conquest against the northern English counties. With the Anglo-Normans distracted with their interventions against Robert II, the Scots renewed their encroachments into Northumbria to annex the region. In August 1091 the monarch returned to England to defend his domains against further incursions from his northern neighbor. He marched his army north, capturing several Scottish occupied towns and strongholds, securing his gains with the construction of a castle at Carlisle. With his demesne under attack, to secure peace the Canmore king agreed to give homage for his remaining English territory and William II consented to return parts of his recent conquests. However, in the following year the Norman ruler refused to honor his pledges and in 1093 Malcolm III again invaded Northumbria, where he was killed during the siege against Alnwick. With the Canmore throne vacant the Scottish sovereign's brother, Donald III, usurped the inheritance rights of his nephew, Duncan, seizing the monarchy by force of arms. Duncan had spent many years in the Norman court as a hostage for his father's pledge of fealty, developing a strong relationship with the English. He now used his influence and friends to negotiate an alliance with William II and, for Norman financial and military support, the Scottish prince agreed to render homage for his realm. In the spring of 1094 he launched his offensive against his uncle, defeating him and capturing the kingdom. The triumph made the English king the defacto overlord of Scotland.

While the Norman court intrigued to gain supremacy over Scotland, in February 1093 William II Rufus became seriously ill. Believing he faced death the king agreed to a reconciliation with the English Church to gain its rights of salvation. The archbishopric of Canterbury had remained vacant since the death of Lanfranc and the crown had continuously impressed its revenues. The prelates proposed the appointment of Lanfranc's student, Bishop Anselm of Bec, as the replacement to Canterbury. Fearing eternal damnation William II granted the request, agreed to fill the vacant dioceses and abbeys and end his campaigns of suppression against the clergy. However, soon after his pledges, he regained his health and quickly ignored many of his promises of reform. Nevertheless, Anselm was confirmed as the new Canterbury archbishop, beginning a period of open contention with the throne.

By late 1093 relations with Robert II had again deteriorated as the duke increasingly demanded his brother's military aid in the recovery of the county of Maine. In March of the following year William II Rufus crossed over to Normandy to personally negotiate a reconciliation. However, no resolution could be found and the English crown began to prepare for war by sending for soldiers from England and recruiting Norman barons and mercenary troops. Operating from his county of Eu William II launched his campaign quickly, capturing numerous fortified towns and castles in the upper Normandy region. However, the hostilities soon favored the duke when he became allied with Philip I of France. The English king countered by forming a coalition with his younger brother, Henry, and his friends and allies. In late December he departed for England, appointing Henry, who had been amply supplied with gold and silver, to continue the campaign. While the English throne retained control over northern Normandy the conflict soon developed into an indecisive stalemate.

In 1095 the crown's troublesome relationship with the English Church evolved into open hostility as Anselm found the demands of his sovereign increasingly impossible to honor. Their dispute centered on the primate's request to travel to Rome to be fully invested in his ecclesiastic office. At the time of the petition there were two popes claiming the Holy See and William II found it politically expedient to recognize neither. If the throne granted permission a claimant would have to be acknowledged and the royal council was not willing to lose the independence of action it had acquired during the schism. Accordingly Anselm was ordered to stay in England under threat of arrest for treason. However, the patriarch continued to intrigue against the Anglo-Norman government while Rufus sought ways to force his ouster. While the English Church had earlier supported Urban II as pope, the Norman regime was uncommitted. However, in 1095 to press his campaign against Anselm, the king negotiated a settlement with Urban II, agreeing to accept him as pontiff in lieu of Clement III in exchange for the right to approve all papal legates to his realm. The Norman court believed it had the freedom to openly attack the archbishop and began to aggressively pursue his removal by appealing to the See of Rome for intervention. A papal envoy was dispatched to England to hear the accusations but no justification for dismissal could be found. Nevertheless, William II pressed his initiative to bring charges of treason. As the dispute intensified the prelate was granted permission to leave his diocese for the archbishopric of Lyons, not returning until the reign of Henry I. However, his Church properties were quickly seized by William II and its large resources diverted to the royal treasury. The English relationship with the Church of Rome remained strained during the balance of William II's rule as he continued to defy the papacy by maintaining sovereignty over ecclesiastic affairs.

While the English sovereign was defending his prerogatives against encroachment by his archbishop, in Northumbria the local earl, Robert of Mowbray, was actively forging a league against the Norman crown's excessive taxes and belligerence. He attracted many of the same Kent rebel lords who had revolted in 1088. The earl was summoned to court to answer charges of treason, but he refused and his properties were forfeited. In the spring of 1095 the king began to mobilize his barons for the seizure of the earldom. The royal army began to advance north, directly challenging Robert by besieging his fortification at Newcastle. In August the garrison surrendered and the campaign was continued against Bamburgh where the earl had earlier taken sanctuary. The castle was placed under investment and, with Robert of Mowbray blockaded, his coalition quickly dissolved. While the fortress remained under siege the earl escaped. However, Robert was soon captured and, when he was threatened with blinding, the Bamburgh defenders submitted. With the fall of the stronghold the entire earldom was under Rufus's occupation and his kingship was reimposed and power strengthened.

In November 1095 Pope Urban II summoned the nobles and knights of Europe to take the crusader cross to free Jerusalem from Saracen occupation. In Normandy the virtues of the holy war were extolled by the archbishop of Rouen, whose preaching inspired Robert II to volunteer. To fund the expenses for his private army he agreed to mortgage his duchy to William II for ten thousand marks of silver for three years. It was further agreed that if Curthose died without a direct heir, the English king would inherit his possessions. The treaty made William II the defacto ruler of Normandy when he received the homage of the local magnates, clerics and towns.

In the spring of 1097 William II sailed to England from Normandy to personally command an incursion against the Welsh who had increasingly attacked his border settlements and fortified towns. Two campaigns were launched into Wales but no major success was achieved and the crown was satisfied with the construction of a series of castles as a marchland defensive barrier.

In November 1094 William II Rufus's figurehead king of Scotland, Duncan II, was overthrown by Donald III. The Norman court had given the deposed House of Canmore sanctuary and Edgar, the current Pretender to the Scottish throne, was a friend and ally of the English regime. During his exile Edgar had begun a political campaign to establish a military alliance with the dissident Scottish warlords and Church and had actively sought Norman financing and soldiers for an invasion. In the late summer of 1097 with his realm at peace William II finally agreed to provide the military forces for the usurpation. Edgar assembled his army of Anglo-Norman and emigrant Scottish troops marching to the north. In October Donald III was defeated and captured and the kingdom was once again under the authority of a vassal to the English crown.

By late 1097 Rufus had imposed his sovereignty over his barons and Church and had secured his English borders. With his brother still absent on the First Crusade, he became determined to press his suzerainty over all western France. In November he sailed to the continent, first reestablishing his personal government over Normandy and then beginning to organize a campaign for the seizure of the county of Vexin, which was claimed by the French crown. An army of Norman magnates and knights was raised with English silver and in February 1098, under William II's personal command, the troops advanced against Vexin. However, the attack was thwarted by the strong barrier of fortifications and little was accomplished. After building and garrisoning a castle at Gisors the Normans withdrew, satisfied with establishing a foothold and presence in the region.

While William II Rufus's initial campaign against the French Vexin had been inconclusive, in April he formed an alliance with Robert of Belleme for the conquest of Maine from the supporters of Robert II. A large army of Normans, augmented with Breton and Flemish mercenary soldiers, was assembled and in early summer the allies marched into Maine, easily occupying the northern lordships. Negotiations were begun with the defenders of Le Mans and under threat of siege the principal city agreed to surrender, securing the seizure of the county and its annexation to Normandy. A Norman administration was established to govern the fiefdom while the king returned to Rouen, having achieved the first step in the quest for dominance over western France.

As the Norman king was involved with the capture of Maine, he negotiated an alliance with William, duke of Aquitaine. The new ally gave William II access in central France and additional protection against the recalcitrant count of Anjou. It further enhanced his influence and prestige among the western lordships to buttress his pursuit for supremacy over the region.

After the triumph in Maine William II redirected his military initiatives back to the conquest of Vexin. In September 1098 a major offensive was mounted against the county but again the attacks stalled before the strong defensive barrier of French castles and fortified towns and only a few minor strongholds were captured. The war was continued into the spring of 1099 before the rivals agreed to a truce. William II had been absent from his kingdom for over fifteen months and his presence was needed to personally preside over his English government. A ruling council of Norman bishops and magnates was established in Rouen to administer the duchy and in April 1099 he crossed the Channel to England.

The sovereign celebrated the Easter season with his court and tended to the task of governing his realm. In June he received reports from his Norman regents that the county of Maine had again rebelled and had replaced his ruling council with the deposed count, Helias. Rufus immediately sailed to Normandy and assembled his regional army, marching against Maine. His troops encountered little resistance and Le Mans was quickly recaptured. The leader of the revolt, Helias, withdrew his remaining loyal knights and infantry to the stronghold of Mayet, compelling the invaders to invest the fortified city. A strong observation force was posted around Mayet while the king returned first to Le Mans to reestablish his administration and then to Rouen. He stayed in Normandy to settle local governmental affairs before embarking for England in September.

Departing to his realm William II first reestablished his government and began to make preparations for the permanent seizure of Normandy. Duke Robert II was expected to return from the First Crusade before the end of the year and William II anticipated his brother having great difficulty in repaying the ten thousand marks of silver he had borrowed for the mortgage of his duchy. During the summer months the royal court remained in southeastern England, close to vessels for a quick cross Channel voyage. While in New Forest he spent his days hunting in the large game preserve that had been established by his father. On August 2, 1100, William II with a small force of nobles including his brother, Henry, set out to hunt deer where, late in the afternoon, he was accidentally killed by a stray arrow. There were suspicions that Henry had murdered his brother to secure the throne but no evidence was ever produced. Rufus had never married and had no direct heir. Robert II Curthose, as the older brother, took precedent over Henry in the hierarchy of succession and could be expected to claim England. Henry needed to seize the government before his brother's impending arrival to ensure his successful usurpation. William II was quickly buried with little ceremony at the cathedral of Winchester after a reign of thirteen years. On August 5 Henry I was anointed with the crown of England in Westminster Abbey.

HENRY I, 1068–1100–1135

Henry was the fourth son of William I and Queen Matilda and was born during the summer of 1068 in England at Selby. The Norman prince spent his early years in the English court of his father, where tutors were appointed for his education. Unlike his older brothers, Henry was highly educated, receiving academic instruction in the letters and religious doctrine, was versed in Latin, and was fluent in both English and French. He was the favorite child of his mother accompanying her on frequent trips to Normandy. Military instructors were provided for his training for knighthood and the lord became skilled in horsemanship and the weapons of the warrior. At the age of eighteen Henry was knighted by his father at Westminster. As the surviving third son of the king he did not expect to share significantly in the spoils of the crown and, accordingly, in late 1086 traveled to Normandy to establish a presence and allies among the local magnates and clerics in the pursuit of his own independent fiefdoms.

In 1087 William I died from the injuries suffered during a pillaging raid into the French lordship of Vexin. At his direction the duchy of Normandy was granted to his eldest son, Robert Curthose the kingdom of England was bequeathed to William and Henry received a large sum of silver and various minor Anglo-Norman lordships that were quickly seized by the new English king. After Robert II's unchallenged assumption of the duchy, Henry remained with his brother's court, joining the Norman governing council.

In 1088 the duke began to prepare for an invasion of England to usurp the regime of William II and, in need of money for the campaign, sold the western county of Cotentin to Henry. The new count quickly established his authority over the lordship, which consisted of nearly one-third of Normandy, as the vassal of his older brother. He organized his local administrative council and governed his demesne wisely, providing stability and security at a time when the remainder of the duchy was beset with anarchy and turmoil under the weak and ineffective rule of Robert II. The well-managed government of Henry won the favor and loyalty of many powerful and influential Norman warlords and prelates and secured his suzerainty.

After the failure of Duke Robert II's planned assault against England and the defeat of the Anglo-Norman rebellion at Rochester in July 1088, Henry crossed the Channel to negotiate the release of his seized inherited lordships. The two brothers met in friendship and the Cotentin count stayed with the English court through the summer months, receiving assurances that his lands would be restored. However when he departed for Cotentin Henry did so without having acquired ownership of his properties from William II.

While Henry was in England rumors had spread through Normandy that he had joined a coalition with William II Rufus and other Anglo-Norman warlords to overthrow Robert II. When the count arrived in the duchy he was arrested on orders from the duke and imprisoned in Bayeux while his estates were forfeited. He remained a prisoner until the spring of 1089 and, after his release, returned to western Normandy, where he had a formidable following among the local magnates. Henry reestablished his overlordship over his former demesne as Curthose became involved in wars against the French on his eastern border. The count brought law and order to the western territories while the rest of the duchy drifted into lawlessness under the continued misgovernment of the duke.

As Normandy was beset with internal chaos and foreign invasions, in England William II began to plot his revenge against Robert II for his involvement in the 1088 rebellion against his crown. In the summer of 1090 he formed a series of coalitions with numerous northern Norman lords and with the payment of English silver they began to harry the duke's lands, capturing many of his minor castles. In November Rouen revolted, joining their militia with the Norman retainers of the English regime. To counter the rising insurrection Robert II summoned his loyal southern vassals and negotiated a reconciliation with Henry and his allies to contend the mutiny in Rouen. The count led the attack, repelling the dissidents from the city and capturing many of their leaders. Among the prisoners was the wealthy merchant and principal commander of the uprising, Conan Pilatus. He was placed in the custody of Henry, who promptly led him to the top of the ducal castle's tower, forcing the conspirator over the edge for his acts of treason. The Cotentin warlord's spirited assault saved the duchy for his brother and won him recognition for his ruthlessness and aggression.

After rescuing the duke from the English crown's sponsored rebellion, Henry departed from Rouen to his lands in Cotentin. While he remained on his estates, in February 1091 William II Rufus arrived in northern Normandy to continue his war against the duchy. His invasion troops were united with the local rebel lords and together their formidable military marched against Rouen. Confronted with an overwhelming military force, the duke was compelled to seek terms. In the ensuing accord the two elder brothers became reconciled and William II was ceded the county of Eu, several seaports and castles and they further agreed to jointly usurp the countship of Henry. The count strongly voiced his protest and began to prepare his defenses. However, he was now deserted by many of his allies and forced to withdraw with his few remaining retainers to the fortified abbey of Mont Saint

Michel. The stronghold was besieged by the united armies of William II and Robert II and with all avenues of reinforcements, food and water blocked, the count was compelled to surrender. In April 1091 he withdrew from the abbey, traveling to sanctuary in France. Henry was once again landless and without sources of income. He stayed away from Normandy until the following year, when his fortunes dramatically improved.

In July 1092 the fortified town of Domfront rebelled against its local Norman seignior, Robert of Belleme, offering allegiance to the exiled Henry, allowing him to assume sovereignty over the castle and the surrounding countryside. Domfront became the focal point of his political and military campaign of revenge against Robert II. Pillaging raids were launched into Normandy and reconciliation talks were initiated with the deposed count's allies and friends in Cotentin. By 1094 Henry had regained much of his lost influence and power in western Normandy through military might and diplomacy. While he was reasserting his overlordship negotiations were begun with William II Rufus, who had earlier broken his alliance with Curthose. As the count increased his pressure on the Norman regime, the English crown agreed to financially aid his private war. The harassing attacks were continued through the summer; however, in December Henry departed from Domfront to join his brother in England to personally solidify their coalition. He remained in the English kingdom into the spring before crossing the Channel to renew the incursions against Duke Robert II.

In November 1095 the First Papal Crusade to regain control over Jerusalem from Saracen occupation was announced by Pope Urban II. Robert II Curthose became resolved to take the crusader's cross and, to finance his personal army, mortgaged his duchy to the English regime. In September 1096 the duke began his overland voyage and William II governed Normandy as regent. His friendly relationship with Henry had continued and he rewarded his brother's service by formally ceding him the Cotentin countship. During the following two years the count frequently joined the Norman army, participating in the campaigns against the French Vexin and Maine in support of his brother's quest for the overlordship of western France.

In the summer of 1100 Henry was with William II's court in the English New Forest region. On August 2 he was part of his brother's deer hunting party when a wayward arrow accidentally killed the king. There was speculation that Henry had murdered his overlord to usurp England, but no evidence was ever produced. Robert II of Normandy was expected to return from the First Crusade later in the year and, as the eldest issue of William I, clearly possessed the superior claim to the throne, which gave rise to the suspicions of assassination. Nevertheless Henry hurried to Winchester to take control of the crown's treasury and at a hastily convened council of barons he was acknowledged as his brother's successor. On August 5 at Westminster Abbey in London Henry I was anointed as the new sovereign of England.

Soon after his investiture Henry I directed his first policy initiatives toward the formation of a stable government and unified kingdom. Many of his loyal Norman allies and friends had lands on both sides of the Channel and he utilized this faction as the center of his English power base. Numerous nobles and prelates from his brother's council were reappointed, while Henry I won the support of others by the granting of estates and titles. Under the reign of William II relations between the crown and Church had remained strained. To foster a reconciliation many of the vacant ecclesiastic offices were filled and the exiled archbishop of Canterbury, Anselm, was recalled. A royal charter of civil rights that promised good government, respect for all laws and an end to oppressive practices was promulgated through the realm. The king's measures were largely successful in securing his sovereignty and the loyalty of the Anglo-Saxons, however, a large party of Norman emigrants still favored the rule of the ineffective and weak Robert II Curthose.

To further strengthen his stature among the Saxon population, in November 1100 Henry I was married to Matilda, the daughter of the king of Scotland. She was a direct descendent of the former English ruling lineage, giving enhanced legitimacy to the new Norman dynasty while the union with a Canmore princess served to solidify friendly relations with the court of Scotland. Matilda had been well educated by the Church and as queen became renown for her many acts of charity and piety. Henry I and his wife developed a close and loving relationship and she played an active role in the monarchy's government, serving as regent during Henry I's absences. Matilda remained loyal to her husband despite his many mistresses, with whom he had at least twenty illegitimate children. The future succession was secured with the birth of a son, William Atheling, in 1103, which had followed a daughter, Matilda, born in the previous year.

As Henry I continued the process of imposing his sovereignty over the recalcitrant Anglo-Norman barons, in September 1100 Robert II Curthose returned from the First Crusade. Many English lords resented the loss of their liberties under the strong government of Henry I and began to conspire with the duke for his seizure of the crown. By July a coalition was formed and he landed at Portsmouth with a large ducal levy to unite with the rogue English magnates, marching north toward London. Henry I mobilized his largely Saxon troops, deploying to block his brother's advance at Alton. As the two armies faced off the king offered to negotiate a reconciliation, pledging to pardon the traitors, pay a yearly pension to the duke and renounce his title to his French demesne while Curthose agreed to disavow his claim to the English throne. The rivals readily accepted the treaty and Robert II abandoned his allies, departing to Normandy. After the dissolution of the insurgent alliance Henry I refused to honor his oath of clemency and ruthlessly attacked the leading Anglo-Norman warlords, isolating and suppressing their dissension. In 1102 the royal court summoned the principal rebellious baron, Robert of Belleme, to answer charges of treason. He refused to respond to the petition, withdrawing to his fortifications to prepare for the regime's assault. The sovereign personally led his retainers against Robert, defeating and forcing him into exile in Normandy. With the conquest of the Belleme lord, all of England accepted the monarchy of Henry I, remaining at peace during the balance of his reign.

As part of the crown's initiative to regain the friendship of the English Church, the deposed archbishop of Canterbury, Anselm, had been reinstated with his diocese. However, he soon reopened the issue of the king's right to invest his own bishops and clerics to vacant offices. The throne refused to relinquish its privilege, ordering the prelate to officially acknowledge its selections or abandon the realm. In 1102 Pope Paschal II formally denied the secular appointment of all clergy offices and ceremonial vesting, which exceeded the Canterbury patriarch's refusal to grant only the act of investiture. The archbishop was sent to Rome to arrange a settlement, but the papacy refused any compromise. During his prolonged absence the regime seized the income from the Canterbury estates. A resolution was finally negotiated four years later when under threat of excommunication Henry I agreed to modify his demands. Under a papal-approved accord the Norman court retained the prerogative to select the churchmen, giving it the effective control over the English Church but ceded the ceremony of consecration.

After his defeat in 1102 Robert of Belleme withdrew to his sizable estates in Normandy to initiate a campaign of insurrection against Henry I. In its suppression of the rebellious Anglo-Norman warlords the crown had forced many of them to abandon their English lands and follow Belleme into exile. A formidable hostile faction rallied to the banner of the baron and increasingly the allies harassed the Norman friends and supporters of the king, especially in his countship of Cotentin. As his magnates came under new attacks Henry I appealed to his brother for protection but Robert II Curthose was unable to check the aggression of his vassals. By late 1104 the English court began to prepare for an invasion to impose its overlordship, using the duke's inability to control the assaults of the rogues as just cause.

In the spring of 1105 Henry I crossed the Channel with a powerful army, landing on the Cotentin Peninsula. He had retained the backing of many of his western Norman allies and they quickly rallied to his cause. To counter his brother's challenge the duke mobilized the forces of the household militia, the troops of Robert of Belleme and other rebellious exiled Anglo-Norman nobles. During the summer the English crown's coalition pillaged the ducal demesne in the west, capturing several fortified towns. However, Robert II refused to openly confront the invaders and in August the king departed for England to settle the ongoing conflict over investiture with Archbishop Anslem, leaving his Norman retainers to continue the offensive. In 1106 Henry I returned to Normandy to personally command the war effort. The campaign of attacks against Curthose's rogue Anglo-Norman warlords was renewed and the ducal lands were again ravaged and burned. In September the English began an incursion against the fortified town of Tinchebray, placing the stronghold under siege. The castle was the property of the duke's principal supporter, William of Mortain, and Robert II was compelled to come to the aid of his vassal. As his soldiers approached Tinchebray, the English monarch maneuvered his forces to block their march. After an attempt to negotiate a resolution, on September 28 the duke's cavalry launched a charge against the infantry of Henry I. The English pikemen thwarted the assault as the king's mounted knights counterattacked to decimate the ranks of the advancing ducal levies. The battle was won in less than an hour and was a decisive victory for the English regime with the capture of Robert II Curthose and the leading rebels. The triumph at Tinchebray reunited the empire of William I, as all of Normandy fell under the sovereignty of Henry I. Curthose spent his remaining twenty-eight years in England as the prisoner of his brother.

The English king stayed in Normandy until the spring of 1107 to fully impose his suzerainty and establish his ducal administration. Among the many decrees published by the ruling council was the creation of a Norman guardianship for William Clito, the young son of the deposed duke. However, the decision resulted in future rebellion as the prince remained in the fiefdom to serve as a rallying cause for the many disinherited warlords he became the leader of a series of uprisings against English occupation.

Departing to England Henry I assumed control of his government, undertaking to settle the outstanding ecclesiastic issues and initiate a series of far reaching re-structuring measures. The throne became fully reconciled with Archbishop Anselm and the vacant bishop and abbot offices were filled. The crown found many able and loyal counselors and advisors from within the Church, which served to bind the two institutions. The realm's judicial system was reorganized with the royal shire courts now supplanting the power of the local barons' courts. The regime's central judiciary, the *Curia Regis*, was expanded to play the dominant role in the administration of justice. The king's laws were enforced throughout the kingdom with both Saxons and Normans receiving equal hearings and trials. The tax collection procedure was revised with the local sheriffs now accountable to the *Curia Regis* for the gathering of all funds. The Court of Exchequer was created to receive and verify the revenue from the sheriffs. Under the new reforms the amounts of money received by the royal treasury was greatly increased. The improvements served to enhance the rule of law and by the end of his reign Henry I was known as the "Lion of Justice."

In 1108 the king of France, Philip I, died and was succeeded by his energetic and ambitious son, Louis VI of Capet, who was determined to regain his lost sovereignty over western France. In March 1109 Henry I returned to Normandy and, in violation of his treaty with the French crown, garrisoned the strategic Vexin castle of Gisors with his troops. Louis VI countered the occupation of neutral lands by launching a series of inconclusive raids into the county of Vexin. To buttress its offensive against Henry I, the Capet regime attempted to provoke civil war in Normandy by forging a coalition with William Clito. Several Norman warlords, including Robert of Belleme, joined together in rebellion to support the restoration of the deposed duke's heir. However, Henry I still retained the loyalty of the majority of magnates and was slowly able to suppress the revolt while keeping the aggression of Louis VI in check. In 1113, with Normandy again secured, the Norman monarch negotiated an alliance with the formidable count of Anjou, Fulk V, to further thwart the French war effort. The allies attacked the Capetian fortifications in Vexin to drive the French back into the Ile de France, compelling Louis VI to seek peace terms. Under the ensuing accord the Capet court agreed to cede suzerainty over Brittany, Maine and Vexin to the English throne.

While the French monarchy had been forced to accept the harsh 1113 peace treaty Louis VI remained determined to bring the western fiefdoms under his domination. In 1116 he formed an alliance with Flanders and Fulk V of Anjou, who abandoned Henry I. To create internal unrest the French encouraged the Norman warlords to revolt in support of William Clito with the promise of military intervention and gold. The allies ravaged the eastern border regions while a powerful faction of Norman nobles rebelled, propelling the duchy into civil war and anarchy. In 1118 the crisis began to turn in the English throne's favor when both Flanders and Anjou broke their coalition with the French. With the Capetian war effort in disarray, in the summer of 1119 Henry I mounted an attack into Vexin and on August 19 decisively defeated Louis VI at the battle of Brenneville. Following the English triumph two years of inconclusive warfare resulted as neither rival possessed the military might to impose his will. Finally, through the intervention of Pope Calixtus II, the two realms agreed to peace terms, with Henry I retaining control over his recent Vexin conquests but allowing his heir, William Atheling, to give homage for Normandy to the French crown.

After finalizing the settlement with France in November, Henry I departed for England with his fleet, however, as the ship carrying his son and successor designate entered the Channel, it struck a hidden rock and quickly sank, drowning William Atheling. The sovereign was without a direct heir, as William Clito became the acknowledged king apparent. Queen Matilda had died in 1118 and to secure the future of the Norman crown the royal council encouraged the king to marry again. In January 1121 he married Adelize, the daughter of the duke of Lower Lotharingia. She was described as a princess of beauty and piety and became a patron of the Church and learning. The union gave prestige to Henry I by uniting the Norman dynasty with a direct descendent of Charlemagne and gave the English government a presence and ally in western Germany. However, the marriage failed to produce the needed successor.

While Henry I remained in England the French king broke the treaty of 1121, forming a coalition with Fulk V of Anjou, William Clito and his supporters to renew his quest for supremacy in western France. In November 1123 the English monarch was once again in Normandy to defend his demesne and forged a counter-alliance with the count of Flanders to secure his northern border. Henry I and the Flemish repulsed the French incursions from their lands and by the following year, under the threat of invasion against eastern France from Henry I's German ally and son-in-law, Henry V, the war entered a stalemate.

As the sporadic conflict against Louis VI continued, the issue of the king's succession was still unresolved. In 1125 Emperor Henry V, the husband of Henry I's sole surviving issue, died and in the following year Matilda joined her father's court in Normandy. With his daughter now a widow and free of allegiance to Germany, the former empress was proclaimed as the heir apparent to secure the future of the Anglo-Norman monarchy. In September 1126 the royal household returned to England where Henry I finalized the inheritance of Matilda by compelling his high barons and prelates to swear an oath of homage to the new successor designate at Westminster on Christmas Day.

The ongoing war with France had remained unsettled and in 1127 the conflict was expanded into neighboring Flanders when the local count, Charles I the Good, was murdered in an attempted coup. Louis VI supported the succession of William Clito as the new count to gain an ally on his northern border and mounted an invasion into the courtship to successfully enforce his will, placing his retainer on the ducal throne, gaining influence and a presence in the strategic region. However, in the spring of the following year, the Flemish towns rebelled with English financial support and encouragement against Clito and the French crown again intervened to secure the lordship for its client-vassal.

While Louis VI was suppressing the Flemish revolt, Henry I began negotiations with Fulk V of Anjou to acquire an ally in his ongoing war with France. As part of the final accord the English court agreed to the marriage of Matilda to the count's son and heir, Geoffrey Plantagenet. The ceremony was held at Le Mans in June 1128. The marriage was a diplomatic success for the king, ensuring a military alliance against France and the possibility of producing a male heir to his throne.

Several months before the marriage of Matilda and Geoffrey, in Flanders the town militias again rose in rebellion against Clito and in support of Thierry of Alsace. Louis VI advanced to the aid of his vassal but in late July 1128 William Clito was killed during siege operations and the French crown was forced to accept the succession of Thierry. The new count formalized his alliances with England and in the following year Henry I and Louis VI agreed to end their war with the Norman regime still the dominant power in western France. With western France at peace in July 1129 the monarch was finally able to depart for England.

Upon arrival in his kingdom Henry I reestablished his ruling council and traveled extensively throughout his realm, personally resolving local disputes, imposing his justice and appointing court officials and vacant church offices. With England remaining at peace and prospering in 1133, he departed to Normandy where at Rouen he joined his daughter, who had recently given birth to a son, Henry Plantagenet. The king was forced to stay at Rouen, as his relationship with his son-in-law became increasingly hostile. Geoffrey demanded the transfer of several Maine-Anjou frontier castles as Matilda's agreed dowry. Henry I refused to cede any territory and the count responded by sacking the fortified town of Beaumont. To thwart future attacks the English sovereign moved south to the border area during the summer to strengthen his defenses. Staying in the region in late November 1135 Henry I became seriously ill while hunting. Over the following days his condition became steadily worse and on December 1 he died at age sixty-seven and after a reign of thirty-five years. His body was first taken to Rouen and finally, in early January, after Henry I was buried in England at the abbey of Reading.

STEPHEN, 1096–1135–1154

At the death of Henry I in December 1135 England was propelled into a prolonged period of civil war as the supporters of his only surviving issue, Matilda, contended for control of the monarchy against the political faction of her cousin, Stephen of Boulogne. Stephen was born in 1096 and was the third son of Stephen, count of Blois, and Adela, the daughter of William I. The young lord spent little time with his father, who left Blois in October 1096 to join the First Crusade to Jerusalem. The count later deserted the expedition during the prolonged Antioch siege and in 1100, under papal excommunication and personal humiliation in France for abandoning his crusader vows, was compelled to return to the Kingdom of Jerusalem. In May 1102 he was killed in the battle of Ramleh, defending Jerusalem against an Egyptian attack. While the crusader warlord participated in the holy war, Stephen spent his early life in Blois and Chartres under the care and influence of his domineering mother, who governed the fiefdom as regent. Following the death of his father the Blois prince was sent to be educated in the kingdom of his uncle, Henry I of England. He was welcomed by the English king, becoming a part of the royal household. Stephen acquired an education as a member of the court, receiving instruction in reading, writing, religion and Latin. Around the age of seven he began military training for knighthood, developing into a skilled mounted warrior and commander under the guidance of experienced masters of arms. After completion of his martial instruction he was knighted by Henry I, joining the English army as a landless vassal of the throne. Stephen traveled with his uncle on frequent military expeditions to Normandy, engaging in numerous campaigns against recalcitrant Norman lords and incursions into the county of Vexin against France.

Stephen became a favorite of the king and was granted the strategic Norman county of Mortain for his faithful services. As the Mortain count stayed with the English court for his loyalty and accomplishments, he was ceded additional lands in both England and Normandy, becoming a powerful and wealthy magnate due to the generosity of his uncle. In November 1120 Stephen's political ambitions changed dramatically when the sovereign's only male heir, William Atheling, was drowned in a shipwreck during a crossing from Normandy to England. William Clito, the nephew of Henry I and grandson of William I, became the rightful successor designate. However, the English throne was at war with Clito and his selection as the new ruler was rejected. Stephen of Blois held similar bloodlines through his mother and a faction of nobles and clerics began to promote his appointment. The count held large estates in England and had remained in high repute with the monarchy, spending most of his days at court where his friendly and easily approachable manner had attracted a formidable following. There was widespread speculation that he would be named to succeed his uncle by the crown's ruling council. Despite Stephen's prominent position, Henry I refused to officially acknowledge any heir but continued to reward him with additional honors and lordships.

In 1125 Stephen was married to Matilda, the daughter of the count of Boulogne, Eustace III. The union was a political agreement secured by the Norman crown to ensure a loyal friend and ally in the strategic French northwestern county. The marriage brought Stephen not only Boulogne but extensive estates in England and a relationship with a direct heir of the former ruling Saxon dynasty. Matilda was described as a princess of intelligence and energy and served as an able advisor to her husband. The marriage resulted in the birth of three sons and two daughters, though none of the children survived to inherit the throne of England.

With the death of William Atheling in 1120 Henry I had only one surviving offspring, a daughter, Matilda, who had been earlier married to the emperor of Germany, Henry V. However, the emperor died in 1125 and in the following year Matilda rejoined her father in England, where the king compelled his high barons and bishops to accept her as the heir apparent. To maintain his favorable position within the royal household, Stephen agreed to recognize his cousin's inheritance. Despite the formal conformation of Matilda's accession, the former empress quickly became widely unpopular among the English lords and clerics for her arrogant and imperious manners. She was resented also for breaking with the long-established historical precedent of only male issues advancing to the kingship and her possible succession met with greater disapproval in 1127 when she married a foreigner, Count Geoffrey Plantagenet of Anjou. As Matilda's standing among the English and Normans declined, Stephen continued to remain a favorite alternative, retaining his political power base particularly among the southern English lordships.

While the count of Boulogne maintained his popular position at court and with the English nobles and Church, the relationship between Henry I and his daughter grew increasingly tense. With the encouragement of his wife, Geoffrey of Anjou became involved with his father-in-law in a hostile dispute along the Maine-Anjou frontier. During late 1135 the king was in southern Normandy, strengthening his border defenses when he unexpectedly became seriously ill, dying on December 1 without re-designating Matilda as his successor.

Count Stephen received notification of his uncle's death while in Boulogne and quickly sailed for England, advancing to London upon landing. He held extensive lands around the city and was widely popular with the local population, who proclaimed him as king. To secure his monarchy he traveled to Winchester to acquire the support of his brother, Henry, who had earlier been appointed as the regional bishop. With the intervention of the Winchester prelate the Church declared its loyalty to Stephen and on December 22 he was formally anointed sovereign of England by the archbishop of Canterbury in Westminster Abbey. In March of the following year, Pope Innocent II formally sanctioned his consecration.

While Stephen was imposing his authority, in Normandy the leading English magnates were negotiating with his older brother, Theobald, for his succession as the oldest surviving nephew of Henry I. However, when the barons received the news of Stephen's coronation they immediately ended their deliberations and hurried across the Channel to acknowledge the new king. Through his quick and decisive actions, Stephen had successfully usurped the monarchy away from the officially recognized heir and outmaneuvered Theobald to assert his reign.

After acquiring the support of the clergy and seizing control of the government, the newly crowned king began to negotiate with his barons to receive their homage. Many of the lords rallied to him but a large faction remained loyal to Matilda. While Stephen was attempting to impose his rule, the Scottish king David I, who had earlier sworn fealty for his English fiefdoms to the former empress, invaded England in favor of her cause and to expand his realm over Northumbria. The Scots quickly occupied many strategic castles and fortified towns, compelling Stephen to hastily raise an army to defend his demesne while his brother led his campaign for acceptance as overlord from the nobility. In February 1136 he advanced north to relieve the investment against Durham. With the approach of the formidable Anglo-Norman forces, David I offered to negotiate a settlement rather than risk his recent gains on the outcome of a battle. In the ensuing Treaty of Durham the Scots were ceded lands and towns along the border region but David I refused to abandon his allegiance to Matilda. With peace restored, while in the northern earldoms, Stephen received the homage of the local warlords and Church to further consolidate his hold on England. In March he utilized his diplomatic success and increased prestige from Durham to summon the great magnates and bishops to his Easter court at Westminster, demanding their oaths of fidelity, completing his formal succession to the monarchy. In return for their pledges the royal court re-confirmed the former grants of their estates, honors and titles.

While Stephen had succeeded in securing the recognition of his ascension to England, he still was faced with sporadic localized rebellions. In Oxfordshire Lord Robert of Bampton revolted, pillaging the neighboring towns and countryside. The king aggressively responded to his act of disobedience by seizing the rebel's castle and lands. With the defiance of Robert resolved, the crown advanced against earl Baldwin of Redress who had broken the peace by occupying the town of Exeter. The earl's fortress was placed under siege and, with his water supplies exhausted, he was compelled to submit. The throne pardoned his acts of dissention but Baldwin soon renewed his revolt from his stronghold on the Isle of Wight. The royal army marched to the coast, again forcing the recalcitrant baron to surrender and for his treason he was exiled to Anjou and his demesne forfeited to the regime. While Stephen's rapid and decisive display of power had subdued the uprisings, his failure to imprison or exact harsh punishment against the rogues, with the resulting implied weakness and lack of resolve, gave cause to future insurgency in favor of Matilda.

Stephen had spent over fifteen months in England establishing his suzerainty, largely ignoring Normandy. In his absence the duchy had erupted into turmoil as the local warlords utilized the lack of a central authority to pillage and subjugate neighboring lordships. As the internal disorder multiplied, the count of Anjou, Geoffrey, invaded the south, occupying several strategic castles. Finally in March 1137 the English king crossed the Channel to his duchy to begin the imposition of his sovereignty. To contend the incursion of the Angevins, the local magnates quickly rallied to Stephen, offering their allegiance and agreeing to end their private wars. The Anjou count had continued his attacks by marching toward the western principal city of Caen. Stephen began his campaign by first securing his eastern borders with a pledge of fealty for Normandy to Louis VI of France. To regain his lost lands, by June he had mobilized a formidable force of Norman knights and foot soldiers augmented with Flemish mercenaries. However, as he advanced against the Angevins the foreign troops mutinied, attacking the Normans and forcing the initiative to be abandoned. The lack of success against Geoffrey caused many of the ducal warlords to withdraw their support for Stephen. He was later reconciled with his vassals through the mediation of the archbishop of Rouen but their relationship remained contemptuous. In November Stephen appointed a ruling council to govern in his name and returned to England. He had only partially asserted his control and departed with his stature and acceptance by the Norman barons and Church seriously damaged, while in Geoffrey a powerful enemy still remained unchecked.

Stephen's lack of will and failure to impose his authority over Normandy and his weak response against the earlier uprisings of Robert of Bampton and Baldwin of Redress encouraged many of his English earls to revolt against his usurpation of the English throne. In the spring of 1138 Henry I's illegitimate son, Robert of Gloucester, renounced his allegiance, declaring homage to his half-sister, Matilda, bringing many of his retainers and allies into the conspiracy. However, the crown was able to contain their rebellion when Robert was forced to remain in Normandy to defend his local estates. The king raised a large army, advancing against the center of the rebels at Bristol, but the campaign soon lost momentum by concentrating on the seizure of only numerous small insignificant castles, allowing the insurrection movement to remain unchecked.

While Stephen squandered the opportunity to crush the Bristol uprising, in Scotland David I had again invaded Northumbria to advance his claims of sovereignty over the border lordships. After an inconclusive campaign in January 1138, the Scots sent a formidable army into the northern counties in April. The Norman court placed their defenses under the archbishop of York, Thurstan, who rallied the local knights and town militias to defend their lands. As David I marched toward York the two armies met at the Battle of the Standards, where the invaders were defeated and compelled to withdraw. Stephen was still engaged against the rebellion of Robert of Gloucester's allies and used his victory over the Scots to quickly resolve the border conflict in order to direct all his resources against western England. To ensure the peace he ceded Northumbria to David's son, Henry, who became a vassal to the English throne. To the crown's loyal barons and prelates, the accord was viewed as a loss of English prestige and territory and a victory for the Scots, further eroding their support for the monarchy.

Despite repeated attempts the Norman throne's war against the Bristol insurgency had remained unresolved. The revolt entered a new phase of belligerence in late September 1139 when Empress Matilda along with her chief ally, Robert of Gloucester, landed on the southern English coast at Arundel with a small contingent of knights. The earl quickly departed for Bristol to raise an army while Matilda stayed secure in the local castle. Upon learning of his cousin's arrival Stephen marched his troops to seize her. However, when he arrived at Arundel, instead of attacking the fortress, Matilda was allowed safe passage to join her rebels in western England on the advice of his brother, Bishop Henry, who was now secretly allied the dissident movement. From the safety of Bristol the empress attempted to rally the lords of England to her cause but initially only a small number of largely disinherited nobles were willing to pledge their allegiance. Nevertheless, despite only limited success, when the earl of Hereford, Miles of Gloucester, declared his support, Matilda gained a powerful and influential landed magnate who, along with Earl Robert, changed the course of the civil war.

During the summer months the king captured several small rebel castles but the empress remained secure at Bristol, where her insurrection grew steadily stronger. While Stephen was achieving some minor successes, the earl of Hereford began the systematic expansion of Matilda's authority and, during the following year, the region west of Gloucester and Bristol to the Welsh border was occupied. With his campaign against the dissidents increasingly failing in late 1140, Stephen attempted to win an ally in Scotland by ceding all of Northumbria free of fealty to David I. The earl of Chester, Ranulf, held a hereditary claim against the lordship of Carlisle, which had been included in the territorial transfer. With the loss of his demesne the earl revolted against the English throne, taking control of Lincoln by force of arms. When informed of Ranulf's attack Stephen assembled his loyal vassals and knights moving north to recapture the fortified town. However, before Lincoln was seized the earl escaped, traveling to Cheshire to secure the intervention of Robert of Gloucester. The allies marched to Lincoln and on February 2, 1141, Stephen advanced from the safety of the stronghold to give battle. In the ensuing engagement he was deserted by many of his retainers, resulting in the rout of his army and his capture.

As the result of the defeat at Lincoln, by March 1141 many of Stephen's friends and allies abandoned him, declaring their loyalty to Matilda. However, to usurp the monarchy she needed to be anointed by the Church in London at Westminster Abbey. Negotiations were initiated with the city's council while the empress made a slow advance to the east from Bristol. In July Matilda entered London but when she demanded the payment of a large sum of money, the Londoners re-affirmed their support for Stephen, driving her from the city. The empress joined her army at Oxford before marching to suppress the rebellion of Winchester, which had deserted her cause. The town was quickly captured but the king's supporters from London, emboldened by their recent triumph, joined forces with the crown's remaining allies, mounting an assault against the rebels. Winchester was besieged by the resurgent troops of the throne, compelling Matilda to counterattack to force her escape. In the ensuing battle her chief ally and half-brother, Robert, was captured, dealing a serious blow to her war effort.

After his seizure Earl Robert was taken to Rochester under the safekeeping of the king's wife. Negotiations for an exchange of the earl and Stephen were soon underway and, through the intervention of Bishop Henry a settlement was arranged. On November 1, 1141 the monarch was released from Bristol and two days later Robert was freed. Stephen quickly reestablished his authority and, under threat of banishment from the Church, many of Matilda's allies deserted her banner. With her forces depleted the empress dispatched her half-brother to Normandy to secure the military aid of her husband. However, he was fully engaged in the conquest of the duchy and refused to send relief. Without assistance from Geoffrey the royalist began the systematic capture of the empress's castles and fortified towns as she became increasingly isolated in the west and her cause continued to lose momentum. In 1145 Count Geoffrey completed his subjugation of Normandy but his army was too exhausted to campaign in England. With the crown's loss of the duchy many Anglo-Norman lords who held lands on both sides of the Channel lost their Norman estates and, to protect their remaining English possessions, were compelled to commit fully to Stephen. Despite the defection of many of Matilda's allies, the violent civil war dragged on until 1147 when Earl Robert died and, without his active support, the empress abandoned her hereditary challenge, sailing to Normandy early in the following year.

With the departure of the empress, the Plantagenet claim to England fell to Matilda's eldest son, Henry. He had earlier been associated with his mother's war against Stephen and in April 1149 returned to contest his rightful inheritance, establishing his court in the southwest at Devizes. During the summer Stephen, along with his son and heir, Eustace, advanced his army against Henry, but many of the crown's allies had grown war-weary and had lost their enthusiasm for campaigning, resulting in an inconclusive incursion. The civil war entered a stalemate with neither rival possessing the military might to impose his will. Realizing that without additional resources and troops he could not win England, in early 1150 Henry sailed to Normandy where his fortunes soon dramatically changed.

As Henry remained on the continent Stephen again alienated the English Church and the papacy over his appointment of a new archbishop to Canterbury. With the support of the local Church many Anglo-Norman lords openly defied the crown, weakening Stephen's authority and military might. As the king's prestige and power deteriorated, Henry was steadily improving his position. In September 1151 Geoffrey Plantagenet of Anjou died and Henry inherited his vast lands in western France. In the following year the duke's military strength was further enhanced when he married the recently divorced Eleanor of Aquitaine. With the marriage, the Norman duke gained control over the formidable and wealthy duchy of Aquitaine but the fiefdom was also claimed by Louis VII of France. The French sovereign formed an alliance with Eustace of Boulogne and Henry of Blois to contend the suzerainty of the duchy, delaying the invasion of England by the Plantagenet overlord. However, by the end of 1152, the Normans had driven the invaders back to their borders and a truce was negotiated, enabling the duke to return to England in January 1153 with a small force of knights and infantry to personally renew his war against his cousin.

While Henry was securing his authority over one-third of France, the civil war in England had largely remained at an impasse, as both rival factions grew increasingly exhausted. In 1152 Stephen attempted to ensure the succession of his family by having his son, Count Eustace of Boulogne, anointed as co-king. However, the Canterbury primate refused to perform the ceremony, leaving the crown only the military option to guarantee the heir's inheritance. In support of Eustace's cause, the king initiated a series of siege operations in the southwest during the summer of 1152, capturing numerous minor castles along with Newbury and investing the great rebel stronghold at Wallingford.

In early January 1153, with his suzerainty of Normandy secured, Prince Henry landed in southern England, again establishing his court at Devizes. After receiving the homage of the powerful barons of Chester, Salisbury and Hereford, the duke advanced to attack the stronghold of Malmesbury. As the castle was placed under siege, the king marched through a severe winter storm to relieve his garrison. However, as he approached Henry's defensive perimeter, many of the royalists abandoned the throne's cause and Stephen was compelled to negotiate a settlement, which resulted in the loss of Malmesbury. This triumph was followed in March by the rebels' occupation of Southampton and in April by the capture of Warwick, as much of the Midlands came under the duke's control. Despite the lightning successes of the dissidents, it was the sudden death in August 1153 of the heir, Count Eustace, that opened the path to a succession resolution.

Disheartened at the loss of his son, Stephen agreed to enter negotiations to find a solution to the devolution of the monarchy while the conflict continued at a sporadic pace. Finally on November 6, the king and Prince Henry agreed to meet, resulting in the ratification of the Treaty of Winchester. Under the accord the duke was recognized as the successor, lands seized during the war were to be restored, castles built during Stephen's reign were to be destroyed and the Norman warlord agreed to give homage to the crown. The two former rivals traveled to London in December to jointly enforce the terms of their settlement and to begin the demolishment of the newly built strongholds.

In April 1154 Duke Henry departed for Normandy while Stephen governed his kingdom independently. He first directed his policies in a successful campaign against the lawlessness and the roving bands of brigands that had evolved during the civil war. The king traveled extensively through his realm, where he was warmly greeted by the local population and his suzerainty was freely accepted. In the autumn the royal court moved to Dover where Stephen suddenly became seriously ill with an intestinal bleeding disorder, dying on October 25 at age fifty-eight. He had reigned for nineteen years of anarchy and civil war to be succeeded by his cousin, Henry Plantagenet.

House of Plantagenet, 1154–1399

The kingdom of England had been plunged into a bloody seventeen-year civil war in 1135 with the death of Henry I and the ensuing power struggle between the two rival cadet branches of the House of Normandy. The conflict was finally resolved in 1153 with the Treaty of Winchester, which recognized Henry Plantagenet as the successor designate. In the following year the last Norman sovereign died and Henry II ascended to the throne. The Plantagenet lineage reigned for nearly 250 years through eight kings. Henry II was the founder of the Angevin Empire, which stretched from the Pyrenees Mountains in the south across western France to the Scottish border. The defense of the empire consumed the regimes of the first three monarchs. By 1214 the inept war and diplomatic policies of the third Plantagenet, John, resulted in the loss of the majority of the French lands and the rebellion of the English magnates, demanding the king govern with their consent. The Barons' Wars were continued during the monarchy of Henry III and were only resolved with their forceful suppression by his son, Edward I. With a peaceful realm, the fifth Plantagenet again attempted to create a unified British Isles by conquering Wales and seizing Scotland. The rule of his son, Edward II, was dominated by the revival of the Barons' Revolt and the emergence of parliament as a representative institution. Under the seventh Plantagenet, Edward III, the struggle against France, which had lain largely dormant, was renewed with the beginning of the Hundred Years War and the re-conquest of the lost Angevin Empire. However, under the misgovernment of the last Plantagenet, Richard II, the fiefdoms in western France were once again squandered and the conflict with the barons re-emerged, resulting in his forced abdication and overthrow.

HENRY II, 1133–1154–1189

With the death of King Stephen in October 1154 Henry Plantagenet inherited the crown of England. His peaceful succession marked the final phase of seventeen years of violent civil war that had erupted between the political factions of his mother and her cousin, Count Stephen of Blois. Henry was born on March 4, 1133, in Le Mans and was the first son of Count Geoffrey of Anjou and Matilda, the former empress of Germany and daughter of Henry I. Two and a half years after his birth his Norman grandfather died and the Plantagenet prince was denied his rightful birthright to the English throne by the usurpation of his cousin, Stephen. In late September 1139 Empress Matilda crossed the Channel to England to contend by force of arms the kingship for her son, leaving the care and education of Henry to his father. Renowned scholars were appointed for the young lord's instruction and he was taught the basics of Latin, reading, writing, law and religion. Henry remained with his two brothers at the Anjou court while Geoffrey mounted an invasion against the English regime's duchy of Normandy, conquering the eastern lordships by the end of 1141. In September of the following year the count agreed to send his son to England with a small force of knights and foot soldiers to bolster the failing war effort of Matilda.

Henry landed on the southern coast, joining the army of his uncle, Robert of Gloucester, where he participated in the capture of several minor castles, gaining his first military experiences. By the beginning of 1143 the Anjou lord became established at his uncle's court in Bristol, where his academic education was resumed. He stayed with Earl Robert for the next two years before returning to Normandy where he actively campaigned with his father in the final phase of the defeat of Stephen's forces in the duchy.

By 1145 all of Normandy had been subdued and Geoffrey assumed the ducal title. Henry remained with his father's court where he became associated with the many governmental initiatives to restructure the judicial process, expand the use of viscounts in local law enforcement and improve the financial system. While he continued to remain in western France, Matilda was attempting to overthrow the English regime in favor of her son's inheritance rights. However, by 1048 she had been defeated and Henry crossed the Channel to renew the campaign against Stephen. The Anjou prince disembarked on the south coast, first traveling to Carlisle in Cumbria to further his cause by meeting with his kinsmen, David I of Scotland. To successfully seize the English throne Henry was in need of allies and he negotiated a treaty of support with the Scots. Under the accord he acknowledged David I's suzerainty over the English northern counties while his uncle recognized his claim to the crown and agreed to wage war against Stephen. Before departing for his power base at Bristol, he was knighted by the king.

In the southwest Henry established his court at Devizes and during the summer launched a series of coordinated attacks against the throne. He sent several of his barons to the north to divert and harass Stephen's forces while his main army attacked the king's remaining southwestern strongholds. By the end of the year the Plantagenet prince had gained firm control over the region but he lacked the resources to seriously challenge the military might of his cousin. In January 1150 he appointed deputies to continue the war and crossed the Channel to Normandy to raise additional troops and finances.

Returning to his father's court at Rouen Henry began to recruit an army and raise money. Soon after his arrival Geoffrey transferred his ducal title to his son and he was recognized as the ruler of Normandy. While the young duke remained on the continent, in England Stephen's power of kingship was steadily deteriorating as his barons increasingly deserted him for the growing fortunes of Henry. However, Henry was forced to stay in Normandy when Louis VII of France mounted an invasion against his eastern border in 1151. The attack was soon contained and a stalemate developed, resulting in a truce. In August the Norman warlord and his father traveled to Paris to settle the final terms of the peace, where Henry gave formal homage for his duchy. During the journey back to Normandy Geoffrey became seriously ill, soon dying. With the death of his father Henry could claim the overlordship of Maine and Anjou in addition to his duchy, giving him ready access to revenue and troops to continue his war against Stephen. Nevertheless, his fortunes improved vastly in the following year with his acquisition of Aquitaine.

In early 1152 Louis VII divorced his wife, Eleanor, duchess of Aquitaine. Henry became determined to expand his growing French empire with the acquisition of the duchy and, with his allies' approval, negotiations were quickly begun for the uniting of the two realms through marriage. An agreement was soon arranged and in May Henry and Eleanor were married. Through the political union the duke gained control over the wealthy and powerful duchy, creating an empire that encompassed much of western France. Eleanor was described as a princess of great beauty and charm, possessing an active intelligence, dominating personality and a strong desire to share in the rule of her husband's demesne. She was appointed by Henry to serve as regent on several occasions during his absences, though never acquiring any real power or influence. The marriage resulted in the birth of five sons, two of whom became sovereigns of England, and two daughters. As the queen's sons grew into maturity and conspired against their father to gain autonomous princedoms, she actively encouraged and supported their rebellions. In 1173 Henry II arrested Eleanor for her intrigues and she spent the next sixteen years under close house confinement. Despite her imprisonment she continued to advise her dissident children never to be reconciled with Henry II.

The 1152 acquisition of Aquitaine did not go uncontested and the French crown responded by forming an alliance with Eustace of Boulogne and Henry of Blois. The allies mounted a coordinated offensive campaign into the Norman duke's lands, delaying his planned conquest of England. Henry quickly marched his troops to the east, first driving Louis VII back into France and then defeating the attack against his county of Anjou. A truce was soon arranged and by the end of the year he was once again ready to invade England.

In early 1153 Henry assembled a small army of knights and infantry, sailing to the southern English coast after an absence of three years. After reestablishing his court and securing the allegiance of his local vassals, he began his campaign to usurp Stephen by marching to attack the crown's strategic castle at Malmesbury. The king responded by advancing through a driving winter storm to relieve his garrison troops; however, many of his royalists deserted and he was forced to agree to a truce, giving up control of Malmesbury. The duke's success encouraged many of the throne's barons to declare their homage to him and by the end of the summer much of the Midlands were under his authority. As Henry continued to gain allies he ended his southern offensive by relieving Stephen's siege against his great stronghold of Wallingford. With the defeat at Wallingford, additional pressure was placed on the regime to negotiate a resolution to the succession. The archbishop of Canterbury acted as the chief peace arbitrator, while the war was renewed at a sporadic pace. However, it was the sudden and unexpected death of Stephen's heir, Eustace, that opened the way to a settlement. Through the relentless diplomacy of the Canterbury archbishop, the two rivals finally agreed to meet at Winchester on November 6, 1153, where the Norman court acknowledged Henry's rights of inheritance and the duke pledged that Stephen would retain the kingship until his death. In the spring of 1154 Henry departed to Normandy, leaving England to the sole rule of his cousin.

In his French demesne the duke secured his absolute sovereignty over the duchy and negotiated a peace settlement with Louis VII to gain acceptance of his overlordship of Aquitaine. In late October Stephen died and on December 7 Henry and his wife crossed the Channel, confirming their formal ascension on December 19 at Westminster Abbey, where he and Eleanor were anointed, beginning 245 years of Plantagenet rule. Henry II was overlord of an empire that stretched from the Scottish border to the Pyrenees Mountains.

Soon after his coronation Henry II began the formation of a central government that had largely been non-existent during Stephen's reign. Thomas Becket was appointed as chancellor and chief advisor for English affairs and loyal magnates were named to the financial and judiciary offices. To limit the power of the barons the Plantagenet throne began the systematic destruction of all illegal castles that had been constructed during the civil war. The few warlords who actively resisted the seizure of their fortresses were soon subdued and their demesne occupied with royal troops. The grants of titles and lands made by Stephen were voided and reissued by the Plantagenet court, ensuring that the lords owed their loyalty to only Henry II and controlled their estates on crown terms. Thomas Becket was assigned to end the widespread lawlessness that had erupted during the turmoil of Stephen's monarchy.

By late 1155 with his kingship secured, Henry II crossed the Channel to his continental lands to defend Anjou and Maine from the usurpation of his brother, Geoffrey. Returning to Rouen the king quickly arranged to meet his Capet overlord in February on the Norman border where he renewed his pledge of homage for all his French possessions, including Aquitaine, thus eliminating Louis VII as an ally for Geoffrey's rebellion. With his brother isolated, his castles were easily subdued and the rebel was compelled to accept a financial settlement in lieu of his inherited lordships. From Anjou Henry II, along with Eleanor, traveled to her Aquitaine duchy, receiving the fealty of the local barons and Church. While he remained in the south, under his encouragement the citizens of the Breton city of Nantes revolted against their ruler, appealing directly to Henry II for protection. The region was quickly occupied and, to forge a reconciliation with his recently defeated brother, the Plantagenet overlord appointed Geoffrey as the local lord, gaining control over the strategic fortified city at little cost. By April 1157 he had firmly imposed his supremacy on his French demesne and sailed for England to contend the growing disturbances on the Scottish border and in Wales.

Upon arrival in England, to ensure his authority, Henry II first renewed his initiative against the few remaining eastern lords that had continued to defy his sovereignty by seizing and occupying their castles with royal troops. With the peace guaranteed, in May 1157 Henry II traveled to Chester to meet with the king of Scotland, Malcolm IV. He had earlier pledged to honor the Scots' suzerainty over the northern counties, but with the overwhelming might of the English military behind him, Henry II demanded the return of the earldoms, offering the smaller lordship of Huntingdon as a substitute. Malcolm IV, still contending rebellion in his Highlands, was forced to accept the harsh terms. After securing his northern border Henry II next moved against the revolt of the Welsh princes, who had reestablished their local autonomy during the long civil war with Stephen. The army was assembled, marching to subdue the northern warlord, Owain of Gwynedd. After a brief, well-planned campaign the Welsh were defeated and the region garrisoned with crown soldiers. In the following year, after a Welsh raid against Gloucester, the English launched an attack into southern Wales, obtaining the homage of the barons to impose Plantagenet rule and end the immediate threat of an uprising from the princedoms.

In August 1158, with his overlordship secured in his British Isles possessions, Henry II departed to Normandy to renew the campaign of expansion in western France. Thomas Becket had earlier negotiated a treaty with the Capet court for the marriage of the Plantagenet heir, Prince Henry, to Louis VII's daughter, Margaret, who was sent to be raised in the English household with the dowry of the eastern Vexin lordships. When the two kings met, the final accord was ratified and Henry II was granted the additional concession of appointing the new ruler for the vacant dukedom of Brittany, which was tantamount to his aggrandizement of the region. Through the diplomatic successes of Becket the English king controlled the majority of western France and had become the most powerful warrior in Europe.

Henry II continued to remain in his continental lands, firmly imposing and consolidating his kingship while beginning preparations in January 1159 to acquire the countship of Toulouse. The southern French county had earlier been part of Aquitaine but the local seigneur, Raymond V, had established an independent fiefdom at the death of Eleanor's father. The English king was determined to enforce his wife's inheritance rights to the area by force of arms. A large Plantagenet army of knights and mercenaries, including Malcolm IV of Scotland and his brother William, was assembled in late June encountering only light resistance as the campaign easily conquered most of the lordship. Count Raymond V withdrew his remaining troops to the capital of Toulouse, appealing to Louis VII for aid. He responded by personally leading reinforcements into the fortified city and Henry II became reluctant to break his fealty vows by directly attacking his overlord. Toulouse was placed under siege but by late September the invading forces had been depleted by disease and the harassing forays of Raymond V. With the approach of winter Henry II was compelled to order an end to the investment. Following the retreat from Toulouse the English advanced to Normandy to continue the war by raiding into the French homeland of the Ile de France, seizing several castles and burning numerous towns. By December the conflict had turned into a stalemate and a truce was quickly arranged. However, the reconciliation and mutual trust that had been developed between the two rivals had been shattered and a state of open hostility prevailed between the thrones for the balance of Henry II's reign.

With the armistice in place Henry II remained in western France, governing his expanding demesne, constantly traveling through the region enforcing his will. The first movement toward a renewal of the sporadic French war occurred in the autumn of 1160 when Louis VII married the sister of the count of Blois, altering the military status quo. The political union secured a powerful and strategic western ally for the French court to mount a coordinated attack against Normandy. Henry II countered the new alliance by arranging the immediate marriage of his heir, Prince Henry, to Louis VII's daughter under the terms of the Treaty of Gisors and with full legal authority occupied the Vexin strongholds. The count of Blois responded to the seizure by preparing for war. However, before he could launch his campaign the Plantagenet king seized his castle at Chaumont on the Loire River. The quick and decisive victory resulted in a lessened French bellicose attitude and in October 1161 a new truce was negotiated.

After the settlement with Louis VII the English monarch returned to Normandy and the personal administration of his vast empire. He traveled extensively throughout his realm, enforcing his laws and justice. Regents had been appointed to govern in England and they sent a constant flow of royal messengers to the king, relating the state of local affairs for his actions. Remaining in Normandy he reorganized the ruling bureaucracies of his many fiefdoms, severely limiting the power of his continental barons and clerics. In April 1161 Henry II named his friend and ally Thomas Becket to the vacant archbishopric of Canterbury gaining control over the powerful English Church, but the appointment resulted in future conflicts for the Plantagenet throne.

In January 1163 Henry II sailed to England, remaining for the next three years. He continued to personally administer his government, moving his court frequently throughout the kingdom. In July 1163 he re-imposed his suzerainty over the recalcitrant Welsh and began a determined effort to end the widespread nonsubmissiveness that centered mainly with the clergy who were not subjected to the crown's justice. In October 1163 Henry II summoned his council to Westminster, where he demanded Thomas Becket and the Church obey his laws. The archbishop countered that he was accountable to only Rome and God and increasingly asserted his independence, defying the throne. After the initial rebuke in January 1164 the king again assembled the great lords and churchmen, ordering the acceptance of the Constitutions of Claredon, which confirmed the dominance of his courts over the ecclesiastic judiciary. Becket verbally agreed to acknowledge the decree but two days later he renounced the declarations, refusing to perform any Church functions. In October the archbishop was put on trial for treason for refusing to accept the Claredon judgments and, fearing for his life, escaped to France.

With Thomas Becket in exile Henry II returned to the governing of his realm and the campaign to enforce his laws and justice. The prerogatives of the existing local courts under the jurisdiction of the barons were replaced with the dominance of the royal judiciary and the power of the sheriffs was expanded as his kingdom moved to peace and prosperity. In 1166 the hostility with the archbishop was renewed when Becket excommunicated the English king and his nobles and attempted through the intervention of Louis VII to secure Pope Alexander III's support. However, the papacy refused to directly confront Henry II and, increasingly isolated, the chief prelate finally agreed to accept the Claredon Constitutions, reaching an uneasy compromise in July 1170. Becket departed to Canterbury from France, where he soon defied Henry II by excommunicating three bishops who had supported the crown during his dispute with the regime. Upon hearing of the conspiracy the monarch became outraged and denounced Becket, encouraging four of his knights to cross the Channel to England and murder the archbishop. The conflict was finally settled when Henry II was forced to do penance and revoked the Claredon decrees to avoid interdiction by the pope.

While Henry II was occupied with his ongoing struggle for control of the English Church in Ireland, the ruler of Leinster, Dermont MacMurrough, was overthrown by a rival warlord and appealed to the English court for military assistance to reclaim his realm. The Plantagenet crown was actively involved with the Becket controversy and could not directly intervene. However, the English barons were granted permission to raise their own private armies to support Dermont's cause. In 1170 the largest and most successful of these independent forces under the earl of Pembroke, Richard of Clare, landed on the eastern coast of Ireland. The Irish princedoms were disorganized and disunited, allowing the earl to quickly overcome all resistance. Pembroke captured Dublin and the eastern coast, establishing a significant presence. Henry II visited Ireland in October 1171, where he received recognition as overlord from his Plantagenet lords. He remained in Ireland to secure his local government and initiate the subjugation of the regional Irish kingdoms before departing to his realm in April 1172.

With England at peace and his authority respected, Henry II crossed the Channel in early 1172 to Normandy, where he quickly resolved the growing border dispute with Louis VII. However, while he had restored order with the French his eldest son, Prince Henry the Younger, began to intrigue to gain his independent rule over England, where he had previously been anointed as co-king. The Plantagenet rebel found an ally in the Capet monarch, who supported and encouraged his insurrection. In March 1173 the young warlord openly revolted against his father and at the urgings of Queen Eleanor was joined by his brothers, Richard and Geoffrey. The malcontents met with Louis VII in Paris, where they granted lands in the Angevin Empire to various dissident lords who agreed to join their war. By the summer there was open rebellion in Anjou, Aquitaine, Brittany and England, while the magnates of Normandy remained loyal to the crown. In August the English king assembled a formidable army of Norman and mercenary soldiers and after an inconclusive assault against the French marched into Brittany to re-impose his overlordship. In September he met with his sons and Louis VII on the Norman frontier, proposing generous financial terms but no autonomous power for a settlement. The offer was refused but the military situation had become stalemated and no additional attacks were made during the year as the war front now shifted to England.

With Henry II occupied with the rebellion of his sons, the king of Scotland, William I, in late 1173 invaded the northern English counties. The initial foray resulted in only the pillaging of the countryside and the capture of Warkworth Castle. In the spring of 1174 the Scots, supported by a large army, again mounted an attack against Northumbria, placing the stronghold at Alnwick under siege. The local English warlords mobilized their militias and vassals, advancing to the relief of the fortress. During their assault on July 13 William I was captured and his forces defeated. The king was taken to Normandy, where he was compelled to accept the Treaty of Falaise, agreeing to give homage for his kingdom. With the signing of the accord, the English gained overlordship for the whole of Scotland.

While the war on the continent remained inconclusive the young Plantagenet co-king dispatched an army of his supporters to raise a rebellion in England, landing on the southern coast in September 1173. However, the local barons and population retained their loyalty to Henry II, decisively defeating the rebel forces at Fornham. With the triumph the revolt in the south quickly lost momentum. Nevertheless, Prince Henry the Younger still had allies in the north, compelling Henry II in the summer of 1174 to return to England to personally direct the campaign against the remaining insurgents. He advanced against the rogues in Northumbria where the royal army easily restored the crown's authority.

At the suppression of his dissident movement in England, Henry the Younger pressed the war against his father by allying with French troops in July 1174 to invade Normandy, attempting to seize Rouen. The Norman capital was placed under siege but despite repeated assaults it could not be stormed. In the following month Henry II arrived with reinforcements from England, driving the weakened French army back across the border. The defeat soon produced peace talks and in September a treaty was signed with Henry II reconciled with his sons and still in total control of his empire. Despite his victory he had been seriously weakened by the financial cost and disruption of his administration, which seriously limited his future expansion plans against France.

Following the accord with his sons the English king remained in Normandy to deal with the local rogue barons who had supported Prince Henry. After re-imposing his authority over the malcontents, despite minor flare-ups, the next five years were generally peaceful and tranquil as Henry II continued to travel throughout his vast empire to ensure against rebellion. However, with the death of Louis VII in September 1180 and the succession of his young, ambitious and charismatic son, Philip II, the war for control of western France was renewed with a new determination and energy.

In the autumn of 1180 the two kings meet at Gisors where the peace was confirmed and the prior treaties between Henry II and Louis VII were renewed. For the next several years Philip II was involved with internal disorders within his family and vassals and it was in his best interest to foster friendly relations with the Plantagenet court. While he asserted his rule, in the spring of 1183 Henry II was compelled to intervene to resolve the private war that resulted from his son Richard's encroachment into the Anjou lands of Prince Henry. The young Henry revolted against his father's interference by plundering his estates, threatening to again plunge the Angevin Empire into civil war. However, the rebel Plantagenet soon became seriously ill and died on July 11 ending the immediate danger.

With the death of the heir, in September 1183 Henry II recognized Richard as the uncrowned successor to the throne, with Geoffrey holding Brittany and John ruling Aquitaine as vassals of their elder brother. Richard resented the loss of his duchy of Aquitaine where he had spent most of his early years and had developed a large loyal following. He found an ally in Philip II, who had assumed full kingship of France and was ready to openly challenge Henry II by making claims for the return of the Vexin region. The peace was preserved when the English king met Philip II at Gisors in December, pledging his fealty for Vexin and Richard was temporarily allowed to retain Aquitaine. However, the French king gave financial and moral support to Henry II's sons, encouraging their continued disobedience.

With his continental lands secured, in 1184 Henry II returned to England where he ruled in relative tranquility for the next two years. He had in place a strong effective administrative and financial system and his laws and justice were respected. While Henry II stayed in England Richard invaded the lands of his brother, Geoffrey, compelling the king in 1185 to cross the Channel to Normandy to personally settle the ongoing private war of his sons. The heir was compelled to relinquish control of Aquitaine to his mother and return to his father's court. With the rebellion of Richard resolved, in April 1186 the Plantagenet sovereign sailed to England, spending the next year governing his empire in peace. Nevertheless, by late 1186 Philip II had again begun to intrigue with Henry II's sons and initiate military incursions against Vexin. As the conflict intensified Henry II re-crossed the Channel to Normandy, where the fragile truce was maintained until July 1188, when the French mounted a large invasion against Berry and Normandy. Richard was ordered to defend Berry while the English king drove Philip II out of his duchy.

Despite the defeat of his campaign the Capet monarch continued to plot to gain the favor of Richard by pledging to support his demands to be formally anointed as the Plantagenet heir. Richard deserted his father, joining a military alliance with the French. In June 1189 Philip II and the Plantagenet rebel advanced against Henry II's county of Maine, easily subduing the lordship and imposing their will. The English king attempted to defend his demesne with a mercenary force but was defeated at Le Mans before withdrawing to the stronghold at Chinon. Continuing their successful attack to the south the French soon conquered Anjou. With his empire in shatters and facing a large army, Henry II was compelled to seek terms. He agreed to appoint Richard as his successor and acknowledged the loss of the recently seized territories.

The years of ongoing wars and family feuds had taken a heavy toll on the king's health and he continued to be weakened from the effects of a high fever. After settling the peace accord he grew increasingly frail from the recent stress of the strenuous campaign and defeats, dying at Chinon in the chapel of Saint Melaine on July 6, 1189. Henry II ruled England for nearly thirty-five years and died at age fifty-six.

RICHARD I, 1157–1189–1199

In 1189 King Henry II was engaged in an ongoing struggle for control of western France when his eldest son, Richard, deserted the Plantagenet House, joining an alliance with the Capet crown. In July Richard was victorious over the Plantagenet army, forcing Henry II to formally recognize him as the rightful successor to his vast Angevin Empire. Richard was the third son of Henry II and Eleanor of Aquitaine and was born on September 8, 1157, in Oxford, England. Until the age of seven the royal prince remained in England before residing with his mother in Aquitaine, where he spent most of his adolescence. In Eleanor's household tutors were provided for the education of her son and he was taught to read and write while studying Latin, letters and religion. He later developed a fondness for church music and wrote poetry. As was the common practice in feudal Europe around the age of seven he began military training for knighthood, excelling in the use of the sword, archery and lance, and was later knighted by the French sovereign. Richard spent long hours hunting deer and wild boar in the dense forest of France, perfecting his martial skills. He was the favorite son of Queen Eleanor and through her influence developed a strong allegiance to Aquitaine. In January 1169 Richard was acknowledged by his father as the duke designate for the lordship. He stayed in the duchy with Eleanor, traveling with her court as she governed the region for her husband. In June 1172 at the age of fourteen Richard was formally consecrated at Poitiers by the archbishop of Bordeaux with the symbols of ducal authority and was recognized as duke, though Henry II still retained the power.

Henry II had earlier designated his eldest issue, Henry the Younger, as the successor to Anjou, Normandy and England, while Richard was granted Aquitaine and the fourth son, Geoffrey, was bequeathed Brittany. Nevertheless, the king refused to relinquish any sovereignty to his heirs and, as they grew older, the lack of independent authority gave cause to rebellion. At the urging of Queen Eleanor, Richard joined the insurrection movement of his older brother. The rebels met in Paris at the court of Louis VII where a formidable alliance was formed with the Capet regime and numerous rogue Angevin warlords, resulting in the agreement to wage war against Henry II's empire. In July 1173 the allies invaded Normandy, where Richard gained his first experiences in battle. However, the attacks against the Plantagenet crown were inconclusive and in September the monarch offered to reconcile with his sons, proposing generous financial terms but no autonomous power. The overture was rejected and the conflict renewed, with Henry II taking the offensive by mounting an assault against Anjou with a formidable army. As his father succeeded in re-imposing his control over large sections of Poitou, Richard assumed his first independent command to contend the throne's incursion. He established his court at Saintes but the fortified city was quickly overwhelmed and the dissident duke forced to flee. The revolt continued unresolved through the summer as Richard's military might steadily deteriorated under the relentless pressure of the Plantagenet counter-campaign. Finally, on September 23, 1174, at Poitiers he agreed to peace terms, accepting a reduced financial settlement and renewed his homage for Aquitaine.

Following his formal submission Richard returned to govern his duchy as the loyal vassal of the crown. The recent civil war with its resulting disruption of central authority had given cause for revolt among his local warlords and the Aquitiane duke was energetically engaged for the next three years with the suppression of their uprisings. The campaigns were Richard's first successful autonomous commands, where he perfected his battle skills. In 1177 he advanced south into Gascony, imposing Angevin supremacy over the recalcitrant lords. However, during much of the following year Henry II was in Aquitaine, personally directing the war effort while the duke played only a supporting role. After the departure of his father to England, Richard assumed control of the government, soon renewing his initiative into Gascony, where in late April 1178 he besieged the great fortress of Taillebourg. The castle was widely believed to be unassailable; however, in less than two weeks the ducal army forced the surrender of the garrison in a devastating and brutal assault. The triumph at Taillenbourg greatly enhanced Richard's reputation as a ruthless military commander, intimidating the remaining Aquitaine rebels into subjugation. At this time he was described by contemporaries as possessing handsome features with blond hair, tall in stature with great strength; a fierce determined warrior who relished in personal combat. He stayed in Aquitaine, ruling the duchy and enforcing his father's rule against sporadic rogue barons, until December 1182 when he was compelled to counter the invasion of his brothers, who were seeking to expand their lands into his demesne.

During the winter of 1182 Henry the Younger and his brother Geoffrey formed an alliance with numerous dissident Aquitaine lords and in February 1183 attacked Richard's lands near Poitiers. The incursion was quickly repulsed and a counter-assault launched by the duke against his older brother's county of Anjou. The war dragged on through the spring and was only settled when Henry the Younger suddenly died. With the death of the heir, as the eldest surviving son, Richard, became the unacknowledged successor designate, which gave rise to growing conflicts with his father.

Henry the Younger had earlier been anointed as co-king and after his death Richard expected to be similarly recognized. However, Henry II refused to formally invest his son with the throne and gave reason to further dissension by demanding that he give control of Aquitaine to his youngest brother, John, while accepting Anjou and Normandy as a substitute. The duke refused to cede any part of the duchy, withdrawing from his father's court to prepare for war. In June 1184 John invaded Aquitaine in a largely punitive raid. When Henry II learned of the attack he ordered both sons to England, where an uneasy peace was restored.

In early 1185 Richard departed from England to Poitou and again assumed control of Aquitaine. However, he was soon engaged in a private war with his brother, Geoffrey, on the border of Brittany. In April the English king crossed the Channel to Normandy and, to end his son's disobedience, demanded Richard transfer authority for Aquitaine to Queen Eleanor. The duke was forced to comply, returning to his father's household in Rouen. Richard spent the next year with the Plantagenet court, taking no major role in the government of the Angevin demesne but playing the part of the obedient son.

In April 1186 Henry II returned to England, ordering Richard to assemble an army to invade the fiefdom of Toulouse and subdue its rebellious count, Raymond V. By the autumn the county of Quercy had been seized from the count and, with the end of the campaigning season, the Angevin troops withdrew to winter quarters. Raymond V appealed to his French overlord for protection but the new king, Philip II, waited until the following year before sending his soldiers against the Plantagenet lands, which allowed the Aquitaine forces an unfettered opportunity to renew their campaign into the lordship. When the French finally launched their encroachment Richard thwarted their attack, compelling Philip II to negotiate a truce with the duke, maintaining control of his conquest. The successful war against Toulouse and the Capet crown continued to demonstrate to the courts of Europe Richard's military skills, enhancing his reputation as an independent commander.

The kings of France had been waging war against their Norman retainers since the tenth century and Philip II remained determined to impose his rightful kingship over the western princedoms. To contend the independence and disobedience of his vassal, Henry II, the Capet overlord began to plot to gain the favor of Richard, meeting with him in friendship. However, the two rivals were soon again at war when the recalcitrant Aquitaine barons rebelled against Angevin control, seeking the military intervention of the French. In support of the rogue Aquitaine warlords' revolt, in June 1188 the Capet crown invaded the county of Berry and the duchy of Normandy. The Plantagenet sovereign responded by personally commanding an army to defend his duchy while Richard was ordered to drive Philip II out of Berry. The incursions were quickly contained in both theatres and, after protracted talks, a truce was arranged. During the deliberations Philip II again began to intrigue with Richard, attempting to form a joint alliance against Henry II by pledging his support for the duke's succession to the Angevin monarchy. The Aquitaine duke accepted the offer, rendering homage to the French throne and preparing his forces for war. In the spring additional negotiations to find a permanent peace were made under the sponsorship of the Holy See but Henry II again refused to recognize Richard as his heir.

In June 1189 the allies, who were joined by many rebellious Angevin barons, launched an invasion against Maine, quickly overwhelming the county. When the Plantagenet monarch attempted to counter the loss of his fiefdom, his army was defeated at Le Mans, forcing his retreat to Chinon with only a few remaining soldiers and supporters. On July 3 the two kings and Richard met where Henry II submitted to the terms dictated by Philip II, agreeing to formally acknowledge his eldest son as heir to his entire demesne in both England and France. Three days later Henry II, suffering from a persistent fever and totally exhausted from his years of near constant warfare, died. Richard I was readily recognized as king of England and duke of Normandy and Aquitaine.

During the years Richard had been struggling with his father to gain his rightful inheritance, in the Kingdom of Jerusalem the Saracen warlord, Saladin, had destroyed the crusader army at Hattin in July 1187 and by October, with the capture of the Holy City, had virtually conquered the Christian realm. When news of the loss of Jerusalem reached the papacy, Pope Gregory VIII immediately issued decrees calling for a new holy war to re-impose Christian overlordship. Henry II met with his eldest son at Le Mans where they agreed to participate in the expedition with the French sovereign. Richard had earlier taken the cross and was eager to begin preparations for the crusade when the sporadic war with Philip II again erupted. However, in July 1189, with his suzerainty over the Angevin Empire secured and peace established with the Capetian crown, he was again ready to initiate the campaign. The Plantagenet family had a tradition of supporting the crusading movement, beginning with the great-grandfather of Richard I, who had been overlord of the Jerusalem Kingdom, and his mother, who had joined the Second Crusade. After installing his governing councils for his French lands, the monarch sailed to England in August. He was enthusiastically welcomed by the population as his court made a slow progression to London, where on September 3 Richard I was formally anointed as king to complete the succession to his father's demesne. With his rule freely acknowledged he began the difficult task of raising the huge sums of money that would be necessary to finance his participation in the Third Crusade. A special tax levy, the Saladin Tithe, had previously been issued and in addition to this revenue Richard I readily sold titles, offices, city charters and estates to generate funds. Huge quantities of war provisions were collected, arrangements were made for a fleet and the army recruited and mobilized. To administer England in his absence two lieutenant generals were appointed; one for the north and the other to govern over the south. In December Richard I crossed the Channel to Normandy, pressing his final preparations. In early July 1190 he met Philip II at Vezelay and together they marched to Lyon, where the French troops traveled separately to Genoa while the English advanced to Marseilles for the sea voyage to Acre in the Latin Kingdom.

At the Mediterranean port of Marseilles Richard I expected to find his navy waiting, but the ships failed to appear and he was forced to advance slowly by rented vessels and overland down the Italian coast to the previously agreed assembly point of Messina, Sicily, arriving on September 22. After an initial friendly welcome by the island's new ruler, Tancred, relations between the two kings quickly deteriorated. Richard I's sister, Joan, had been married to the former sovereign of Sicily but he had recently died and when her brother demanded the return of her dowry and inheritance Tancred refused. Conveniently for the Plantagenet monarch the population of Messina soon attacked his troops and he countered by ordering the seizure of the town to hold as ransom. The Sicilian overlord was compelled to agree to pay Joan's bequest and a peace treaty was quickly ratified. The crusaders were forced to spend an uneasy six months on the island due to the frequency of winter storms in the Mediterranean Sea and were not able to sail to Acre until early April 1191. Philip II left Messina in late March with the English following the next week.

During the voyage to the Crusader Kingdom, the English fleet became dispersed by a late seasonal gale and three of the vessels were lost near Cyprus. When Richard I arrived at the island he quickly became involved in a dispute with the local king, Isaac Comnenus, who held the crews from the wrecked ships for ransom. The crusaders mounted an attack against the Cypriot army and when Guy of Lusignan, the deposed ruler of Jerusalem, arrived with reinforcements from Acre the island was soon conquered and Isaac expelled. English governors were appointed to administer the kingdom and Richard I sailed on June 6, landing at Acre two days later. The rapid capture of Cyprus secured the crusaders' lines of communication while providing a useful base of food supplies for operations in the Latin Kingdom.

Prior to departing for the Christian Kingdom, on May 12, 1191, Richard I was married in the Cypriot Chapel of Saint George to Berengaria, the daughter of King Sancho VI of Navarre. The political union with the northern Spanish kingdom gave the Plantagenet crown a highly useful ally on its southern border and a source of troops to be utilized against rebelling warlords in Aquitaine. She was described by contemporaries as a queen of beauty, nobility and wisdom. Soon after their marriage Berengaria traveled to Acre, staying in the Crusader realm during Richard I's military campaigns. During the time in the Holy Land the monarch and his wife became estranged and never fully reconciled, as each lived separate lives. The marriage produced no issue, which gave cause to claims of Richard I's homosexuality, though no supporting evidence was ever found. He did have at least one adulterous affair, resulting in an illegitimate son, Lord Philip of Cognac.

When the English army arrived at Acre they were warmly welcomed by the local Christian soldiers and the forces of Philip II, who had taken personal command of the expedition. The ongoing Acre investment had been previously initiated by Guy of Lusignan, but he lacked the military might to seize the stronghold. After taking charge of the stalemated siege the French overlord had spent the last month preparing his troops for an assault against the castle but had waited for the English to make a combined attack. Relations between the two kings had been strained at Sicily and deteriorated still further when Richard I offered to pay more to all willing to join his army. Their rivalry was intensified when the Plantagenet commander attempted to begin independent negotiations with Saladin, the leader of the Saracens, while their discord was made worse by the illnesses of both rulers. As the contention deepened, the holy warriors continued their offensive operations, finally breaching the defensive walls forcing the Acre garrison to surrender on July 11.

Soon after the occupation of the fortified port, the disputes between Richard I and Philip II again erupted. The Capet king was anxious to return to his realm to renew the campaign of expansion of his demesne into western France and utilized the triumph at Acre as just cause to abandon the holy war, sailing for home in early August. After the departure of Philip II, the sole command of the crusade was quickly assumed by Richard I. He was impatient to begin the march to Jerusalem, but Saladin continually delayed implementing the terms of the Acre surrender. After ten days of waiting it became certain that the Moslems were not going to honor the treaty. The crusaders had to determine the disposition of the approximately 2500 Acre captives who could not be cared for and guarded or released to rejoin the Saracens. A war council was assembled where they agreed that the only option available was the mass murder of the hostages, which was carried out over a three-day period.

With the elimination of the prisoners Richard I was finally ready to begin his campaign to Jerusalem, leaving on August 22 on the coastal road to Jaffa. The line of march was designed to give maximum protection to the slow-moving baggage train, which was positioned on the seaward flank with the cavalry and infantry on the landward side. Soon after leaving the security of Acre the crusaders came under the harassing sorties of Saladin, however, Richard I refused to allow his men-at-arms to counterattack. The advance was made difficult not only by the constant assaults of the Saracens but also from the lack of food and water and the intense heat, which caused the death of many soldiers. As Richard I approached the town of Arsuf, Saladin drew his troops into battle formation, launching an attack to block the approaches to Jaffa. Again the Plantagenet commander refused to permit his forces to respond, but as the Moslem onslaught intensified two knights broke ranks and charged. Richard I responded by ordering a counter-assault, which broke the Saracen sally, driving them from the battlefield. After a brief day's rest the crusaders resumed their holy war, reaching the strategic seaport of Jaffa, which was quickly fortified with walls and ditches. With the capture of the town the English king secured a base of operations that could be easily re-supplied from the sea and allowed direct access to Jerusalem.

The crusaders spent the next months consolidating their conquest while Richard I began negotiations with the Saracen leader, demanding the return of the Holy City. During the course of the deliberations with Al-Adil, the brother of Saladin, the two rivals developed a cordial relationship, becoming friends. When the ultimatum for Jerusalem was rejected the king softened his advance by proposing the marriage of his widowed sister, Joan, to Al-Adil, with the two ruling Jerusalem and the recently conquered coast as co-sovereigns. However, Joan refused to marry a Moslem and the offer was withdrawn. The talks were continued but no resolution could be found.

After the failed peace deliberations, in late November Richard I revived his war initiative to capture the Holy City. Marching through winter rains the crusaders came to within fifteen miles of the city when he halted the army's advance, calling a council of war with his senior commanders. The strength of his forces had been severely weakened during the march to Jaffa and by the renewed harassing attacks of Saladin against his exposed lines of communications. With his military might already depleted and with many of his remaining troops also pilgrims who planned to return home after the seizure of Jerusalem Richard I believed that he could not hold the city if captured. Given the reality of the military situation, he ordered a withdrawal back to Jaffa.

Upon arriving on the coast the crusader leader departed to Acre, leaving his army at Jaffa, where the immediate countryside was occupied and fortified with a series of strongholds. From the north new negotiations were begun with the Saracens and an accord in principal was arranged. During the spring Saladin delayed ratifying the treaty, which would have partitioned Jerusalem into separate Moslem and Christian zones and allow the retention of the already conquered coastal towns. However, when Richard I received news that his presence was needed in England to protect his sovereignty against the encroachments of his brother, John, and as the talks with the Moslems remained at an impasse, he became resolved to make another attempt to capture Jerusalem. The decision was greeted by the crusaders with great enthusiasm and preparations were quickly made. Returning to his base camp at Jaffa the Christians set out on June 7 for the Holy City, arriving at Beit Nuba five days later, where a forward base of operations was established for the final assault. However, as the Saracens renewed their harrying sorties, the campaign began to bog down. With the advance stalled dissension soon broke out in the army, with the French knights demanding an immediate attack against Jerusalem and the English king increasingly doubtful about the prospects for success and concerned about exposing his forces to ruin. A war council was appointed, where the decision was made to again abandon the initiative and withdraw to the coast. On July 5 the disheartened crusaders began their march after coming to within twelve miles of their goal.

Soon after arriving in Jaffa Richard I renewed his negotiations with the Saracens through Al-Adil. As the talks continued, in July 1192 the English monarch returned to Acre, leaving a small garrison to defend the fortified town. With the major body of the army in the north, Saladin seized the opportunity to launch an assault against Jaffa, quickly capturing the outer defensive works. Messengers were sent to Richard I and he immediately collected a small force of knights and infantry, sailing south on July 31st arriving at the fortified port the next morning. The crusaders immediately attacked and were joined by the garrison troops to drive the Moslems from the city. Saladin launched a counter-sortie five days later but he was driven off after two days of hard fighting, with Richard I energetically leading the charge.

While the Plantagenet monarch remained in the south, new negotiations were initiated through Al-Adil. Finally in early September a three-year truce was ratified, which allowed Christian pilgrims unfettered access to the holy sites in Jerusalem and the retention of the captured coastal cities and surrounding countryside. With the agreement finalized on October 9, 1192, Richard I left the Holy Land, never to return. Before departing from Acre he established a new ruling government with Henry, count of Champagne, as the king of the reborn Kingdom of Jerusalem. The Third Crusade failed in its primary objective to free the Holy City from Moslem occupation, but Richard I reestablished a large part of the former realm, which remained under Christian control for much of the next one hundred years.

Richard I sailed for France at the beginning of the winter storm season and as his ship approached the northern Adriatic coast, it was caught in a gale and wrecked. As the king made his way overland through southern Germany, he was seized by the local duke, Leopold of Austria. The duke had been a part of the German contingent at the Acre siege and had developed a hostile relationship with Richard I. When Leopold learned of Richard I's presence in his lands, he took the opportunity to gain his revenge for the Plantagenet's prior insults by holding him for ransom. However, his overlord, the German emperor, Henry VI, claimed custody when informed of Richard I's capture. The Plantagenet sovereign was transferred to the emperor, who demanded the payment of a huge indemnity, which was slowly collected in England and the Angevin French fiefdoms. By January 1194 the required amount had been paid and he was freed, finally arriving in England in March.

While the Plantagenet overlord had remained in the Kingdom of Jerusalem, Philip II had returned to France, renewing his attacks against the Angevin Empire. He had seized the Vexin county and much of eastern Normandy prior to Richard I's release from captivity. In England the brother of the sovereign, John, had openly rebelled, occupying several castles in the northern lordships. After learning of the payment of the king's ransom, many of the rogue earls surrendered before his return. Upon landing on the east coast Richard I immediately initiated a campaign against the few isolated dissidents, marching to seize the castle at Nottingham, which had continued to defy his authority. On March 25 the fortress was attacked and, after bringing up siege engines, the defenders capitulated. The remaining rebels were quickly overcome and, following the end of the revolt, he traveled to Winchester, summoning his barons and prelates to formally acknowledge his monarchy and government. On April 17, in a grand and elaborate ceremony, Richard I appeared before his vassals in full royal regalia to signify his unquestioned assumption of power. After imposing his authority over England he sent troops into Wales to regain his lost suzerainty and friendly relations with Scotland were renewed when William I offered homage for his northern English fiefdoms. With his kingship secured Richard I prepared to leave for France to regain his lost lands, appointing the archbishop of Canterbury, Hubert Walter, his regent before sailing in May.

After landing in Normandy the Plantagenet army launched its attack in the south against Philip II in Anjou and by the end of 1194 the county, along with Aquitaine, were back under Angevin control. After the loss of his southern conquests the French king agreed to a truce, which remained in place until the summer of the following year. With the expiration of the peace accord several months of sporadic warfare followed, where Richard I's forces regained the lordship of Berry and parts of Poitou. In December the two rivals again met to negotiate a permanent resolution. The Treaty of Louviers was ratified in January 1196, which gave the Angevin overlord most of his father's former demesne, but the French retained the Vexin countship and sections of eastern Normandy.

With the peace restored to his borders, in April Richard I began to conspire to gain control over the dukedom of Brittany by demanding custody of the young heir, his nephew Arthur. However, the Breton lords had regained a large measure of local autonomy during the sovereign's prolonged absence on the crusade, rebelling against his intervention. Arthur was secretly taken to the court of Philip II, where he was given sanctuary. Richard I claimed that the French had broken the Treaty of Louviers and began construction of a large castle at Gaillard, which would protect the approaches to Rouen. By July the fighting had resumed as the Plantagenet overlord seized several fortified towns. With the renewal of the conflict Richard I began a diplomatic initiative to secure allies to encircle and isolate the Capet crown. An agreement was reached with Raymond VI of Toulouse whereby his private militia was to join the war against Philip II while the English regime agreed to abandon its claim of suzerainty over his county. Military alliances were also forged with the count of Boulogne and Baldwin IX of Flanders. With his coalition in place the Plantagenet king began to prepare for a decisive assault by bringing troops from England and hiring additional mercenaries. During the first half of 1197 the Angevins were engaged in only limited sporadic skirmishes. However, in August Baldwin IX mounted an attack against the French city of Arras. When Philip II advanced to the relief of the garrison, his army was defeated and he was compelled to agree to a truce, acknowledging the loss of additional lands.

After ratifying the peace accord Richard I continued to strengthen his military might by bringing additional levies from England and in July 1198 secured an additional ally to further isolate the Capet crown when his nephew and friend, Otto of Brunswick, was elected as the new king of Germany. In September the truce was broken by Baldwin IX's capture of the castle at Saint-Omer. The initial encounter quickly led to a retaliatory raid into Normandy by the French and Richard I took to the field, seizing several border fortifications. After an indecisive series of limited engagements, a new armistice was again ratified.

Despite the occasional eruption of fighting the agreement remained unbroken and in early 1199 the peace treaty was renewed as both rivals agreed to a five-year extension under papal-sponsored negotiations. With his borders secured Richard I took the opportunity to travel south to Aquitaine and reimpose his sovereignty. While he stayed in Chinon the viscount of Limoges rebelled against Angevin overlordship and Richard I quickly mounted a campaign against the rogue strongholds to enforce his will. At the castle of Chalus the garrison refused to surrender and was personally placed under siege by the Plantagenet king. He remained actively engaged on the battlefield. While during a sortie Richard I was struck in the left shoulder by the bolt from a crossbow. The wound was deep and in the following days gangrene set in, as he grew increasingly weak. Richard I died on April 6, 1199, at age forty-two and with a reign of ten years. Before his death he acknowledged his brother, John, as successor to the Angevin Empire.

JOHN, 1167–1199–1216

In early April 1199 John succeeded to the Plantagenet crown of England and the Angevin Empire when his older brother, King Richard I, was killed during siege operations against a rebellious vassal. John was born in the evening of December 24, 1167, at Oxford and was the fifth son of Henry II and Eleanor of Aquitaine. Soon after his birth he was taken to France and placed under the custody of the abbey of Fontevrault, remaining for the next six years with little personal contact with his father or mother. In July 1174 the Plantagenet prince joined the monarch in his English household, where he gained his first exposure to court life and politics. Returning to France John was soon put under the care of his eldest brother, Henry the Younger, where his academic and military training was begun. In 1182 he crossed the Channel to England, becoming a part of the family of Henry II's chief judicial official and advisor, Ranulf de Glanvill, where his formal education was renewed and expanded. Glanvill appointed prominent scholars and over the next three years John received intense instruction in Latin, religion, literature and law.

While the young Plantagenet lord was in England, his brothers rebelled against Henry II, attempting to establish their own independent realms. John remained loyal to his father and was rewarded with the grant of several small fiefdoms and castles in England and France. In June 1183 Henry the Younger died, advancing the second son, Duke Richard of Aquitaine, into the role of successor designate. The king demanded that his new heir relinquish his personal control over Aquitaine and transfer the duchy to John. Richard refused to obey his father's command and John was ordered to raise an army to seize the region. In August 1184 he invaded the county of Poitou, but after pillaging the countryside, his troops were compelled to withdraw when confronted with the superior military skills and might of Richard. As the Aquitaine warlord continued his attacks, Henry II intervened to force a peace between his sons, allowing Richard to retain Aquitaine and appointing John to a lordship in Ireland.

In 1170, acting under royal charter issued by Henry II, English barons had begun the conquest of Ireland by seizing control of Dublin and the eastern coastline. In the following year the king received acknowledgement from the victorious invaders as their overlord. To expand the domains of the crown and establish a private fiefdom for himself, in the spring of 1185 John sailed to Ireland with a large expeditionary army. However, the local Irish warlords refused to engage in open battle, causing the Plantagenet prince to withdraw in frustration, having gained neither glory nor new territory. Early in 1186 John returned to his father's English court with his plans for subjugation in shatters. Nevertheless his fortunes were soon revived with the death of his second brother, Geoffrey of Brittany.

In August 1186 Geoffrey was killed in a jousting tournament and John became second in line for the throne. The death of the Brittany duke resulted in a re-distribution of Henry II's demesne, which expanded the inheritance of the youngest son at the expense of Richard. The Plantagenet heir became enraged at the reduction of his birthright, revolting against his father and forming an alliance with the French crown. In the ensuing war the allies invaded the Angevin Empire, defeating the English king and compelling him to accept their terms. Soon after his son's triumph, in July 1189 Henry II died, exhausted from the many years of campaigning, and was succeeded by Richard I. Late in his brother's rebellion John had joined his cause and readily offered homage to the new monarch.

John was married in August 1189 to Isabella of Gloucester, the daughter of William, earl of Gloucester. The union had been arranged by Henry II thirteen years earlier to provide estates for his youngest son. John and Isabella were ill-suited to each other, spending little time together and living in separate households. During their marriage John was repeatedly unfaithful to his wife, having numerous mistresses and illegitimate children. In 1200 he divorced Isabella to marry Isabella of Angouleme in a political arrangement that gained the Plantagenet throne a strategic Poitou lordship in Aquitaine. The union resulted in five children, including the future successor, Henry III.

After recognizing Richard I's kingship, in late 1189 John sailed with the royal court to England, where his brother was beginning to raise huge sums of money and mobilize and equip an army for the Third Crusade against Jerusalem. As Richard I began his preparations a regency government was established to rule during his absence, but John was denied any appointment to the new administration. Instead he was granted the Norman countship of Mortain, taxes from six English counties, and numerous lesser fiefdoms and ordered to leave England for three years.

In July 1190 the king departed for the Kingdom of Jerusalem while John settled on his Norman lands. However, he soon began to intrigue against Richard I's Plantagenet regents, influencing his mother to intercede on his behalf to sponsor his return to England. Late in the year the Mortain count landed in England and immediately began to conspire with the local dissident barons. John quickly established himself as the leader of the opposition faction, threatening to plunge the realm into civil war. When Richard I learned of the deteriorating political situation, he dispatched the archbishop of Rouen as the new viceroy with full powers to rule in his name. Under the forceful leadership of the prelate, order was restored as the rebellious warlords deserted John, pledging their allegiance to their absent overlord.

With his plans for territorial aggrandizement thwarted, in 1191 the Mortain count crossed the Channel to Normandy and began to plot with the French king, Philip II, to usurp Richard I's continental possessions. John forged an alliance with the Capet regime after the English monarch was captured and held for ransom in Germany on his way home from the crusade. Under the terms of their accord the army of France invaded Normandy while John attempted to raise a revolt in England. However, in February 1194 Richard I was released from his imprisonment and the Mortain lord was compelled to end his conspiracy and seek reconciliation for his acts of treason. John met his brother in Normandy where he was pardoned, though his numerous lordships and castles were forfeited. The disgraced and landless prince became a part of the Plantagenet court, joining the Angevin army in the war against the Capet crown for control of western France. He remained loyal to the throne and was rewarded for his military services in 1195 with reinstatement to the countship of Mortain. While the sporadic conflict against Philip II wore on, John continued to support his brother's cause but unexpected events in early 1199 propelled him to the suzerainty of the Angevin Empire.

In April 1199 Richard I was in Aquitaine at Chinon when the viscount of Limoges revolted against Plantagenet sovereignty. He quickly mobilized a local army, marching to re-impose his authority. The viscount's castle of Chalus was placed under siege; however, during the assault Richard I was fatally wounded, appointing John as his successor to the Angevin Empire before his death. Soon after learning that his brother was dead, the heir designate advanced to Normandy where he was readily acknowledged as duke. While he remained in Rouen, a small faction of Richard I's former English advisors agreed to offer the monarchy to the Plantagenet prince. On May 27, 1199, John was anointed king of England in Westminster Abbey as the Church, nobility and shires accepted his inheritance to the crown.

While John was freely recognized as overlord in England, Normandy and Aquitaine, the remaining princedoms in the Angevin Empire gave homage to Arthur, the young son of Geoffrey of Brittany. After securing his English sovereignty the Plantagenet king sailed to France to enforce his birthright. However, while he was occupied with the imposition of his reign over the rebellious vassals, Philip II attempted to take advantage of the internal turmoil and uncertainty to renew his war of expansion. The Capetian regime mounted an aggressive campaign into eastern Normandy, seizing much of the region. By May 1200 the conflict had evolved into a stalemate and the two rivals met at Le Goulet to find a reconciliation. Under the terms of the ensuing treaty John was recognized as the successor to Richard I's continental fiefdoms, Arthur was granted Brittany as the vassal of the Plantagenet crown and the French were ceded the Norman countship of Vexin. Despite agreeing to Arthur's assumption of the Breton duchy, when he returned to claim his lands, the young lord was seized by retainers of his uncle and later murdered while John retained direct control over the lordship. While the French throne accepted the aggrandizement of Brittany, the peace was soon broken with John's political marriage to the daughter of the count of Angouleme.

Several months after his settlement with France, John divorced his first wife to marry Isabella of Angouleme. The union with the strategic county in the heartland of Aquitaine brought him an influential ally and friend while enhancing his presence and prestige among the frequently recalcitrant local warlords. However, in 1202 the lord of Lusignan appealed to Philip II, claiming he had been previously betrothed to Isabella and that John had falsely charged him with treason. The Capetian king was anxious to renew the war against the Angevin Empire and as John's overlord for his continental lands, summoned him to Paris to answer the accusations. The Plantagenet sovereign refused to appear at court, thereby forfeiting his French possessions under feudal law.

In the summer of 1202 Philip II launched his armies against northern Normandy, capturing numerous towns and castles while in the southern Angevin Empire the Capetian allies mounted successful attacks into Anjou and Touraine. As the French were gaining victories, John established his court in Maine and sent envoys to England to raise additional cavalry, foot soldiers and money to defend his demesne. In July, with his forces reinforced, he led his troops into Anjou, reasserting his authority over large parts of the county. With the loss of his offensive's momentum in the south, Philip II abandoned his recent Norman conquests, withdrawing to the French border. The war continued into the autumn with a stalemate soon developing. However, during the winter, Philip II succeeded in forging an alliance with numerous lords in Anjou and Brittany to strengthen his campaign against the Plantagenet regime. In early 1203, as the conflict was renewed, the Capet soldiers again marched against Normandy while the Bretons advanced into the southern Norman region and large sections of western Aquitaine rose in revolt. With his military resources dispersed throughout the area, John was unable to thwart the allies' invasions. Philip II made steady progress in the north and in March 1204 seized the great castle at Gaillard, the key defensive barrier to Rouen, despite a combined naval and land relief attempt engineered by John. With the loss of Gaillard, support for the Angevin cause dissolved and by early summer all of Normandy was under the French crown's control. After the collapse of the duchy John's remaining warlords in Maine, Anjou and Brittany soon deserted him to give fealty to Philip II. Eleanor of Aquitaine managed to retain the loyalty of many of the local seigneurs for her son. However, with her death in April 1204, the duchy was lost to the Angevin overlord. By the end of the year John's continental empire had been reduced to Calais and the small Gascony enclave on the southwest coast centered on Bordeaux.

The Plantagenet king had stayed in England during the final phases of the ongoing French war funneling money, war stores and troops to the continent. With the loss of his lands he remained determined to regain his Angevin Empire and in 1205 initiated measures to return to France. To protect eastern England from a cross–Channel attack, under the crown's direction the navy was reorganized and enlarged while the coastal defenses were reinforced and a permanent royal army created. By the summer of 1206, with his shoreline secured, John was prepared to mount a campaign against the French. He landed his forces at La Rochelle and, after collecting mercenary soldiers, launched an assault into Poitou and Anjou, capturing the fortified city of Angers. However, as John advanced north his offensive drive lost momentum and he was compelled in October to negotiate a two-year truce with Philip II, with the Plantagenets retaining their recent conquests.

After imposing his sovereignty in Gascony and in parts of Poitou, John departed to England to continue his diplomatic and military campaign to revive the Angevin Empire. When he inherited the English crown in 1199, the monarch had re-appointed the archbishop of Canterbury, Hubert Walter, as his chief minister. The prelate was an energetic and capable administrator who had been largely responsible for raising the vast sums of revenue that the regime needed to finance the French wars and had acted as regent in the king's absences. However, in July 1205 Walter died and the throne's choice of a replacement to the archbishopric of Canterbury resulted in a serious breach with the papacy.

After the death of archbishop Walter, in late 1205, disregarding the throne and existing precedent, the Canterbury monks chose their sub–Prior Reginald as the new primate. To secure the legality of their selection, he was sent to Rome for confirmation from Pope Innocent III. When John learned of the clerics' actions, he demanded the appointment of his friend and advisor, John de Gray, as the new archbishop. As the dissension grew the Holy See intervened, ordering new elections and proposing its own candidate, Stephen Langton. In late 1206, under papal instructions, the Canterbury clerics elected Langton to the archbishopric. In June of the following year Langton was installed as the chief prelate and John responded by confiscating the estates of Canterbury in defiance of the See of Rome. The conflict escalated further when the papacy declared an indiction against England and excommunicated the king. The pope's actions were soon followed by the Plantagenet crown's seizure of all Church properties and revenues.

While the crisis with Innocent III remained unresolved, in 1209 John initiated measures to fully protect his borders with Scotland. The Scottish king, William I, had long pressed his birthright to the northern English counties of Northumbria and Cumbria and had encouraged his Lowland warlords to pillage the cross-border lordships. To impose his authority John assembled a formidable English army, marching north with the objective of invading Scotland. However, at the approach of the Plantagenet forces, William I, who lacked the finances and military means to resist the attack, offered to negotiate a peaceful settlement. The two monarchs met at Norham, where the Scots agreed to pay a large indemnity and abandon their claims against the English lands.

In 1210 after the successful intervention against Scotland, John became determined to assert his full feudal authority over the rebellious Plantagenet lords of Ireland. In 1171, after conquering eastern Ireland and offering homage to Henry II, the English barons had largely ignored the royal government, creating numerous nearly autonomous private princedoms. In June 1210 John sailed to Ireland with an army of English knights and mercenary soldiers to subdue his vassals. After establishing his court at Dublin, he marched against his recalcitrant warlords, easily compelling their submission with the might of his military. The ruthlessness and determination of the campaign ensured his Irish-Anglo retainers remained loyal for the balance of his reign.

As the Plantagenet throne was imposing its sovereignty in Scotland and Ireland, the Welsh prince, Llewelyn, had secured his supremacy over the northern fiefdom of Gwynedd. He had earlier given fealty to John, but with the English occupied with foreign campaigns, he revolted to gain his independence. Soon after his return from Ireland the king invaded Wales, but Llewelyn retreated into the mountains to harass the English army with small skirmishing attacks. Frustrated at the lack of success, the Plantagenets withdrew, mobilizing a sizable force of reinforcements for a second incursion. The Welsh rebels were unable to resist the might of the new assault and Llewelyn was compelled to sign a humiliating peace treaty, agreeing to an English occupation and the construction of new castles. Despite the regime's initial success, the loss of territory and national pride rallied the whole of Wales into a united rebellion as the Gwynedd prince formed an alliance with Maelgwyn of Deheubarth to drive John from his conquest and compel him to entirely abandon his campaign.

After returning from Poitou in October 1206 John had instituted a determined policy designed to secure and strengthen his English kingship to facilitate his future recovery of the lost Angevin demesne. However, the conflict with Pope Innocent III over the appointment to the archbishopric of Canterbury had remained unresolved. The papacy's indiction against England had been largely ignored by the royal court and in December 1212 the Holy See moved to increase the pressure on the Plantagenet regime by forming an alliance with Philip II of France for a combined papal–Franco invasion of England. In the summer of the following year the Capetian army began to assemble on the English Channel coast. As the threat of the intervention grew into reality, the English government intensified its negotiations with Innocent III, agreeing to terms previously proposed. On May 13 the papal legate accepted the offer and John pledged to recognize Langton as archbishop of Canterbury, to pay a large indemnity and become a vassal of the papacy for England and Ireland. With the dispute finally settled, the Pope withdrew his support for the cross–Channel attack, forcing Philip II to abandon the campaign. By offering his homage to the See of Rome, John had diplomatically thwarted the danger of invasion and gained an influential ally for his planned war against France.

With the dispute with the Holy See resolved, the papal indiction and excommunication bulls were withdrawn and John was free to negotiate a series of alliances for the campaign against Philip II. The Plantagenet court sent envoys to the Holy Roman emperor, Otto IV, who was eager to join the invasion against France to address past disputes. The count of Flanders and various dissident French warlords also agreed to join the growing coalition. In early 1214, prior to his cross–Channel departure to initiate the war, the king appointed the bishop of Winchester as his regent to govern with an advisory council of chief prelates. On February 2 he sailed for La Rochelle with an army comprised mostly of mercenaries and only a small contingent of English knights. John planned a large two-pronged assault against Philip II with the northern allies of Otto IV along with the rebel French magnates, attacking from Flanders while he marched toward Paris from the south. The Plantagenet forces landed in La Rochelle in late February and soon began the re-conquest of the southern Angevin countships, encountering little resistance from the local seigneurs who pledged fealty to their former sovereign. By June John had advanced north into Anjou, capturing the capital of Angers. After garrisoning the city he moved west to besiege the castle at La Roche-au-Moine. While the Plantagenets were detained with the investment, Philip II sent his son, Louis, into the Loire Valley to harass and obstruct the English encroachment. The delay at La Roche-au-Moine allowed Prince Louis the time to mobilize the local barons and together with his small complement of royal troops he launched an attack against John. At the approach of the French soldiers, the Poitou lords in the Plantagenet army refused to fight their former overlord, deserting the expedition. John was compelled to abandon his initiative, returning to La Rochelle in early July, surrendering all the gains of the southern war to Louis of Capet.

While the English were being driven back to La Rochelle, in Flanders the northern wing commanded by Otto IV mobilized for the campaign against Paris. In July the massed allied army began their march as Philip II was advancing north to contend the invasion with the main body of his troops. The two forces met at Bouvines on July 27 with the battle initiated by an attack against the French rearguard. Philip II quickly re-positioned his heavy cavalry, ordering a charge against Otto IV's right flank, which quickly broke the coalition's formation, causing the center of its line to collapse. The encounter was a decisive victory for the French king, securing his conquest of the Angevin Empire. The defeat at Bouvines forced John to come to terms with Philip II and in September he agreed to a five-year truce with the Capet regime, retaining all its territorial gains in western France. In October the Plantagenet sovereign returned to England to face the brewing storm of dissention from his increasingly rebellious barons.

When John sailed to France in February 1214, he had appointed the bishop of Winchester, Peter des Roches, to govern the kingdom. During the king's absence the bishop had maintained control over the English lords but his harsh administration was widely unpopular, which caused resentment to be directed against the royal council. During John's campaign of 1214 des Roches's government had met with increasing dissent from the northern earls over the imposition of new taxes to finance the Angevin re-conquest. The heavy appropriations imposed to wage war against a foreign realm where the English knights had little personal interest were a major cause of their coming rebellion. Prior to their overlord's return after the defeat at Bouvines, the warlords had formed an informal coalition, asking the crown to accept the liberties previously granted by Henry I and rule in the manner of the Anglo-Saxon kings by the consent of the nobility. Following his arrival from France in January 1215, the high magnates met with John in London to confirm their charter. However, the Plantagenet regime delayed giving any response and appealed to Pope Innocent III for his intervention. In April the Holy See issued a proclamation supporting the English throne, ordering the barons to pay the taxes. The league members responded by preparing for civil war.

At the end of April the rebel magnates assembled their troops, marching to confront the king. John sent emissaries to determine their demands but again he rejected their petition of liberties. Despite one final attempt to resolve the revolt through papal arbitration, in May the estates of the recalcitrant lords were forfeited to the crown, marking the beginning of the Barons' War.

The first hostilities of the civil war were initiated at Bedford in May as the rogue army advanced to London under the command of Robert fitz Walter. On May 17 the city gates were opened to the barons and the capital was occupied. The success at London encouraged additional nobles to join the conflict as the rebellion spread to the southwest and Midlands. As prospects for a wider war grew, the royal court dispatched the archbishop of Canterbury to forge a truce agreement, arranging for John to again meet personally with fitz Walter and his rebels. In early June the king traveled to Runnymede to begin reconciliation talks with his dissident vassals and through a series of negotiations regained the homage of the majority of them. The peace was to be guaranteed by the Great Charter or Magna Carta, which defined the civil liberties of all Englishmen and the feudal rights of the monarchy. To further ensure the end of the uprising, John agreed to replace numerous unpopular government officials and establish a committee of twenty-five barons to monitor and protect the interest of the nobility. However, not all of the English earls had agreed to the terms of the Charter and their combined dissent soon led to the renewal of the magnates' war.

After Runnymede a new alliance of rebel earls still not satisfied with the pledges of the king was organized and they began to fortify their castles in preparation for war. The dissidents in London refused to return the city to the crown's authority, intending to hold it until John fulfilled his promises. The conflict escalated further when rogue troops began to assemble around London as John recruited mercenary knights and infantry and petitioned Innocent III to annul the Charter. At the end of September the pope's revocation order was published in England, signaling the resumption of the Barons' War. The Plantagenet sovereign opened his offensive campaign by capturing the great stronghold at Rochester and numerous lesser fortresses were soon under his control as he aggressively pressed the attack. With the success of their revolt threatened, the barons appealed to Philip II of France, inviting his son, Louis, to usurp the English monarchy. While the coalition negotiated with the French court for its military intervention, John mounted a devastating assault against the northern rebels, destroying their fortifications and burning their lands. After its successful foray the royalists turned south to confront the expected arrival of Prince Louis and his French soldiers.

In May 1216 Louis of Capet landed unopposed in England and was quickly acknowledged as monarch by the dissident lords as they increasingly deserted John. By the end of the month London and the eastern counties had given homage to the Capetian heir. After gaining control over Winchester the Anglo-French forces marched north to besiege the port of Dover. By late August John's sovereignty had been reduced to only the western and Midland lordships. In the autumn he mobilized a new army of loyal earls and mercenaries, launching a well-planned counterattack, attempting to re-impose his authority by seizing the eastern earldoms. However, by October after raids against Lincoln and Norfolk he grew increasingly ill and weak from the effects of high fever and dysentery, dying at Newark Castle on October 18 at age forty-eight and after a reign of seventeen years. John was succeeded by his nine-year-old son, Henry III.

HENRY III, 1207–1216–1272

At the death of King John in October 1216, Henry III succeeded to the crown of England in the midst of a bloody civil war that threatened to destroy the Plantagenet dynasty. Henry was the first son of John and Queen Isabella of Angouleme and was born at Winchester on October 1, 1207. He spent his early years in the royal castles under the immediate care of a court-appointed governess. His education and military training were begun around the age of seven by prominent English scholars and knights. However, in the autumn of 1216 his father unexpectedly died and the nine-year-old Henry III inherited the kingdom of England.

At his ascension to the throne the young king was readily acknowledged as the rightful heir by only the western and Midland lordships, while the northern English counties were under the control of the local barons and the east coast and London swore fealty to Prince Louis of France. With his realm in shatters Henry III was anointed at Gloucester Cathedral on October 28, 1216, in the presence of his few supporting prelates and magnates. According to the wishes of his father, Henry III was placed in the immediate protection of the papal legate, Gualo, who provided for his continued education and care. The powerful office of regent was assumed by the able and experienced earl of Pembroke, William Marshal, who had faithfully served the three previous sovereigns. With the kingdom divided by civil war, to regain the loyalty of the dissident earls Marshal quickly enacted needed financial and judicial reforms and declared the administration's intention of ruling under the provisions of the Magna Carta. Many rebels abandoned the Anglo-French alliance, preferring the weak and uncertain central government of the regency period. With its military might bolstered by the defections and with the full support of the papacy, the Plantagenet regime under Marshal began the re-conquest of the occupied countships in the spring of 1217. While the Pembroke earl was assembling his army, the Anglo-French forces marched against the fortress at Lincoln after failing to seize the royal stronghold at Dover. In May the Plantagenet troops under the personal command of the regent counterattacked the French and their English allies at Lincoln. In the ensuing battle Louis was defeated and compelled to seek peace terms. In September the Treaty of Kingston was signed by the Capet prince who agreed to end his war and return to France for an indemnity while the English rogue warlords were reconciled to the crown for their pledges of homage.

The royal triumph at Lincoln signaled the end of the First Barons' War and the beginning of a phase of reunion. Under the spirited leadership of the Pembroke earl, order was generally restored to the realm, the king's justice was enforced and taxes collected. While Marshal was re-asserting the regime's prerogatives, Henry III remained under the protection of his tutors, taking little part in his kingdom's affairs. In 1219 William Marshal died and the regency's authority was now divided between the new papal legate, Pandulph, justiciar Hubert de Burgh and bishop Peter des Roches of Winchester. With the loss of the dominating Pembroke earl, a power vacuum developed in the court, creating an atmosphere for a weak and ineffective government. In the absence of a strong administration, baronial unrest once again renewed, threatening to disrupt the peace. The unity of the ruling directorate was further reduced in 1221 when Pandulph was recalled to Rome, causing open conflict between de Burgh and des Roches as they contended for total control of the crown's council. The justiciar formed a political faction with the archbishop of Canterbury, Stephen Langton, while the bishop of Winchester became allied with numerous dissident barons. De Burgh was able to impose his will and assume the regency with the aid of the chief prelate and his threats of excommunication. However, he continued to govern a rebellious England where the law was only maintained by frequent punitive expeditions.

In January 1227, at age nineteen, Henry III assumed the kingship free of any restrictions. To preserve the peace he broke with the former regent's practice of actively confronting the earls' rebellions and instituted a policy of conciliation and toleration with the nobility. The Magna Carta was re-issued, resulting in the acknowledgement by the crown that tax levies now required the consent of the magnates. With the barons temporarily pacified and the regime's authority respected, Henry III became determined to re-conquer the Plantagenet lordships in France that had been lost by his father and during the de Burgh administration. In 1227, to pursue the subjugation of the western French counties, the English government negotiated an alliance with Peter, duke of Brittany, and other dissident French warlords who were waging war against the Capet sovereign, Louis IX. The English king sent a small army under the command of his brother, Richard, to Gascony to join the war effort. However, the coalition was soon dissolved under pressure from the Capet attack and Richard could only secure a two-year armistice. At the expiration of the truce Henry III dispatched emissaries to the French court to discuss a permanent peace. However, no settlement could be found and in 1229 the throne began to assemble a large force of knights and foot soldiers for an expedition to Brittany in support of Duke Peter. In 1230 Henry III landed in western France, joining his troops with the Bretons. To press their campaign against Louis IX the allies launched an assault into Poitou but the incursion failed to achieve any significant gain as the local lords remained loyal to the French realm. In September the English abandoned the invasion in frustration, sailing home.

When Henry III assumed his personal kingship in 1227 he was physically described as of medium height with a stocky appearance and exhibited a generally friendly nature. He was a pious follower of the Church of Rome, a patron of the arts and letters and had proven his courage on the battlefield. However, the king had limited natural military or administrative aptitude, was weak-willed and a poor judge of character. He possessed little of the personal traits that had made his descendents great generals and skilled governors.

The cross–Channel expedition to Poitou had achieved little and had been a financially costly foreign invasion that was greatly resented by the English nobility. The king blamed his chief minister, de Burgh, for much of the mismanagement, threatening to charge him with treason. Their relationship deteriorated further over the issue of ecclesiastical prerogatives for the papacy. Henry III was devoted to the Holy See and fully supported its right to tax the English Church and appoint clerics to local benefices while de Burgh held the opposite populous position. The Plantagenet monarch disregarded the advice of his minister, allowing Rome to name its nominees to English religious positions. As the number of foreign-held church offices increased, there were riots against the pope's appointments. The throne's chief advisor was accused of involvement in the uprisings and Henry III dismissed him from the council, naming the bishop of Winchester, Peter des Roches, as his replacement.

The new minister was a Frenchman from Poitou and soon after assuming his office he selected his native Poitevins to positions in his new administration. There was an influx of foreigners rushing to des Roches's ministry in search of favors, royal appointments and honors as the Plantagenet government came increasingly under alien domination. The English nobles grew resentful at the loss of their participation in the court and in 1234 a coalition of English barons under the archbishop of Canterbury appealed to Henry III to expel the Poitevin faction from the realm. As the threat of rebellion grew he was forced to dismiss des Roches and his allies, attempting to rule independent of advisors.

As Henry III was attempting to solidify his administration, he was married to Eleanor, the daughter of Count Raymond IV of Provence, on January 20, 1236, at Canterbury Cathedral. The union was a political arrangement to foster a close connection to Louis IX of France, who was married to Eleanor's eldest sister. They proved to be well suited to each other, developing a happy and loving relationship. Eleanor became totally devoted to her husband, traveling to France to raise troops and money for his wars against the barons. It was through the queen's relationship with the Capet court that French literature, art and Gothic architecture developed in England. The marriage resulted in five surviving children, including the heir, Edward, born in 1239.

Soon after taking control of his government Henry III ignored the provisions of the Magna Carta and ruled without the advice or consent of his earls, in the manner that was currently popular on the continent. He began to fill his court with French officials, which alienated the regime from the nobility. The influx of foreign office seekers was further exasperated by the monarch's marriage to Eleanor of Provence. The new queen was the daughter of the French count, Raymond IV, and soon after the ceremony her many Provencal relatives flocked to her household, seeking favors and English lordships. Two of Eleanor's uncles received high positions in the Church while two others were appointed counselors to her husband. The demands from the many alien compatriots of Henry III's wife, his extravagant lifestyle and the many grants of money to the Church placed a severe strain on the royal treasury at a time when the throne was estranged from its principal sources of revenue. The English barons complained increasingly at their lack of representation and presence in the administration and their heavy tax burden.

As the dissent among the English earls slowly grew, Henry III again began to negotiate with rebel French warlords for a joint campaign against Louis IX to recover his aggrandized lordships in the western county of Poitou. In early 1242 the royal court attempted to raise money and soldiers from the English nobles for the continental war, but they refused to grant any new taxes or support his foreign invasion. The Plantagenet expeditionary force was compelled to sail to Gascony in May on the limited funds from the king's personal treasury, which placed the initiative's success in jeopardy due to the lack of supplies and troops. Landing at Royan Henry III joined his small army with the rogue barons under the command of Hugh of La Marche and together they marched into Poitou. On July 22 the allied advance guard encountered the French near the Charente River crossing in the city of Saint James. The Anglo-French deployed into battle formation, occupying the left bank of the river, expecting a frontal assault across the town's bridge. However, positioned on the opposite side, Louis IX quickly forded the river by boats and pontoon bridges, aggressively attacking the flank of the unsuspecting allies. In the ensuing battle of Taillebourg the Capet army overwhelmed the coalition, compelling its retreat to the city of Saintes. The French continued their assault, defeating Hugh, while the surviving English, including Henry III, escaped to the safety of Bordeaux. The Plantagenet king remained in Gascony until April 1243 before agreeing to a five-year truce and departing to England. The war in Poitou ended in total defeat, resulting in the loss of respect and prestige and an additional strain on the royal treasury.

While the French policies of the Plantagenet court had ended in failure, the crown achieved a measure of diplomatic success with the resolution of the ongoing marchland conflict with Scotland. The Treaty of York was personally negotiated between Henry III and the Scottish sovereign, Alexander II, to end the repeated attacks between the northern English earls and the Lowland warlords. Under the provisions of the accord the boundary between the two realms was established at the Tweed River and the Solway Firth and future cross-border forays were prohibited. Despite the terms of the settlement relations along the frontier continued to remain strained, with sporadic skirmishes. As the Northumbrian barons began to increasingly raid into the Lowlands, the Scots responded by initiating the construction of a network of castles along the border. With the threat of war escalating Henry III marched north with a large army to impose a permanent peace. However, an invasion of Scotland was averted by a hastily arranged meeting between the two kings where the Treaty of York was renewed and the détente was to be secured with the marriage between the Scottish heir and a daughter of Henry III. The English throne also agreed to respect the territorial limits and independence of Scotland.

While order had been ensured along the Scottish border, the Welsh had continued to resist English subjugation. Under the leadership of their warlords the Welsh launched forays into the marchlands and successfully defied the Plantagenet crown's attempts to impose its sovereignty. To end the border war in 1234 Henry III negotiated an agreement with the warring princes that produced a period of relative calm despite isolated skirmishes. However, the ongoing status quo was shattered in 1246 when the recognized Welsh overlord, David ap Llewelyn, died and, with the lack of a central authority, Henry III seized on the lack of an unified regime and army to mount an invasion to reassert his rule. Under the military might of his attack the local lords were forced to submit to the English under the Treaty of Woodstock and large sections of the eastern principality were annexed directly to the Plantagenet throne. Nevertheless, despite his initial success, as Henry III became increasingly occupied with the rebellion of his barons, the Welsh prince, Llewelyn, forged a series of alliances with the fiefdoms and by 1257 had driven the English occupiers from Wales. The Plantagenet court was compelled to recognize Llewelyn's dominion over the princedoms and confirm his title as prince of Wales and autonomous ruler. Wales was lost to the English until the reign of Edward I.

Throughout his monarchy Henry III remained submissive to the papacy, continuing to support its ecclesiastic rights to tax the English Church, and routinely sent large grants of money to Rome. In 1250 at the encouragement of Pope Innocent IV, the English monarch took the cross, declaring his intention of going on a crusade to recapture Jerusalem. In preparation for his holy war he began to collect large sums of money but at the request of the Roman Church, the funds were diverted to aid its conflict against the Hohenstaufen family for supremacy of Sicily. For his financial support Innocent IV appointed Henry III's second son, Edmund, as the king of Sicily. However, the kingdom still had to be conquered and for the military expedition the Plantagenet crown needed additional taxes from its nobles. In April 1258 Henry III summoned the Great Council of barons to Oxford to request a subsidy for his Sicilian campaign. The magnates under the leadership of Simon de Montfort, earl of Leicester, refused to grant any new levy and took the opportunity to put forward a series of reform measures. They demanded the court's foreign favorites be exiled and replaced with English lords, the appointment of a baronial council to control the realm's finances, the reorganization of the government and the formation of an interim committee to prepare a plan for the Great Council's approval in June. Henry III was overwhelmed by the determination and solidarity of his vassals and was forced to agree to all their conditions.

When the English magnates met in June they passed a charter of reforms known as the Provisions of Oxford. The measures placed various functions of the crown's government and the king's household directly under the control of baronial committees that were responsible to the Great Council and not the monarchy. The realm's chief advisors were to be appointed by and responsible to the nobles. The kingdom was to be administered by a permanent council led by Simon de Montfort that was to rule in the name of the monarch. Lacking the financial support and military means to resist the earls, Henry III was compelled to reluctantly accept the new charter. However, the Provisions soon proved too cumbersome and ineffective, resulting in internal dissent among the warlords. While the earl of Leicester and his advisors struggled to restore order and the law, rebellions erupted in numerous lordships as Henry III began to plot to regain his lost prerogatives. He utilized his cordial and close relationship with the papacy to induce Pope Urban IV to absolve the Provisions of Oxford and in January 1264 Louis IX was persuaded to arbitrate the growing conflict, finding in the king's favor. As the Plantagenet throne began to slowly restore its authority the barons responded with civil war.

As rebellion spread throughout his realm, in March 1264 Henry III summoned his loyal vassals to assemble at Oxford while the dissidents mobilized their militia at Northampton. In April the Plantagenet troops scored the first victory of the renewed Barons' War by capturing Northampton while Simon de Montfort, with his main force, was subduing the south. Despite the initial success, on May 14 the royal army was decisively defeated at Lewes in Sussex where Henry III and his heir, Edward, were captured. With the seizure of the king a rebel council took control of the government, headed by de Montfort. Henry III was placed under house arrest and his sovereignty reduced to the status of figurehead monarch. To solidify his usurpation and gain the support of the English towns and counties, the Leicestser earl convened a meeting of an enlarged Great Council or Parliament, which included church officials, shire knights, and burgesses from each large city, in addition to the high lords. However, the new representative form of government alienated many of the leading barons, who deserted the administration to return to the royalist party. Henry III's rising fortunes were further revived in May 1265 when the warrior-prince, Edward, escaped from captivity to assume authority over his father's restoration campaign. Under the command of the charismatic warlord, many of the nobles flocked to the Plantagenet banner and on August 4, 1265, the rogues were decisively destroyed at Evesham and de Montfort killed. The triumph at

Evesham enabled Henry III to reimpose his unfettered kingship and over the next two years he aggressively pursued the remnants of the revolt. In the summer of 1267 Edward subdued the last of the dissenters at Ely to end the Second Barons' War.

With his authority recovered Henry III revoked the limitations placed on his power by the Provisions of Oxford and returned to his form of absolute rule. The surviving members of the rebellion were hunted down and their lands forfeited to the throne. Following the victory over the barons the governing of the kingdom was increasingly assumed by Prince Edward and, under his capable administration, law and order were re-imposed and the crown's finances put on a firm footing. After reestablishing his sovereignty, in 1267 the king authorized the issuance of the Treaty of Marlboro, which placed certain restrictions on his prerogatives in favor of the nobility. Henry III devoted his last years to the construction of the new abbey at Westminster, which was completed in 1269. By 1272 he had grown frail and weak from age and the years of combating his recalcitrant earls. Henry III died on November 16, 1272, at age 65 and after a reign of 56 years to be succeeded by his heir, Edward I.

Edward I, 1239–1272–1307

At the death of King Henry III in November 1272, his eldest son, Edward, succeeded to the throne of England while returning home from a crusade to the Kingdom of Jerusalem. Edward was the oldest surviving issue of Henry III and Queen Eleanor of Provence and was born on June 17, 1239, in London at the Westminster Palace. He was named after Edward III the Confessor, who was the patron saint of his father. Soon after his birth a separate household was established for the infant prince at Windsor Castle. Edward spent his childhood with his brothers, sisters and the children of other noble families in the pious and cultured Plantagenet court. He grew up in a loving and caring environment, developing a deep and enduring affection for his parents. Tutors were provided from the royal court for his education and he received instruction in reading, writing, Latin, French, the arts and sciences. However, the focus of the training was the development of his military skills. Around the age of seven Edward began his preparation for knighthood under the guidance of experienced masters of arms, where he learned to use the lance and sword while becoming proficient in archery and horsemanship.

In 1249 Edward was granted the southwestern French duchy of Gascony, but he remained in England while the government of his demesne continued under the crown's appointed viceroy. The Gascons had a long history of defiance to English occupation and in 1252 Henry III, along with the Plantagenet prince, traveled to the fiefdom to personally intervene to find a resolution to the ongoing conflict. The king met with the leading warlords where a settlement was negotiated, with the thirteen-year-old Edward playing only a ceremonial and nominal role. In the following year the Gascon nobles again rose in open revolt while, to the south Alfonso X of Castile threatened to invade the duchy to press his hereditary claims of sovereignty. Henry III was again compelled to sail to Gascony to end the danger of war and, after reimposing his authority over the local vassals, began deliberations with the Spanish court. To secure the southern border the English envoys proposed the marriage of Edward to Eleanor, the sister of Alfonso X, in exchange for the Spanish renouncement of all rights to Gascony. In March 1254 the treaty was signed and in November, after traveling to the Castilian capital of Burgos, Edward was knighted by the Spanish monarch and married to Eleanor. To provide the income for an adequate household in addition to Gascony, Henry III granted his heir Ireland, occupied Wales and lesser English lordships, which he was to administer as a retainer of the throne. Following the wedding ceremony the Plantagenet lord stayed in Gascony for the next year to gain his first practical experiences in the management of the royal duchy.

The marriage between the fifteen-year-old Edward and Eleanor of Castile was a political arrangement between the two courts designed to protect the southern border of Gascony and provide a strong ally for the Plantagenets against an increasingly bellicose France. Despite being a negotiated union Prince Edward and his wife were well suited to each other, developing a life-long loving and caring relationship. She was described as a princess of beauty, piety and grace and became totally devoted to her husband, evolving into a trusted and influential advisor who actively participated in the government of the realm. The future Plantagenet dynasty was secured with the birth of the fourth son, Edward, in 1284. The king expressed great sorrow at Eleanor's death in 1290, which was exhibited by a series of twelve crosses to mark the route of her funeral procession from Lincoln to Westminster Abbey.

In November 1255 Edward departed to England from Gascony where he soon became directly involved with the ongoing dissent in his newly acquired Welsh lands. However, his harsh policies and disrespect of the local population forced the magnates to rebel under the charismatic leadership of Llewelyn. The Welsh prince succeeded in uniting the warlords to his war effort and by 1257 the entire principality was under his authority, forcing Edward to abandon his fiefdom.

While Edward was directing the crown's failed campaign against Wales, the English barons revolted against Henry III, demanding control over the kingdom's finances and administration through a baronial council. The king was compelled to accept the Provisions of Oxford and his son only reluctantly gave his approval. Following the magnates' triumph Edward broke with his father over his weak response and lack of resolve, joining the dissident faction under the leadership of Simon de Montfort. Henry III learned of his son's alliance with the rebel lords while in Paris in February 1260 and hurriedly sailed to England to impose his authority over Edward. After his pledge of homage to the throne, the prince was sent as viceroy to Gascony where he stayed until early 1261. However, he continued to be estranged from Henry III and, after ending his governorship of Gascony, traveled to France, participating in numerous military tournaments and festivals. Edward did not return to England until the outbreak of the Second Barons' War in 1264.

With the renewal of the barons' revolt Edward crossed the Channel to England and was quickly reconciled with his father and the Plantagenet cause against the rebels. He was given command of the crown's forces in the west, where he captured several castles and plundered Gloucester. In April 1264 the warrior-prince united his soldiers with Henry III's cavalry and infantry to storm the stronghold at Northampton. After continuing his pillaging attacks against the western lordships, the Plantagenet lord joined his father at Lewes to confront the dissidents' main army. In the ensuing encounter on May 14 Edward commanded the right wing of the royalists, initiating the battle with a bold but impetuous charge against de Montfort's London contingent, which quickly succeeded in driving the rogues from the field. However, the heir failed to control his men-at-arms as they aggressively pursued the fleeing Londoners. His division's absence from the battlefield allowed de Montfort to overwhelm Henry III's remaining troops, capturing the king. Upon his return to Lewes Edward refused to abandon his father and freely surrendered to the insurgents.

With his victory at Lewes, de Montfort established a new government dominated by dissident barons, with Henry III acting as figurehead sovereign. Edward remained the prisoner of the rogue magnates and was held at several castles before being taken to Hereford in March 1265. Once established in Hereford he was able to make arrangements with local supporters for his escape and late in May managed to gain his freedom. Edward assumed command of the royalist cause and soon mobilized a formidable military force. Confronted with a resurgent Plantagenet campaign the insurgent earls increasingly deserted de Montfort. After gaining a minor victory at Kenilworth the prince advanced against the main militia of Simon de Montfort at Evesham. On August 4 he outmaneuvered the surprised rebels, completely destroying their army and killing de Montfort.

After the triumph at Evesham Henry III once again claimed the kingship, revoking the restrictions of the Provisions of Oxford to return to a government of absolute rule. He adopted a policy of revenge against the surviving rogue magnates, sending Edward to attack their castles and estates. During the next two years the Plantagenet prince forced the submission of London and seized the great insurgent fortifications at Dover and Kenilworth. Peace was finally restored with the surrender of the last remaining dissident stronghold at Ely to end the Second Barons' War. After his success over the rebels Edward increasingly assumed the independent administration of England while beginning preparations for a crusade against the Saracens in Jerusalem.

In June 1268 Edward took the crusader's cross and for the next two years raised money, troops and war provisions for his holy enterprise while leading the king's government. He agreed to unite his small English crusader army with the primary expedition commanded by Louis IX of France, who had gained approval for the Seventh Crusade from the papacy. In August 1270 the Plantagenets sailed for Tunisia to join the main war effort. However, when he landed at Tunis, with the death of Louis IX, the French had already concluded a peace treaty with the local emir and were preparing to abandon their campaign. The English warlord refused to accept the agreement, planning to sail with his English soldiers to the Crusader Kingdom. However, due to the lateness in the year and the constant threat of Mediterranean storms, he was compelled to spend the winter in Sicily with the French crusaders before renewing his personal holy war in the spring.

After nearly two hundred years the once formidable Kingdom of Jerusalem had been reduced to a thin coastal strip centered on Acre that was under constant assault from the Egyptian Mamelukes in the south and the Mongols in the north. In April 1271 Edward sailed to Acre with his English army, arriving as the Saracens were besieging the fortified city. After landing his troops the Plantagenet crusader relieved the attack against Acre and began to mount raids against the Moslems. Nevertheless due to the limited size and strength of his military forces, he was able to only launch sporadic sorties but did manage to seize the holy city of Nazaraeth. With a small army and the native Christians beset with internal discord, Edward was compelled to end his crusade and negotiate a settlement with the Egyptian sultan, Baibars. However, soon after agreeing to a ten-year truce, the English warlord was stabbed with a poison dagger by a member of the fanatical sect of Assassins. The wound was serious and he nearly died. However, after the infected area was excised, Edward made a steady recovery. By September he had fully regained his health and with the peace in place the warrior-prince departed for England.

Edward sailed from Acre to Sicily, spending the winter as the guest of the island's king. While in Sicily he learned of the death of his father and his acknowledgement by the nobility and Church as sovereign. In his absence a regency government was established and the once rebellious barons now freely respected the new administration's assumption of power. In the spring of 1273 Edward departed from Sicily, first arriving in Rome, spending time with Pope Gregory X, reporting on his holy war against the Saracens, making plans for a new expedition and arranging for an extension of the tax levy against the English clerics to finance his Acre crusade. From the See of Rome he slowly advanced through northern Italy into France, participating in numerous jousting tournaments and being lavishly entertained. By the summer he had established his court in his duchy of Gascony, which was again in open rebellion. Edward I stayed in the fiefdom for nearly a year, reasserting his sovereignty, finally returning to England on August 2, 1274. Landing at Dover the king traveled to London where on August 19 he was anointed and crowned as Edward I.

During Edward's formative years he developed into a formidable warrior and skilled diplomat and administrator. He gained widespread renown in England and in the European courts for his triumphs in jousting tournaments and exploits during the crusade of 1270. The king remained committed to the crusading movement, planning to renew the campaign against the Saracens in Jerusalem. For most of his life he was an active hunter, especially with falcons, and enjoyed playing chess and games with dice. As Edward I assumed the kingship he was described by contemporaries as extremely tall at over six feet and possessing great physical strength, mental resolve and determination.

After undertaking his personal rule the king reorganized his administrative council, appointing his own representatives as court officials. To fully impose his kingship he soon ordered a realm-wide survey of the county governments to determine the crown's prerogatives that had been usurped by the local royal officials and the degree of abuse and corruption that the populace had been subjected to by the sheriffs. To redress the findings a Parliament was assembled in April 1275, which produced the First Statute of Westminster. The decree was a new codification of the law, based on the Magna Carta, covering a wide range of legal issues. While the immediate results of the Parliament were limited, it did provide a demonstration of Edward I's intention to enforce his rights and justice.

Soon after his coronation Edward I had received the pledges of homage from his vassals with the exception of Llewelyn of Wales. Despite numerous summonses the prince refused to appear at the court of his overlord to offer fealty. As the Welsh leader continued to ignore his feudal obligations, at the Parliament of October 1275 the king declared his intention of imposing his sovereignty over the recalcitrant Welsh. Nevertheless, during most of the following year, the English throne was involved with diplomatic initiatives to prevent its involvement in the war between France and Spain, becoming distracted from the Welsh conflict. After settling with the warring European rivals, to avoid invading the Welsh principality, in October 1276 the crown again demanded Llewelyn's appearance at the Westminster Parliament. However, when he asked for hostages to ensure his safety, Edward I began military preparations for war. During the period prior to the invasion the borderland was made secure to protect against raids and in July 1277 the English army was assembled at Worcester. While the sovereign's brother, Edmund, earl of Lancaster, commanded a second contingent of troops to the south, the main force under Edward I launched the campaign from Chester against the principal strongholds in Snowdonia. With the Plantagenet navy blocking all access from the sea for reinforcements and war provisions and under the regime's relentless drive from the east, Llewelyn was compelled to surrender and give homage.

With peace restored to the Welsh marchlands Edward I returned to the personal government of his realm. Semi-annual parliaments were held and the crown's laws and justice enforced. In foreign affairs, relations with France improved with the meeting between the two kings in May 1279 while Spain continued to be a friend and ally. The sovereign became occupied with the daily, routine administration of the kingdom until March 1282 when the brother of Llewelyn, David, attacked the royal castle at Hawarden, causing the whole of Wales to erupt into revolt against English subjugation. The Welsh warlord had earlier supported the English cause in the 1277 war against his brother and had been rewarded by the Plantagenet throne with grants of land in Snowdonia. However, he became disgruntled at the size of his new territory and lack of respect shown him by the court's officials. When Edward I received news of the rebellion, he ordered his borderland earls to assemble their retainers and hold the Welsh attack in check while he summoned his vassals and recruited mercenaries. By August the Plantagenet army had been mobilized and the king advanced his campaign against David in Denbigh while a second force marched into southern Wales against Llewelyn, who had recently joined the war in support of the uprising. Edward I's offensive made little progress during the autumn as the soldiers of David withdrew into the mountains, compelling the English to temporarily abandon the incursion. However, while the northern Plantagenet troops took up defensive positions, in the south Llewelyn mounted a surprise sortie against the royal castle at Hereford. As the Welsh were besieging the stronghold the garrison commander launched a surprise assault from the fortress, outmaneuvering and killing the prince in the ensuing battle. With the death of their charismatic leader the southern Welsh quickly lost their enthusiasm for war and by December had become pacified. Nevertheless David still remained a formidable enemy in Snowdonia.

During the winter months Edward I continued to recruit additional troops and stockpile supplies for his campaign. By mid–January he had amassed a powerful army to renew his attack against northern Wales. Facing the overwhelming military might of the English, David was forced to withdraw into the mountains with the king's cavalry in close pursuit. Finally in June the Welsh captain was seized and after a trial suffered the traitor's death of being drawn and quartered. With the execution of David all organized resistance ended and the crown officially annexed the whole of Wales into the Plantagenet kingdom. To protect against future rebellions Edward I began the construction of a formidable network of castles to encircle the Welsh with a ring of English power. To more fully integrate the principality into the Plantagenet governmental structure, Wales was brought under the regime's existing legal system with royal agents assuming all administrative functions. The sovereign remained in his new colony during much of 1284, traveling throughout the princedom personally imposing his control. There was one final uprising in June 1287, which was quickly quelled, fully enforcing royal authority.

Following the successful conquest of Wales Edward I returned to England, entering London in April after first visiting the eastern counties to assert his kingship against the recalcitrant local lords. While in the capital a parliament was held in June, which issued the Second Statute of Westminster, dealing with the rights of property owners. Edward I stayed in England, administering his government and justice, until May 1286 when he crossed the Channel to France to render homage for his duchy of Gascony to the new Capet sovereign, Philip IV. From Paris the English court traveled to Gascony where the nobles were again in open rebellion against Plantagenet authority. Edward I spent the next three years in his duchy, advancing through the lordships, imposing his rule over the magnates and towns while encouraging the development of commerce and enacting laws to promote economic growth. By the time he left Gascony a fully functioning and respected government had been put in place and his sovereignty was enforced. Due to his prolonged absence lawlessness and abuses in the English legal system began to grow and the king was forced to return to his realm to personally impose his control. Under Edward I's forceful administration his justice and laws were soon honored. For the next three years England remained peaceful and prosperous while relations with the European courts continued to be cordial. However, the death of the young queen of Scotland and the increasingly bellicose foreign policy of Philip IV of France in 1294 soon propelled the Plantagenet throne into years of hostility.

After consolidating his kingdom Philip IV directed his territorial ambitions against the English-held duchy of Gascony. As a pretext to war the Capet crown summoned its Gascon vassal, Edward I, to Paris to answer charges of attacking its vessels and seaports. The English king's brother, Edmund, earl of Lancaster, was sent to arrange a resolution of the escalating conflict. An agreement was soon negotiated and under the treaty France was allowed the temporary occupation of several border castles and the future inheritance of Gascony was to be settled by the recently widowed Edward I's marriage to the sister of Philip IV, with their issue assuming the sovereignty of the duchy. Despite ratifying the accord the French court soon declared its Plantagenet liegeman a rebel and his lands forfeited. When Edward I learned of Philip IV's actions he began to prepare for war to retain his demesne. A parliament was summoned where a new tax levy was granted to finance the conflict. During the summer of 1294 an army was mobilized, sailing to Gascony in October under the command of the earl of Lancaster. However, after re-conquering several key strongholds in the north, the Plantagenet forces failed to drive the French from the duchy as Philip IV's soldiers continued to press their offensive.

While his host struggled in Gascony Edward I began a diplomatic campaign to isolate France by forming an alliance with the count of Flanders, Guy I de Dampierre, the duke of Brabant and several lesser magnates. In April 1297 Edward I crossed the Channel to Flanders, uniting his military forces with the Flemish in an attempt to divert the war effort away from Gascony with an attack against northern France. To counter the coalition's new initiative Philip IV invaded Flanders, quickly defeating the Anglo-Flemish faction. Following the French victory Edward I was compelled to negotiate a truce. Both regimes found it mutually advantageous to extend the armistice several times until 1303 when a peace treaty was signed. Under the terms of the settlement, which were highly favorable to the English due to the Capet court's ongoing hostilities with Pope Boniface VIII over the Church's secular rights, Edward I offered liege homage to Philip IV for Gascony while the French throne recognized the English claim to the duchy and agreed to withdraw its occupation troops.

While the Plantagenet forces were struggling to gain supremacy during the Anglo-Franco War, Edward I remained in England to personally impose his suzerainty over Scotland. In 1290 the Scottish queen, Margaret I, died without a direct heir, propelling the kingdom into the danger of civil war as rival families contended for the vacant throne. To find a peaceful resolution the Scottish regents petitioned Edward I to arbitrate the disputed succession. He agreed to reconcile the issue only if the claimants would first give homage to him. As the threat of open conflict mounted the Scots were forced to accept the demeaning stipulation. In May 1291 the candidates met with the English king at Norham Castle, pledging their loyalty and presenting their individual claims to the realm. After eighteen months of sporadic deliberations and acting through a parliament of Scottish and Plantagenet electors, the inheritance rights of John Balliol were judged the superior. In late November 1292 he was invested with the Scottish monarchy and on December 26 gave fealty to the English crown.

During the ongoing arbitration parliament Edward I had won the right to temporarily occupy key Scottish castles on the pretext of providing security for the kingdom. However, after the enthronement of the new king, he refused to abandon his control of the strongholds and began to encroach in local legal activities, claiming the right to judge all appeal cases of disgruntled Scottish lords. At first Balliol reluctantly agreed to the interference in his internal affairs, However when the English crown demanded that he serve as a liege vassal with the Plantagenet army in Gascony, the Scots reacted to the humiliation by negotiating an alliance with France and preparing for war.

As the level of Scottish border hostilities intensified and war with France again threatened, in November 1295 Edward I summoned the Model Parliament to Westminster, so called because of its widespread representation from the nobility, Church and commons, to provide finances for the coming conflicts. By early the following year troops and supplies had been assembled and in March the Plantagenet throne began its invasion of Scotland while soldiers were sent to Flanders to buttress the initiative against the French. The first objective of the campaign against Balliol was the seizure of the strategic port of Berwick, which was stormed and brutally sacked. After garrisoning and strengthening the castle's defenses, the English marched north along the coast to capture Dunbar. At the loss of the fortified city Scottish resistance withered and the major strongholds at Edinburgh, Roxburgh and Stirling were soon in the king's hands. On July 10 John Balliol formally surrendered the kingdom to his Plantagenet overlord. After stripping him of his monarchy Edward I advanced unopposed through Scotland and on August 23 received the homage of the local lords and clerics. English officials were appointed to govern the realm and the strategic fortresses were garrisoned with royal troops. Scotland was to be administered as an annexed colony of the English regime.

Edward I's uncontested march through Scotland had effectively eliminated all organized resistance. However by 1297, as the English administrators plundered and brutalized the Scots, independent bands of insurgents began to retaliate. In the western lordships, acting under the banner of their deposed king, rebel warlords led by William Wallace launched a series of small raids against the occupation forces. As the successes of their revolt grew the English crown sent an army to reimpose its authority. Under the command of the earl of Surrey, in September the Plantagenet troops advanced against the dissident strongholds. However, as they approached Stirling Bridge their vanguard was isolated and destroyed by Wallace, compelling the earl to abandon his campaign. The triumph at Stirling Bridge galvanized the Scottish resistance movement and by the end of 1297 the gains of the English conquest had been reversed in all but the strongest fortifications.

While the emboldened Scots were reestablishing their local government and autonomy, Edward I was summoning his vassals and hiring mercenaries to assemble a powerful new army for a second invasion of Scotland. In July 1298 he launched the campaign by marching north from Roxburgh with his formidable military force. Advancing toward Edinburgh the English encountered the waiting rebels of William Wallace at Falkirk. The Plantagenets were deployed for battle and, through the skillful use of his cavalry and archers, the king completely routed the troops of Wallace. After the Falkirk victory Edward I turned his host to the southwest into Carrick to counter the rebellion and growing popularity of Robert Bruce who, along with John Comyn, had been newly elected as co-Guardians for Scotland, replacing the disgraced Wallace. At the approach of the English, Bruce was compelled to withdraw to the security of the Highlands while the crown's soldiers ravaged and burned his lordship. After pillaging through Carrick Edward I abandoned his attacks and retired to Carlisle as his food supplies became exhausted. However, despite the success of the war effort the Scots refused to submit and much of the kingdom was still unconquered.

Edward I remained determined to fully enforce his overlordship in Scotland and, ignoring the mounting rebellion of his parliament and growing international pressure from the papacy and Philip IV against the conflict, in 1301 he again began to prepare for a new invasion. By July two armies were assembled for a double-pronged attack with the king personally commanding the eastern campaign and his heir, Prince Edward of Caernarvon, directing the western offensive. As the main English force advanced into eastern Scotland from Berwick, the Scots refused to give battle, compelling Edward I to deplete his energy and resources in fruitless pursuits. Finally, with its troop strength reduced by disease and desertion, the Plantagenet throne under a papal-sponsored initiative agreed to an eight-month truce. In February 1302 Edward I departed to England after a frustrating and failed attempt to impose his absolute sovereignty.

In January 1303, after ensuring peace with France by negotiating a resolution to their ongoing conflict over Gascony, the Plantagenet crown began to make preparations for the renewal of the conquest of Scotland. By May two formidable armies were mobilized with Prince Edward of Caernarvon again commanding the western attack while the king led the campaign up the eastern coast. Advancing from Roxburgh Edward I's forces encountered little organized resistance and by early 1304 most of the region was firmly under his authority. In February the Scottish guardian, John Comyn, surrendered the kingdom and along with the prominent magnates gave homage. In August Edward I returned to England after occupying the major towns and strongholds with troops and appointing a viceroy to govern his new acquisition.

After the forced submission of Scotland the king established his court at Westminster, holding a series of parliaments to address the growing problems of poverty and lawlessness brought on by the prolonged period of war. Despite his advancing age he continued to travel through his realm to personally administer his government and justice. During the final years of his monarchy Edward I had so fully imposed his sovereignty over his English earls that he could now safely renounce the Magna Carta and rule without baronial restrictions. While the Scottish campaign of 1303 had enforced English suzerainty, Robert Bruce began to intrigue against the occupation forces and by March 1306 had ignited the kingdom into open revolt. Ignoring his frail health Edward I became resolved to again personally dictate his authority over his recalcitrant vassals. By June an invasion army had been assembled and the aging monarch began his slow advance north by litter. While he struggled toward the border a large contingent of knights was sent forward and they renewed the war of subjugation by defeating Bruce at Methven. As the offensive was pressed into Scotland Edward I's health grew increasingly worse and he died on July 6, 1307, at age 68 and a reign of nearly 35 years.

EDWARD II, 1284–1307–1327

Edward II was the sixth Plantagenet king of England, succeeding to the throne at age twenty-three with the death of his father in July 1307. The prince was born in Wales at Caernarvon Castle on April 25, 1284, and was the fourth male offspring of Edward I and Queen Eleanor of Castile. The first two male issues of the sovereign had died during infancy and soon after Edward's birth he became heir to the English crown with the death of the third son, Alfonso. He spent his early childhood largely separated from his father and mother, under the care of court-appointed guardians. As the successor apparent Edward I took a special interest in his education and at an early age provided tutors for his welfare and preparation for kingship. He was taught to read and write and to speak French, English and Latin; he studied religion and received instruction in the social graces of music, dancing and court etiquette. However, like the nobility of the medieval era, the core of his training centered on preparation for warfare. Under the watchful supervision of seasoned knights, the prince of Caernarvon was instructed in the battle skills necessary to command the royal army. Nevertheless, despite the stern dictates of his father, Edward developed little interest in military affairs, choosing to master the common skills of farmers and craftsmen and spend his days occupied with his lowborn favorites. He evolved into a competent equestrian but disliked the martial sport of jousting, preferring hunting and horse breeding.

While Edward continued his education England had been at war with France for three years for control of the duchy of Gascony with little success and in 1297 the king sailed to Flanders to personally command his army against the Capet throne. Edward I's absence afforded the heir his first opportunity to assume authority of the government, gaining political experiences as the nominal regent through an advisory directorate. During Edward I's absence, acting through his son, the council took measures to quell escalating baronial unrest due to the harsh demands required to fund the French conflict and the renewal of rebellion by the Scots against English occupation. In March 1298 the Plantagenet monarch departed from Flanders, again assuming sole responsibility for the administration of his realm. The nearly fourteen-year-old Edward withdrew from all court functions, traveling to his castle at Langley where he engaged in a period of youthful debauchery. On his return from the continent Edward I had brought with him Piers Gaveston, the son of a trusted Gascon ally and friend, as an official companion for his heir. The close relationship that quickly developed between the two youths at Langley colored the remainder of Edward of Caernarvon's life.

During Edward I's absence in Flanders, in 1297 the Scots under William Wallace rose in revolt. Upon his return the king led several campaigns north to assert his authority. Nevertheless Scotland remained undefeated and defiant. The young Edward had taken no part in these expeditions but in 1300, as the English army again advanced to enforce the crown's will, he joined his father to gain his first military exposure. In June the large force of knights and infantry marched into southwestern Scotland where the prince took part in siege operations and gained his initial combat experiences, leading the rearguard. The invasion ended in disappointment as the Scots refused to give battle and in November the sovereign, along with his son, who had conducted his duties well, abandoned the incursion, departing to England. Edward of Caernarvon was rewarded for his actions in Scotland with the grant of Wales and the title of prince of Wales.

The Plantagenet military campaign of 1300 against Scotland accomplished little and, in the following year, the king again set out to suppress the rebellion. The invasion was planned as a double-pronged attack, with Edward I leading the eastern army and his son commanding the western wing. In July the prince of Wales advanced with a large well-equipped force from Carlisle into the southwestern Scottish lordships. However, as in the previous year, the Scots withdrew, refusing to engage the English in battle and after a fruitless six months the heir returned to England with his father after the regime arranged an eight month truce. Though the results of the incursion were disappointing, Edward of Wales had performed well with his first opportunity at independent command. Following the second Scottish offensive he again spent much of the winter at Langley with his favorite companion, Piers Gaveston.

After repeated attempts to impose his sovereignty over the Scots, during much of 1302 the king and his heir were personally involved in preparations for a new invasion. Large quantities of war supplies were amassed, mercenary troops hired and the royal army mobilized as Edward of Caernarvon again prepared to lead the western arm of the planned two-pronged attack. Away from his involvement with the Scottish war effort, he presided over parliament on behalf of his father, attended to the needs of his personal estates and renewed his decadent encounters. As the plans for the campaign continued, Edward I became determined to remain in the north to relentlessly harry the rogue kingdom into subjugation. In May the two military forces launched the incursion, which lasted until the next year as the Scottish lords finally and reluctantly agreed to give fealty under the constant destructive pressure of the crown's initiative. In the ensuing settlement the prince played a prominent role in the peace negotiations.

Following the successful year in Scotland Edward returned to Langley with his lowborn friends and during early 1305 rejoined the royal court, expanding his participation in the administration of his father's realm. However, despite their apparent cordial relationship, Edward I grew increasingly displeased with the close association of his son and Piers Gaveston. In June he vented his anger by exiling the heir from all governmental activities and denying him access to the royal treasury over a seemingly trivial poaching of a deer. He was not reconciled with the throne until October as the revolt again erupted in Scotland under the charismatic leadership of Robert Bruce. In June 1306 Edward of Wales marched north in advance of his aging father to confront the newly crowned Scottish king. However, before the royal army had reached the border, Bruce had been defeated. Nevertheless, the prince had managed to arrive in time to participate in the seizure of Kildrummy Castle. Edward of Caernarvon remained with the troops through the campaigning season, pursuing Scottish subjugation before departing south for the winter.

Despite the apparent reconciliation between Edward I and his son, in January 1307 new contention developed over the heir's request for a countship for Piers Gaveston. The king had become increasingly alarmed at their intimate relationship, resulting in the banishment of Piers from England. In May 1307 Edward of Wales traveled with his favorite to Dover for the forced exile to France.

After Gaveston departed the Prince of Wales returned north to rejoin the king in the ongoing Scottish war. However, soon after reaching his father, Edward I died and on July 7, 1307, Edward II was acknowledged as the successor to the throne of England, receiving the pledges of homage from his lords and Church. His first official act was to recall the exiled favorite from France and Gaveston joined the royal court in August at Dumfries, Scotland, where he was granted the extensive and wealthy estates of Cornwall and named earl. The entitlement was customarily reserved only for members of the royal household and its bequeathal greatly offended the nobility at the perceived elevation of the Gascon's status. The Scottish revolt was still unresolved but Edward II displayed little interest in pursing the war, appointing viceroys to continue the subjugation campaign while he remained involved with his lowborn friends from the security of the Scottish castles. In October 1307 he traveled back to England to confront the escalating animosity of his magnates, who were rebelling at their exclusion from the royal council in favor of the king's companions.

Before directing his policy against the rebel barons, in January 1308 Edward II crossed the Channel to Boulogne for his wedding to Isabella, the daughter of King Philip IV. The marriage had been arranged by Edward I in 1298 as part of a greater treaty ending the prolonged war in Gascony. The English monarch and his wife were unsuited for each other, resulting in an unhappy and strained relationship. His rumored homosexual affair with Piers Gaveston, along with his outward displays of affection toward the Gascon, doomed their early years to failure. However, after the favorite's death, a mutual accommodation was found. Despite the apparent reconciliation, when Hugh Despenser became Edward II's first minister in 1322, a new estrangement quickly erupted. Isabella was described as a princess of grace and cultivation with a strong and determined will. The future of the Plantagenet throne was secured in 1312 with the birth of the future Edward III and was followed by three additional children.

While Edward II was making his final preparations for his wedding ceremony to Isabella of France, he further alienated the magnates by arranging for the marriage of Gaveston to his royal niece and naming him as regent during his absence across the Channel. The acts of estrangement against the nobility were continued during the coronation ceremony as Piers was again appointed to prominent roles, lavished with gifts and the personal attention of the monarch. Gaveston further contributed to the growing discord with his overbearing and pretentious manner. Finally, in the April 1308 parliament, the barons united to demand the exile of the Gascon. Under threat of force by arms, the king agreed to his favorite's banishment to Ireland as viceroy.

As Edward II watched Gaveston's departure, he became determined to use every means to secure an end to his exile. He quickly adopted a policy of bribes and grants of land and titles to the rogue lords, winning back a significant faction. The political campaign was successful and by the summer of 1309 the king had regained enough baronial support to recall Piers. However, the Gascon soon returned to his arrogant and extravagant ways, again unifying the magnates against the royal court. Rallying against Gaveston by early the next year, the barons were strong enough to demand the establishment of a committee of twenty-one nobles, called the Lords of Ordainers, to reform the government.

While the Ordainers gathered to draft their ultimatum, the Plantagenet sovereign returned to his political strategy of dividing the earls with bribes and favors but the solidarity of the insurgency movement held firm. Following this initial setback he attempted to unite the nobility to the monarchy by announcing a new invasion against Scotland. Again few lords answered the summons and the campaign resulted in only the pillaging and burning of the Scottish countryside. While Edward II continued his attacks in Scotland against Robert Bruce, the committee remained in England, producing a charter of forty-one measures of reform dealing with finance, administration and good government. However, the principal articles dealt with the misrule of the crown's advisors and in particular the demand for the banishment of Gaveston. The unified magnates threatened civil war unless the throne implemented the Ordinances without delay. Finding himself with little support the king was compelled to accept the provisions and in early November 1311 his Gascon favorite sailed from England into exile. However, Piers was back with the royal court before the end of the month as Edward II openly defied his barons, who responded by preparing for war.

Early in 1312 the rebellion movement rallied around the wealthy and powerful Thomas of Lancaster and under his direction the private armies of the barons assembled to defend their rights under the Ordinances. As the rebel forces gathered, determined to enforce their will, the king, along with Piers, fled north to Scarborough Castle but no magnate came to their defense. In an attempt to raise troops, Edward II and his favorite agreed to separate, with Gaveston remaining in the castle while the sovereign traveled to York. The Scarborough stronghold was quickly invested by Thomas of Lancaster and Piers was compelled to surrender under terms, which allowed his fate to be determined by parliament. However as the captive made his way south, he was forcibly seized by Guy Beauchamp of Warwick and taken to his fortress where the earl was soon joined by the lords of Lancaster, Arundel and Hereford. The four warlords declared Piers Gaveston guilty of treason against the realm and sentenced him to be executed at Blacklow Hill on June 19, 1312, by beheading. When Edward II learned of the death of Gaveston he began to immediately plan for his revenge.

The return of Gaveston in November 1311 had energized the rogue warlords but with his death their unifying cause had been eliminated and quickly their alliance began to disband as the lords of Pembroke and Despenser, along with their allies, rejoined the crown. Nevertheless, Thomas of Lancaster retained the loyalty of a significant faction, remaining a threat to the Plantagenet throne. Under the direction of Lancaster a large force of dissident nobles marched against Edward II in London. However, no attack was ordered as both warring parties agreed to begin peace discussions. In order to resolve the ongoing dispute, which had reached a stalemate, the king petitioned his father-in-law, Philip IV of France, to intervene. Philip IV sent his brother, Louis, and together, with two papal envoys, a compromise settlement was negotiated. Under the October 1313 treaty the earls of Lancaster, Warwick, Hereford and Arundel admitted their guilt in the death of Gaveston and Edward II agreed to issue a full pardon to the four earls and their allies. Despite the apparent accord it was an uneasy peace, as Edward II maintained his determination to seek retaliation against the murderers of his favorite and regain his lost authority. However, before directing the power of the monarchy against the rebels he first had to settle the ongoing Scottish war for independence.

While the English crown had been preoccupied with the internal disorder of the rebel barons, Robert Bruce had consolidated his sovereignty over Scotland. The Scots had seized most of the English-occupied towns and castles with the exception of Stirling, which was under siege. To re-impose Plantagenet rule over Scotland, in June 1314 the royal army assembled in the north at Berwick with many of the most powerful earls in attendance to march to the relief of Stirling. As Edward II's forces advanced across the borderlands, Bruce mobilized his militia near Bannockburn and had ample time to select the battle site and coordinate his plan of attack. On June 23 the English advance guard made its first contact with the well-prepared Scots and immediately the knights charged the defensive lines. The assaults of Edward II's mounted troops were thwarted by the long pikes of the northmen and, as night fell both armies still held the field. To find open ground to more effectively deploy his superior heavy cavalry, during the night the king ordered his forces to shift forward. However in the morning, as the Plantagenet soldiers were reforming their lines, Robert Bruce launched a surprise attack to catch Edward II's host unprepared. The infantry was steadily driven back and began to break despite the repeated charges of the English men-at-arms. As his battle-line collapsed, after fighting bravely, Edward II was compelled to abandon the engagement making his escape to Berwick.

The military defeat at Bannockburn was a political disaster for Edward II. In September he was compelled to meet with the Committee of Ordainers in York, where the earl of Lancaster demanded the full acceptance of the Ordinance Articles and the reorganization of the government and royal council. The Plantagenet king had been largely abandoned by his allies and forced to accept the rebels' ultimatum as he was reduced to the puppet of the oligarchy Lancaster regime. However with the breakdown of central authority, private wars erupted in the north and along the Welsh borderlands. The Lancaster administration proved unable to quell the ongoing disruptions and, as crop failures added to the general misery, by 1318 his rule had been discredited and his primacy deluded. While his realm slipped into near anarchy Edward II did all he could to encourage the dissent as his power was slowly regained. He turned increasingly to the lords of Pembroke and Despenser in an attempt to regain full sovereignty as they formed a political faction in opposition to Lancaster known as the Middle Party. Through their initiatives many of the kingdom's powerful earls and prelates rallied to their cause. To peacefully end the ongoing discord, the Middle Party began negotiations with Thomas of Lancaster and in August 1318 a treaty of reconciliation was signed at Leake. Under the settlement, the Ordinances were reinstituted and a permanent governing council appointed, comprised of members from both parties. However in the formation of the committee Lancaster was outmaneuvered and was represented by only one minor magnate to reduce his influence still further. In early 1319 Edward II sanctioned the actions of the Middle Party, hoping to utilize it to destroy Lancaster, the murderer of Piers Gaveston.

The accord at Leake gave the outward appearance of a once again united kingdom and in June 1319 the English throne directed its policy toward the subjugation of Scotland. A large well-prepared military force was mobilized and the campaign launched by advancing against Berwick. The realm's most powerful earls, including Thomas of Lancaster, answered the king's call to arms. However, the siege against Berwick failed and, as the raiding Scots of Robert Bruce struck deep into England, defeating the regime's militia at Myron, the invasion had to be abandoned. The military expedition had been a total disappointment and Edward II blamed Lancaster for his lack of support, which served to further weaken the rebel baron's authority and influence.

Following the abortive Scottish campaign the prominence of Pembroke was replaced in the royal council by the Despenser family and in particular by Sir Hugh the Younger. By 1320 Sir Hugh had become the new favorite of the king, who granted him the Welsh marchland lordship of Glamorgan and many expensive gifts. Soon after acquiring his new estates the ambitious Despenser attempted to expand his territorial holdings by claiming neighboring Gower, but his actions were resisted by the now unified march lords, led by Roger Mortimer. Edward II gave his full backing to Sir Hugh as the Marchers attacked Glamorgan, while appealing to Thomas of Lancaster for military aid. A new league headed by Lancaster was quickly formed to confront the crown's party. After ravaging the Welsh lordships, as the Lancaster alliance's troops advanced against London, the civil war spread to much of the Midlands. With an overwhelming show of military might and under danger of being deposed, the rebels compelled Edward II to exile the Despensers and accept new controls over his rights to freely govern. Despite the success of the coalition the Plantagenet sovereign remained defiant in his resolution to regain his lost prerogatives and punish the Lancaster earl.

Throughout much of 1321 an uneasy peace developed between the two rival factions. However, late in the year as tensions escalated, the king marched his army against the border lords. As additional warlords joined his cause the Despensers were recalled from their brief exile. With the encouragement of Hugh of Glamorgan, Edward II continued his assaults against the Welsh marchland magnates and, with the absence of the Lancaster faction in the north and the capture of the local leader, Roger Mortimer, by early 1322 he had regained control over the region. Having imposed sovereignty over the rebellious west, the Plantagenets directed the campaign against Thomas of Lancaster, who remained in the north plotting for military aid from Robert Bruce. The royal troops were advanced in pursuit of Lancaster and on March 17, 1322, the earl's forces were defeated at Boroughbridge and Thomas seized. On March 22, after a short trial presided over by Edward II, the earl was condemned as a traitor and sentenced to death by beheading. The surviving rebel leaders were relentlessly pursued and executed.

With the elimination of the Lancaster alliance Edward II regained his full sovereignty over the kingdom as the Ordinances were repealed at the May parliament. The Despensers were rewarded for their services with the granting of an earldom for Hugh the Elder and much of south Wales for Hugh the Younger. The parliament enacted various reforms that his royal council proposed as Edward II once again claimed the full support of the English magnates. To retain the favor of the nobility the assembly of 1322 also approved measures from the Ordinances dealing with the government's administration and confirmed its rights to be consulted by the king.

In June 1322 the truce with Scotland expired and Robert I responded with a large pillaging raid deep into England. The Plantagenet throne countered with a campaign against Berwick. However, the castle defenders resisted all assaults and Edward II abandoned the siege to plunder the Lowlands. As the king was retiring south, at Old Byland he was unexpectedly attacked by Bruce and, along with the queen, barely avoided capture. The humiliation at Old Byland left northern England unprotected and open to additional Scottish forays, which led to the opening of peace negotiations. No final resolution resulted from the initial discussions, though a thirteen-year truce was ratified.

With his northern border lands secure and no threat of internal rebellion Edward II could direct his crown's policies toward the consolidation of his power. Under the able direction of his favorite and chief minister, Hugh of Glamorgan, the governmental and financial problems were addressed. The offices of exchequer and chamberlain were revamped and made to work with greater efficiency and independence. Ongoing foreign commercial activities were reformed, resulting in an expansion of trading opportunities with Flanders and France. The initiatives brought better government and growth in the largely agriculture-based economy as Edward II's rule became more widely accepted.

While England remained at peace and returned to prosperity, in France King Philip V unexpectedly died in 1322 to be succeeded by his brother, Charles IV. Under feudal custom Edward II was now required to appear before his new overlord to give homage for the French duchy of Gascony. Nevertheless, before he could travel to France, Charles IV renewed the campaign against the Gaston region that had remained unresolved since the rule of Philip IV and the local English viceroy aggressively responded by attacking across the border. Charles IV countered by declaring the Plantagenet fiefdom forfeited to the Capet crown. As the possibilities of war escalated the papacy intervened, suggesting Isabella, the wife of Edward II and sister of the French monarch, as a suitable envoy to negotiate a peace settlement. After the execution of the earl of Lancaster in 1322, she had secretly become the center of opposition to Hugh Despenser as many English lords resented his overbearing and opulent manner. Despite her intrigues the queen was sent to the French court of her brother in March 1325, where she successfully persuaded Charles IV to abandon his occupation of Gascony, provided the English sovereign offered homage for the duchy. While in Paris Isabella became the focus of the outlawed English rebels and among the exiled party she met Roger Mortimer, who had escaped from the Tower of London three years earlier. The queen had previously known Mortimer and their relationship quickly developed into a love affair. Together with the English rogues they began to plot an invasion and overthrow of the Plantagenet throne.

The possibility of war with France still remained unresolved, pending the required pledge of homage by Edward II. He was reluctant to leave England and agreed to send his son as a surrogate. In September the thirteen-year-old prince Edward traveled to France to perform the required oath. However, once under the control of Isabella, she refused to permit the heir to return to his father. By the following year Charles IV had tired of his sister's scandalous affair with Mortimer and ongoing intrigues, forcing them to leave his realm. The party in opposition soon found refuge in the nearby court of Hainault, where a marriage agreement was arranged between Lord Edward and the daughter of the local count. With the funds from the dowry the queen was able to raise an invasion army of mercenaries and in September sailed for the Suffolk coast with Mortimer and her son to seize the crown of England.

After landing in England Isabella and her army were met with little armed resistance as she advanced against London and the Plantagenet court. At the approach of the queen and Prince Edward, the Londoners quickly renounced the king in favor of his wife. With the loss of his principal city Edward II, along with the Despensers, abandoned all resistance, traveling to the base of their power in the west. After consolidating her authority and appointing her son as governor of the realm, the rebel league marched against the fleeing monarchy as the Despensers and the crown's allies were hunted down and executed. On November 16, 1326, Edward II was seized at Neath Abbey in south Wales and transferred to the security of Kenilworth Castle.

While Edward II remained in captivity Isabella and Mortimer summoned a parliament in the name of Prince Edward to meet at Westminster in January 1327 where the king was officially deposed under six Articles of Desposition. To give greater legality to the assembly's actions a deputation was sent to Kenilworth to obtain his voluntary abdication. Initially Edward II refused to surrender the throne. However, when the parliament threatened to deny his son's rightful inheritance to the English realm, he agreed to the demand and on January 16, 1327, renounced his monarchy.

In late January 1327 the fourteen-year-old prince Edward was crowned as the king of England. Soon after the coronation of his son, the deposed monarch was transferred to harsher confinement at Berkely Castle. Edward II's continued presence in England presented a constant threat to the new and unsure regime, serving as a rallying point for future rebellion. Edward III was too young to rule independent of his mother and her lover and, as Roger Mortimer began to assume the dominant role in the royal council, he was increasingly resented by the lords and commons. As the popularity of the government steadily declined, in July an attempt was made to rescue Edward II, which succeeded for a brief period before his recapture. Mortimer grew concerned over a future successful escape, ordering the murder of the ex-king to safeguard his usurpation of power. On September 21, 1327, the Plantagenet court announced that Edward II had died of natural causes. The exact manner of his death was never disclosed or determined.

EDWARD III, 1312–1327–1377

As the result of baronial rebellions, in early 1327 King Edward II was forced to renounce his monarchy in favor of his fourteen-year-old son, Prince Edward. The future Edward III was born on the morning of November 13, 1312, at Windsor Castle and was the first child of Edward II and Queen Isabella. Several days after the heir apparent's birth he was named as the earl of Chester and granted numerous estates and castles. He was educated by private tutors appointed by the royal household, receiving instruction in reading, writing, French, English, Latin, religion, and the social graces of music, dancing and court etiquette. Unlike his father Edward enthusiastically participated in martial sports and enjoyed jousting and field sports. In preparation for knighthood he received military training under the guidance of experienced masters of arms in the handling of the lance, sword and crossbow, while becoming a skilled horseman.

While the young earl of Chester grew into adolescence, England was beset with the weak and ineffective rule of Edward II and the ongoing revolts of the barons, which threatened the future of the Plantagenet monarchy. The royal council was dominated by a series of court favorites who further alienated the nobility by their overbearing and pretentious manner. By 1325 the rebel lords had rallied around the queen and, while on a diplomatic mission to the French court she raised an invasion army for the dethronement of her husband. The thirteen-year-old prince played only a passive part in the rebellion, serving as a figurehead to give legitimacy to the new regime. On January 15, 1327, Edward II was officially deposed by the Westminster Parliament and twelve days later his son was crowned as Edward III.

On February 3 the new king presided over his first parliament, which created a ruling regency council dominated by the queen and her lover, Roger Mortimer, to govern the realm for the underaged Edward III. Soon after establishing the machinery of government, to redirect attention away from the recent usurpation of power, the guardians turned their first policy initiative toward a renewal of the war against Scotland. In April 1327 a large military force began to assemble in the northern city of York under the nominal command of Edward III. He had played a sheltered role in the armed overthrow of his father and after his recent knighting was anxious to gain his first combat experiences. As the Plantagenet army began its advance the Scots under Robert Bruce again employed their tactic of refusing a direct confrontation and instead harried the English line of march. After weeks of pursuing the elusive Scottish cavalry, in late August the monarch was compelled to abandon his campaign, having gained either victory or glory. The Scots had again thwarted the military might of the English crown with their strategy of evasion. Following the withdrawal of the Plantagenet troops Robert I ravaged deep into the northern English counties, finally forcing the court of Edward III to offer peace negotiations. After five months of deliberations, in March 1328 the Treaty of Edinburgh was signed, which guaranteed the sovereignty of Scotland and established the border between the two realms.

In January 1328 Edward III was married to Philippa, the daughter of Count William V of Hainault. The marriage was part of the larger political agreement that had been earlier negotiated by Queen Isabella to ensure the finances for the invasion army for her usurpation of the English crown. Edward III and his queen were well suited for each other, developing a close and loving relationship despite his numerous infidelities. Philippa played an active role in the Plantagenet court and government, accompanying her husband on many of his foreign campaigns. Through the years the queen became a trusted unofficial advisor to Edward III. As a continental princess and through her association with her Flemish relatives, Philippa brought to England the latest in letters, arts and music, using royal patronage as a means to acquire prestige and power for the regime. She imported foreign authors and sponsored English poets, including the young Chaucer. The marriage resulted in twelve children, seven sons and five daughters, securing the succession of the Plantagenet throne with the birth of Edward, the future Black Prince, in 1330.

While Edward III was directly involved with the Scottish war, the royal court came under the supremacy of Roger Mortimer as he eliminated all but his friends from the ruling council. He was considered a usurper by the established peerage and his indignant and opulent lifestyle further alienated the nobility. By late 1328 a party in opposition, which was led by Henry of Lancaster, began to form against the newly created earl of March. As the Lancaster faction grew in strength Mortimer began to attack and pillage their lands and, with custody of the young king, maintained his control over the realm. While Edward III continued to be loyal to his mother and, through her to the March earl, the rebel league remained impotent. However, in early 1330 Mortimer began to plot to eliminate members of the royal family in an attempt to seize the monarchy for himself. As the threats against the Plantagenet regime intensified, Edward III, with the encouragement of Henry of Lancaster and his allies, mounted a counter-conspiracy and on October 19, 1330, during a meeting of the Great Council, personally arrested the earl of March. A proclamation was issued the next morning announcing that Edward III had assumed personal authority for his government while summoning a parliament to address the grievances of the kingdom.

The following month the parliament met at Westminster, where Mortimer was condemned to death for his acts of treason against the realm. The king exacted little personal revenge against the March earl's retainers, taking many of the more talented lords into his administration, signaling his intention to rule with an unified nobility under a policy of toleration and inclusion. To further unite the magnates Edward III cancelled all the grants of lands issued by the regency, returning the property to the rightful owners and rewarding his friends with gifts of titles and estates. The decrees issued at the Westminster Parliament were intended to set the tone for the style of the new government.

Over the next two years Edward III consolidated his sovereignty, working to unify his nobles and bring peace and prosperity to the kingdom. During the period of internal reconciliation he maintained friendly relations with Scotland while building up his authority and military might. While he steadily united his realm, the Scottish Lowland warlords had continued to raid into the Plantagenet border counties with impunity in violation of the Treaty of Edinburgh. With a just provocation established, Edward III directed his first foreign policy initiative at re-securing his suzerainty over his northern neighbor. To better facilitate the conquest a treaty of mutual cooperation was ratified with Edward Balliol, the son of the deposed Scottish monarch, John Balliol. Balliol had earlier forged an alliance with Scottish dissidents and needed the powerful English military to overthrow the Bruce kingship. In November 1332 he appeared before the crown to acknowledge the Plantagenet sovereign as his overlord. In May 1333, in support of his new ally, Edward III launched his invasion from York with a large well prepared and provisioned force personally trained by the king. The formidable army was directly under the command of Edward III, who advanced the campaign against the stronghold at Berwick. The castle was invested and, as the siege wore on, in July the Scots mounted an attack to relieve the city's garrison. However, as their troops marched south they were outmaneuvered and routed at Halidon Hill by the Plantagenet militia. The victory compelled the Berwick defenders to surrender and, with the fortified port's seizure, the northern English lordships were freed of Scottish occupiers. Soon after the triumph at Halidon Hill Balliol, backed by a strong contingent of Plantagenet infantry and cavalry, invaded Scotland, usurping the monarchy forcing the boy-king, David II, to flee to France to once again impose English overlordship over the recalcitrant Scottish lords.

While the Plantagenet crown maintained a sizable military presence in Scotland to enforce the reign of its vassal, the royal council began to take measures to address the escalating hostility of France. In 1337, war with the new Valois king, Philip VI, who had succeeded his cousin, Charles IV, threatened to erupt when the French army invaded the English duchy of Gascony. Edward III countered first with a diplomatic initiative directed at denying the Valois court allies in Flanders and Germany. Through the liberal use of money the Flemish counts and Rhinish lords agreed to support the English invasion of France. Edward III laid claim to the French regime through his mother's birthright as a sister of Charles IV, directly challenging the legal right of Philip of Valois to the throne to signal the beginning of the Hundred Years War. Before departing for the continent a regency council was named to govern the realm and parliament summoned to approve the campaign and provide revenue.

In 1338 Edward III sailed to Coblenz to formally sign the treaty of alliance with the German and Flemish warlords. In the following year he launched his attack but the French withdrew to the south, refusing to give battle, content for the allies to deplete their war supplies and treasure. The Anglo-German army spent the remainder of the year ravaging the countryside but, with his money exhausted, the Plantagenet king was compelled to abandon the campaign and return home. After two years of warfare the English invasion had failed to achieve any tangible results and had left the crown heavily burdened with debt.

In early 1340 the royal court crossed the Channel to London and Edward III again assumed his personal rule, summoning a parliament to address the unresolved grievances of the Church and barons and raise new revenues. At the assembly he successfully settled the dissident of the nobles and prelates and with the grant of taxes made preparations to renew the French war. However, before he could return across the Channel the Valois throne began to assemble a large navy for a counter-invasion of England. While the French fleet remained inactive on the Holland coast near Sluys, the Plantagenets quickly collected every available vessel, sailing to engage Philip VI's flotilla. From his flagship, *Thomas*, Edward III personally directed his heavily armed squadron against the still-anchored French warships, destroying virtually the entire armada on June 24, 1340. The triumph at Sluys ended any danger of Valois naval activities directed at England but it in no way diminished their military might.

Following his success at Sluys Edward III landed his army in Flanders, joining his allies to renew their offensive against France. The Anglo-Flemish troops advanced against the great stronghold at Tournai, which was placed under siege. While the investment wore on, during the summer the English pillaged the surrounding towns and countryside, attempting to lure Philip of Valois into open battle. Despite the occasional small skirmish the French refused a general engagement. By October, receiving little military or financial aid from his kingdom and with the campaigning season drawing to a close, the English sovereign agreed to a papal-sponsored truce, which was later extended several times. In late November he returned to London after another unsuccessful campaign, which was blamed on the lack of support from the governing Plantagenet council.

After reestablishing his personal rule Edward III began a political campaign to address the corruption and lack of competency in his ministers and secure unfettered revenues. The chief counselors were replaced and many local ineffectual officials were dismissed. However, many of the bureaucrats were members of the Church who strongly opposed the throne's decrees, demanding a parliament be called to defend their rights. Under the leadership of the archbishop of Canterbury the nobility and commons rallied to defend the clergy and, as the discord intensified, Edward III was forced to summon parliament. To mollify the oppositionists and gain much needed new money he agreed to grant concessions, allowing the assembly more control over taxation and a greater consultation role.

As the Plantagenet court was appeasing the unrest of Parliament, war preparations were continued. However, before returning to France Edward III was compelled to intervene in Scotland, where his vassal-king, Edward Balliol, had been overthrown by the forces of David II and much of the kingdom re-conquered. In October 1341 the royal army marched north to re-impose Plantagenet overlordship. However, with time and as their allies, the Scots withdrew, refusing to confront the English, resulting in another fruitless campaign. With the onset of winter the king retired to London with most of Scotland still under David II's sovereignty.

While the initiative against Scotland had diverted the English crown away from its major war effort in France, Edward III gained a new opportunity to renew the Hundred Years War when the duke of Brittany died without a direct heir. The ducal title was claimed by John of Montfort and Charles of Blois, who was an ally of Philip VI. The Brittany magnates and Church favored the Montfort duke and he was proclaimed the rightful successor. Charles of Blois countered by appealing to his overlord, Philip VI, for military aid, signaling the beginning of the Breton War of Succession. When the French threatened to invade the duchy John offered his liege homage to Edward III for his intervention. In early 1341 the Valois army crossed into Brittany, seizing the northern lordships while the English were distracted with their campaign against Scotland. It was not until the following year that Plantagenet troops began to arrive in Brittany and in June Edward III's soldiers began their first attack. Marching from Brest to the north the Anglo-Breton forces succeeded in capturing several fortified towns, however, the advance stalled as the Blois count counterattacked.

Edward III had remained in England, raising additional soldiers and money for the Breton initiative and in late October sailed to Brest with reinforcements and to take personal command. Contingents of troops were sent to again attack the strength of the Frano-Breton alliance in the north while the king marched to the south to besiege the fortified port of Vannes. With the exception of the major strongholds, which continued to resist the assaults of Edward III, by December most of the duchy was in his hands. While the unconquered castles remained under investment Philip VI finally arrived with a formidable army, forcing the scattered Plantagenet troops to relinquish their recent gains and retire toward Brest. The French again refused to offer a general engagement, content for the allies to deplete their energy and treasure. With the war again turning into a stalemate and with winter approaching, a truce was signed under papal sponsorship.

With the armistice in place Edward III returned to London in February 1343, determined to create a ruling council that could provide the revenue and administer the kingdom to allow him the freedom to wage war against the Valois court unfettered with concerns about his realm. The government was reorganized and revitalized with able new ministers who assumed the responsibility of managing the regime and dealing with the potentially rebellious Church and nobility. Freed from the burden of daily operations Edward III began to plan for a renewal of the Hundred Years War.

While the incursion into Brittany continued to languish, resulting in no resolution, to force the decisive confrontation that the throne needed, a double invasion of France was prepared. The first arm of the campaign was to be directed against the duchy of Gascony, which was under increasing danger of being seized by Philip VI, while Edward III was to personally command the second wing from Normandy against the Ile de France region. In the summer of 1346 a sizable expeditionary force was dispatched from Gascony to harry the Loire area. In July the king landed in Normandy to burn and pillage the countryside and towns and threaten Paris, once again attempting to lure the French into a pitched battle. As the Plantagenet army demonstrated along the Seine and Somme rivers, Philip VI summoned his vassals, marching to challenge the English. At the approach of the French Edward III established a strong defensive position protected by a dense forest on the right and a river on the left near the town of Crecy. On August 26 the Valois advance guard began the battle by charging Edward III's well-fortified lines of dismounted knights and archers to be thrown back. After the initial failure the main body of French cavalry advanced as wave after wave were cut down by the English longbowmen. The bloody encounter lasted into the night when the Valois monarch was finally compelled to order the withdrawal. The battle at Crecy was a total triumph for Edward III with over ten thousand French casualties while his losses were considerably less.

Following the victory the Plantagenet war council directed the campaign north against Calais to secure a French bridgehead for future attacks and allow a safe harbor for the crown's Channel shipping interest. The town was strongly protected by high walls and garrisoned with seasoned troops, making a direct assault impossible. Edward III was forced to build trench lines and prepare for a long siege designed to starve the defenders into submission. By the summer of 1347 food supplies became exhausted and, with Philip VI unable to assemble a relief army, the town surrendered. With Calais in his hands the Plantagenet king strengthened the port's defenses and established a permanent colony by bringing new residents from England. Following the capture of Calais both rivals had become exhausted by the war and in September agreed to a truce arranged by Pope Clement VI. The armistice was extended numerous times as the Black Death devastated both France and England, bringing an end to active campaigning.

While Edward III had remained in France and distracted by the siege at Calais, in Scotland David II prepared to break the ongoing truce by mounting an invasion of the northern English lordships to support his Valois ally. In October 1346 the Scots launched their assault, seizing numerous lightly defended border fortifications and plundering the countryside. As the Bruce monarch continued his pillaging raid south, the local town militias began to assemble around the Plantagenet throne's northern lieutenants, the archbishop of York and Henry Percy. As the English marched north the two armies clashed at Neville's Cross on October 17, 1346, where the Scots were routed and their king taken prisoner. The victory secured the border counties, allowing Edward III to direct all his resources and energies against France.

In 1348 the Black Death entered England through the seaports, bringing disastrous consequences: severe depopulation, social disruptions, loss of tax revenues and economic depression. As the kingdom struggled to recover, military campaigning was halted and through papal intervention attempts were made to find a resolution to the ongoing war with France. However, no peace treaty resulted and in 1355 the Plantagenet throne renewed its offensive after the new French monarch, John II, failed to extend the truce. Edward III sent his son, Edward, Prince of Wales, from Gascony on a highly successful raid to ravage the Loire and Toulouse regions. In the following year the king again attempted to draw the Valois crown into open battle by harrying Normandy and threatening Paris. Advancing from the Calais enclave the English initiative soon floundered as the French attacked their rear and lines of communications, forcing Edward III to withdraw after a short fruitless campaign. After the failed northern invasion of his father, in July the Prince of Wales launched a second lightning foray from Gascony into the Loire Valley. After plundering the lightly protected area, in September Edward began to retire toward Bordeaux when the formidable army of John II blocked his line of march. Widely outnumbered he was compelled to take a defensive position near the town of Poitiers on a ridgeline that was quickly fortified. On the morning of September 19 the French heavy cavalry began the battle by charging against Edward's formation of men-at-arms and archers. The initial assault was repulsed, to be followed by several additional attacks that all failed to penetrate the English defenses. Finally, in desperation, John II personally commanded the final sortie with a strong contingent of dismounted knights but his advance was thwarted and he was taken prisoner. Following the victory at Poitiers the French sovereign was taken to Bordeaux to discuss terms for a permanent resolution to the war and set the conditions for his ransom. With a papal legate acting as intermediary, a two-year truce was ratified and in May 1357 John II was sent to London to facilitate the ongoing negotiations.

After John II arrived in England peace discussions were resumed, with papal legates shuttling between both rivals. In May 1358 a proposal was accepted by Edward III, which granted him a large cash indemnity and nearly all of western France, but the Valois government delayed any decision. A second offer was put forward the following year by the English court, demanding all of western France and a sizable ransom while the king agreed to renounce his claim to the French monarchy. In May 1359 when the proposition was received by the Valois Estates-General, it was rejected as too severe.

With the failure to reach a peace treaty, Edward III began to prepare for the renewal of the campaign to force a final settlement with a demonstration of his military might. In late 1359 a well-equipped and provisioned army advanced from Calais with the objective of seizing the strategic city of Rheims in eastern France. In November the stronghold was placed under investment after the garrison defiantly refused to surrender. As the siege wore on the Plantagenet troops suffered terribly in the harsh winter conditions and early in the new year the attack had to be abandoned. The king now redirected his initiative south into the duchy of Burgundy, which was brutally plundered before returning to threaten Paris. As before the French refused to offer battle and, after devastating the countryside and unprotected towns, Edward III agreed to open peace negotiations. After two weeks of discussions the Treaty of Bretigny was signed in May 1360, which granted the Plantagenet crown the western one-third of France free of all fealty and set the final amount of the ransom for John II while the English throne agreed to renounce its claim to the Valois monarchy.

After finalizing the Treaty of Bretigny Edward III departed to London to begin the difficult task of asserting his sovereignty over the recent acquisitions. The French population openly resisted the Plantagenet occupation and the accompanying heavy taxes, making the implementation of the peace accord impossible. Slowly the English hold over the new territories became tenuous and, when the duchy of Gascony revolted in June 1368, the new French king, Charles V, declared war and claimed full suzerainty over the English-occupied demesne.

Before renewing hostilities the Valois government initiated a diplomatic campaign to isolate its Plantagenet foe. Flanders withdrew its support for Edward III when the French king arranged the marriage of his brother, Philip, to the daughter of the local count. Castile abandoned Edward III when Charles V sent his soldiers to buttress Henry of Trastamara against the pro–English Peter II in their ongoing Spanish civil war. Brittany was won over when the new Breton duke, John V, found it more politically expedient to support the Valois court. While the English were losing their continental allies the Scottish border attacks again erupted as the Lowland warlords raided into the Plantagenet northern counties and the Bruce monarchy negotiated a new military treaty of mutual cooperation with France to further dilute Edward III's international strength.

With the English alliances shattered, to enforce his sovereignty over the disputed Gascony duchy, Charles V invaded the lordship, seizing the border region. At the resumption of the Hundred Years War Edward III responded by launching two formidable cavalry raids, sending his son, John of Gaunt, to plunder Normandy while John Chandos ravaged central France. The forays succeeded in inflicting a large amount of damage but they failed to bring Charles V back to the negotiating table.

While the Plantagenet campaigns were producing no tangible results, the French began a program of tax exemptions, promises of land and titles combined with intimidation and armed encroachments to win the loyalty of the English-occupied lordships. Edward III's French towns and lands now came under increasing assaults as the local warlords deserted his rule and the Valois army expanded its war effort. Under the new French initiative, by 1372 the Poitou region was lost.

As Charles V energetically and relentlessly pressed his military and political initiatives, the isolated Plantagenet king remained in England, growing increasingly inactive and withdrawn with age. The management of the government was largely handled by his ministers and, without the forceful personality of Edward III, parliament grew more independent, openly challenging the royal power. The kingdom had suffered financially through the years of constant war and the effects of the Black Death, making it difficult for the council to raise fresh taxes to defend its possessions in France. The prolonged period of economic slowdown, harsh taxes and the perceived opulent and extravagant spending of revenues by the crown and its advisors resulted in the growing unpopularity of the regime. As the realm became worn out from the conflict in France, the throne and parliament welcomed the papal-sponsored two-year truce of 1375, with Edward III only retaining control over Calais and a coastal strip in the southwest centered on Bordeaux.

While the parliament became more militant Edward III refused to summon its members until financial needs forced the April 1376 session. In the so-called Good Parliament the merchants and shire knights united to refuse any new requests for money until significant administrative reforms were announced and the regime's advisors dismissed. Edward III was forced to accept the harsh terms, marking the first time the commons had set the political agenda.

After the April 1376 parliament Edward III's grasp of the government grew weak and ineffective while his son, John of Gaunt, duke of Lancaster, assumed personal control of the realm. In the autumn the Lancaster duke replaced the newly appointed ministers and restored the former administration in defiance of the Good Parliament. The crown's council grew increasingly unpopular with the commons and prelates in early 1377 when a new parliament under the direction of John voted a poll tax to finance the budget shortage and attempted to seize ecclesiastical rights of the Church. As the unrest grew riots erupted in London and Gaunt was forced to flee. Edward III remained isolated at Richmond as his once peaceful and united kingdom slipped toward dissension, unable to personally intervene. He had suffered from several strokes in his last years and as his health worsened King Edward III died on June 21, 1377, at age sixty-four after ruling for over fifty years.

RICHARD II, 1367–1377–1399–1400

After a reign of fifty years Edward III died in 1377 to be succeeded by his grandson, Richard II. The future king was born at Bordeaux in the English duchy of Gascony on January 6, 1367, and was the second son of Edward, Prince of Wales, and Joan of Kent. With his father frequently absent on military campaigns he grew up in a household dominated by his loving and devoted mother. In 1371 Richard's older brother unexpectedly died and the young lord was now second in line to the monarchy. He had spent his first four years in Bordeaux. However, with his new importance to the Plantagenet succession, Richard was sent to live in England at his family castles at Berkhamsted and Kennington. Prince Edward appointed tutors for his son's education and he was instructed in reading, writing, languages, religion and the social graces of dancing, singing and court etiquette. However, his academic education was secondary to the preparation for knighthood, where Richard of Bordeaux received training routinely in the handling of the lance, sword and crossbow and the equestrian skills of a mounted warrior. At the age of six, acting through an advisory council, he gained his first exposure to politics with his appointment as regent while the king and his father campaigned in France.

In June 1376 Prince Edward died and his nine-year-old son assumed the role of heir apparent. Richard was paraded before the parliament, where he was recognized as the successor and in November he was officially named Prince of Wales to further buttress his rights of inheritance. While Richard remained on his family estates under the immediate care of his mother, on June 21, 1377, Edward III died and his grandson was acknowledged as the new Plantagenet sovereign. On July 16 he was crowned at Westminster Abbey as Richard II in an elaborate coronation planned by his uncle, John of Gaunt, duke of Lancaster. The ceremony was designed to usher in a new era of mutual cooperation and union between the institution of the monarchy and the kingdom.

Following the enthronement a regency council was chosen to administer the realm in the name of the minor king. The new ministry was dominated by parliamentary members who had united to exclude the ruling oligarchy Lancaster faction and as such was a compromise government of differing political interests, resulting in a stagnant and ineffective guardianship. While the regents struggled to provide adequate finances and address the mounting grievances of the kingdom, the young Richard II remained under the direct control of his mother, who utilized her position at court to exercise considerable behind-the-scenes power to promote the interest of her son.

The first years of Richard II's reign were dominated by the unsuccessful struggle against France and the ongoing difficulty of raising adequate revenue to fund the government. Several military campaigns were launched against the French. However, they failed to achieve any meaningful results and only added to the budget shortfall. By 1379 the English ruling council faced a severe financial crisis. In an attempt to create a new source of funding the regency, with the approval of parliament, approved the creation of an universal poll tax. The levy was widely unpopular and strongly resisted throughout the kingdom. The unrest was heightened in the following year when a more severe second poll tax was introduced. The assessment was met with widespread avoidance and, as the throne's agents pressed the collection process, rioting erupted in the southeastern lordships to begin the Peasants' Rebellion of 1381. By May a great army of dissenters was assembled and, under the command of Wat Tyler, advanced toward London, demanding an end to their oppression and an expansion of the Magna Carta to break the bondage of feudalism. As the rebels marched to the capital they turned into a mob, destroying property and murdering the local population. While the rioters mutinied with impunity, Richard II's regents maintained their impotency from the safety of the Tower of London. By the time the dissidents reached London the residents were in a panic, demanding protection from the regime. As the danger mounted the ministers remained indecisive and it was finally the king who announced his intention to personally meet with the peasants' leadership. He conferred with Tyler and his lieutenants on June 14 readily agreeing to all their terms. However, the rogues refused to disperse and the chaos continued. On the next day a second conference was hastily scheduled at Smithfield where a show of crown military might was planned. As Wat Tyler approached Richard II, the mayor of London stabbed him to death. The capital militia now attacked, surrounding the rebels to destroy the momentum of the Peasants' Revolt. Over the next month the principals of the movement were tracked down and executed to fully reimpose the supremacy of the Plantagenet monarchy.

Following Richard II's personal triumph at Smithfield, the ruling authority of the kingdom continued under the current feeble regents. However, to create a more effective administration, a parliament was summoned for November to address the ongoing misgovernment and to make changes in the royal council. At the November assembly the existing ministers of the regency were replaced largely with magnates loyal to John of Gaunt, who had returned to court after his brief self-imposed exile. Through the new appointees the Lancaster duke now became the power behind the throne. While his uncle set the crown's policies the sixteen-year-old king amused himself by surrounding his immediate household with a group of favorites who, through their frivolous and opulence, alienated the governing peerage. However, from this band of royal retainers a political faction had begun to form which increasingly opposed the initiatives of the ruling barons.

In 1378 the Gaunt government had begun a series of negotiations with various European courts for the marriage of the young king and in late 1379 an agreement was reached with the German emperor, Wenceslas. The political accord was signed to forge a closer relationship with the rich and powerful continental empire and to foster a future military alliance against France. On January 20, 1380, Richard II married Anne of Bohemia, the daughter of the former emperor Charles IV. The new queen and her husband soon developed a loving and close relationship, with Anne frequently traveling with her husband on his many journeys throughout the realm. As a German princess Anne had been raised in the wealthy court of the Holy Roman Empire and possessed great charm, intelligence and an interest in the arts and letters. She became a trusted advisor of Richard II and often interceded with the royal council to plead for mercy for numerous lords accused of serious crimes. The queen died prematurely at age twenty-eight from the plague without producing a successor to the Plantagenet throne.

As Richard II reached adulthood he was physically described as possessing handsome muscular features and was over six feet in height with long, flowing, blondish hair. He became an energetic patron of the arts and letters, sponsoring Chaucer and other English poets. However, he showered the bulk of his favor on Westminster Abbey, with lavish gifts and the renovation of the church. Under the influence of his two continental wives the king introduced a more formal and elegant style to his court and was credited with instituting the use of the handkerchief.

While Richard II remained under the tutelage of the regency council, across the Channel the French continued their relentless and successful campaign to recover sovereignty over the English-occupied territories in Gascony. In 1382 two attempts were made to thwart the war effort of the new Valois king, Charles VI, by sending an invasion army to aid the Flemish and a second to buttress the Portuguese in their ongoing struggle against Castile, an ally of France. However, both initiatives ended in failure and an embarrassment to the governing baronial faction. The Flemish and Portuguese expeditions served to crystallize the confrontation between the two rival political parties of the sovereign and John of Gaunt. Richard II had played no role in the foreign policy of the Gault regency, which further enhanced his desire to secure his independent rule. As he pressed to gain his kingship, a series of plots was instigated against the Lancasters, which further increased the mounting hostility. It was only through the intervention of the queen mother and the archbishop of Canterbury that a fragile reconciliation was attained.

As the Plantagenet court was beset with an internal power struggle, in France the Valois crown had renewed its alliance with Scotland, sending troops to Edinburgh for a joint invasion of the English border counties. While the Franco-Scottish army prepared for the coming campaign, the Lancaster government mounted a pre-emptive strike in an attempt to thwart the anticipated attack. In July 1385 the royal levies and the private retainers of John of Gaunt and the barons assembled at Newcastle with Richard II in personal command. As the English advanced the allies withdrew north, refusing to risk defeat in a decisive encounter. In frustration the royal forces plundered the eastern Lowlands. However, no major battle occurred and, in defiance of his uncle's strategy to continue the war, a retreat was ordered by the king. The expedition achieved no victory or personal glory for Richard II but did deter the Franco-Scottish incursion.

The fragile peace between Richard II and John of Gaunt had been further damaged by the recent Scottish war. After his return to London the king seized upon the prospects of a foreign enterprise to at least temporarily rid himself of his uncle to enhance his quest for independence. Through his marriage the Lancaster duke had a claim to the vacant Castile crown and his nephew actively sponsored an invasion of Spain to aid John's pursuit of a separate throne. A parliament was assembled in the autumn to approve the necessary funds for the campaign but the commons refused any money unless the Church also matched their grant. The prelates protested at the encroachment into their ecclesiastic prerogatives but, under pressure from the royal party, finally agreed. The commons pressed their success by demanding that their king no longer petition the assembly for revenue to administer his household and provide a periodic accounting of his expenses. At this perceived threat to his personal privileges, he angrily refused, dismissing the parliament. However, Richard II had the necessary money for his uncle's foreign adventure and with the absence of the dominant force in the Lancaster faction he was now able to overcome the opposition and assume his autonomous rule.

With John of Gaunt engaged with his personal war for a crown in Spain, the king's youngest uncle, Thomas of Woodstock, duke of Gloucester, assumed control of the Lancaster party. Thomas had already had several hostile encounters with his nephew and each fostered a strong hatred for the other. Unlike his older brother the Gloucester duke was overly ambitious and totally absorbed by greed and self-advancement. Three months after the departure of John of Gaunt from the political scene, a parliament was assembled to address the threat of a French invasion on the English homeland. The Gloucester faction gained widespread approval by seizing on the danger to masquerade as the kingdom's protector to weaken the authority of Richard II's new regime. With a lack of popular support the king's inner circle was directly challenged by Thomas of Woodstock in a baronial power play, demanding the dismissal of the Plantagenet's chief advisors. Richard II initially defiantly refused. However, under threat of dethronement he was forced to agree and the government was placed in the hands of a parliamentary committee known as the Lords Appellant, led by the Gloucester duke.

Despite the triumph of the Gloucester party, the king delayed the ouster of his ministers, raising troops to defend his prerogatives. Thomas of Woodstock responded by mobilizing his private retainers and, joined by the earls of Arundel and Warwick, moved to oppose the crown in London. At the approach of the overwhelming rogue military force, Richard II agreed to the arrest of his council. However, his closest ally, Robert de Vere, escaped to the north, recruiting an army to reassert the Plantagenet's will. As de Vere marched south he was intercepted at Radcot Bridge by the Gloucester coalition, which augmented by the arrival of the soldiers of Henry of Bolingbroke, defeated the royal forces. Following the victory the barons advanced to virtually imprison Richard II in the Tower, where he was compelled to approve a parliament in early 1388 for the trial of his counselors and friends on charges of treason.

The so-called Merciless Parliament met on February 3 at Westminster, where Richard II's inner counselors were quickly found guilty and sentenced to death. The full control of the government was now in the hands of the Gloucesters and the king was forced to sanction the proceedings of the hostile ministry while he plotted his revenge. In power the new administration governed the realm as poorly as the prior guardians and, when Richard II finally acted to assert his authority, they found little popular support. Under the Appellants the conflict against France was renewed but they suffered a series of embarrassing military defeats while the border unrest with Scotland again flared up. The foreign campaigns with their accompanying need for funds caused a break in their accord that had been forged with the parliament, which encouraged Richard II to openly rebel. In May 1389 during a meeting of his ministers the king suddenly announced that he was of the age of majority and was assuming his full sovereignty, replacing the Lords Appellants with a ruling directorate of his choosing. Under the new council a series of initiatives and reforms was acted upon to enforce his supremacy over the nobles and relieve the suffering of the population, which brought peace and stability. A truce with France was negotiated, military expenditures were reduced and the taxes were lowered resulting in an economic revival.

Having imposed his supremacy Richard II undertook a number of measures to rebuild the shattered authority of the Plantagenet monarchy. To give the appearance of personal power a private company of knights was hired as a bodyguard and, to raise his dignity, he introduced a more formal and elaborate court life based on the continental style. Richard II created an atmosphere of magnificence and opulence to glorify and set his throne apart from the barons and commons so as to rule in a more autocratic manner. To govern more independently, attempts were introduced to gain financial freedom by making tax levies permanent. The actions undertaken were all non-provocative as he endeavored to maintain peace with the magnates, Church and the population. In November 1389 when John of Gaunt returned from his failed Spanish campaign, he was welcomed back to the new administration, becoming a trusted advisor, friend and elder statesman. As a sign of stability the disgraced Appellants, Woodstock, Arundel and Warwick, were invited back to the council, though they exerted little influence.

While Richard II's assertion of his kingship had brought a new order and prosperity to England, the Hundred Years War had remained unresolved. In 1392 the Plantagenet crown sent the duke of Lancaster to France to negotiate a final settlement to the ongoing conflict. A truce soon ensued from the talks with Charles VI's government and over the next two years the deliberations were continued, finally yielding the Truce of Lelinghen. The treaty did not finalize all the outstanding issues. However, it did result in many years of peace. John of Gaunt was fully supported throughout the mediation process by the king, who had little personal interest in fighting a foreign war.

Despite the general calm that prevailed throughout the realm, there were occasional uprisings by the local lords and population. In 1392 the residents of London rose in revolt against Richard II's request for money and in the following year the earldom of Chester rebelled against the area's high unemployment. To retain peace with parliament the king attempted to stay on good terms with the restless barons. However, the earl of Arundel continually challenged their mutual accord, remaining a potential source of instability.

In the summer of 1394 Richard II began preparations for an expedition to Ireland to re-impose Plantagenet sovereignty over his recalcitrant English vassals and the Irish warlords. In October the royal army was assembled and, with the king in personal command of over four thousand troops, sailed across the Irish Sea to Waterford. The first objective was to subdue the Leinster monarchy but its ruler, Art MacMurrough, refused to offer battle and only limited non-decisive skirmishes resulted. With no prospects for a military victory Richard II opened talks for a reconciliation, which ended with the Irish agreeing to meet in Dublin. In November Richard II was in Dublin, where he reasserted his personal kingship over his local lords, who, through the years of neglect from London, had increasingly grown semiautonomous. The Irish Lordship was reorganized and a new Plantagenet governing body was appointed, which pledged to obey the will of Richard II. Through the intervention of the Anglo-Irish a series of negotiations was held with MacMurrough and the regional Irish kings and chiefs, who were persuaded to offer homage to the English crown.

However, while the sovereign was successfully reimposing his rule over the Irish lordship, a religious uprising known as the Lollards necessitated his return to England in May 1395. The movement had its origins in the corruption and heavy financial demands of the Church and the need for reforms. As the archbishop of Canterbury struckback at the heretics, threatening civil war, they found support among the more liberal nobles of the court, who petitioned parliament for redress. When Richard II arrived in London the Lollard members of his council were compelled to swear an oath to refrain from all future religious activities but he took no further actions against the reformers, who withdrew from their aggressive campaign for change. By his quick and decisive response Richard II ended the threat of religious war between the earls and further imposed his power over the realm.

In 1394 John of Gaunt had arranged the Truce of Lelinghen with France but no final resolution to the Hundred Years War had been found. After his return from Ireland Richard

II again sent his ambassadors to renew the negotiations for a more permanent settlement with Charles VI. However, the deliberations reached an impasse over the issues of the French claim for Calais and English demand for financial reparations. While no compromise could be found, both parties were agreeable to a twenty-eight year truce that was to be ratified with the marriage of the recently widowed Richard II and Isabella, the seven-year-old daughter of the French king. In March 1396 the wedding ceremony was performed by proxy and the treaty finalized. The long-term truce assured peace with the ancestral enemy and, with the Plantagenet's domestic initiatives, the discontent of the barons and commons had been largely contained, allowing Richard II to feel secure on his throne. From a position of power he could finally direct his revenge against the Lords Appellant, who had earlier seized his government and humiliated him in 1388.

In July 1397 Richard II finally struck back at his uncle, Thomas of Woodstock, and the earls of Warwick and Arundel, personally arresting them on charges of treason. Thomas was sent to Calais, where he was murdered on orders from the court; Warwick was exiled to the Isle of Man under heavy guard; and after a short parliamentary trial Arundel was condemned to death for his conspiracy. The two remaining former Appellants, the earl of Nottingham and Henry of Derby, in recent years had become faithful allies and friends of the throne and no retribution was taken against them. With his old enemies eliminated Richard II began to take measures to strengthen his kingship and weaken the influence of the barons. There were new grants of land, titles and lavish gifts to secure the loyalty of the nobility. In the January 1398 Shrewsbury Parliament he was voted the authority to rule as a virtual dictator with the concession of a permanent income, which eliminated the need to summon future parliaments. An enemies' list was compiled of those considered disloyal and a threat and they were forced to pledge loyalty to the crown. As the tyrannical regime intensified, Richard II, who was always surrounded by his personal bodyguard of Cheshire archers, grew increasingly feared and hated.

In December 1397 the king's cousin, Henry Bolingbroke of Derby, was exiled for ten years for his alleged involvement in a plot to seize the throne. In the following year his father, John of Gaunt, died and the banishment of Bolingbroke was extended for life and the great Lancaster properties were forfeited to the Plantagenet court. While Henry began to quietly intrigue from Paris with a small party of allies to regain his seized estates, Richard II announced plans for a second expedition to Ireland. Since his May 1395 departure from the island, the Irish had broken their fealty, renewing their raids against the English settlers. The monarch began to assemble his troops to reassert his rights as overlord and to avenge the death of his appointed successor designate, Roger Mortimer, who had been killed in battle against the rebellious Irish warlords. In late May 1399 the Plantagenet infantry and cavalry crossed the Irish Sea to the port of Waterford. After landing Richard II launched his attack to subjugate the ruler of Leinster, Art MacMurrough. The Irish again reverted to their tactic of refusing to engage in a pitched battle and, after two weeks of fruitless campaigning, the offensive was abandoned. Following the failure to subdue MacMurrough the Plantagenets advanced to the safety of Dublin, where in early July Richard II received the news of Henry Bolingbroke's landing in England. The royal army was quickly re-assembled and marched south to Waterford where the fleet had been anchored. By late July Richard II was back in the kingdom, anxious to muster his allies in defense of his monarchy.

Upon arriving in England the royal court was informed that Henry's small invasion force had been enthusiastically joined by most of the great barons and the northern and eastern lordships were under his authority. As the Bolingbroke campaign gained momentum the king was beset with mass desertion from within his immediate faction and compelled to flee to the safety of northern Wales. On August 11 he arrived at the unassailable Conway Castle, where he soon received envoys from the Bolingbroke alliance. Richard II remained confident that he could rally the once faithful Welshmen to his banner and refused to discuss any terms of surrender, but did agree to meet with his cousin to discuss a settlement. However, as he rode out from the safety of the Conway fortress, the king was seized and taken to Henry at Flint Castle as his prisoner.

A proclamation was issued in the name of the monarch, summoning a parliament to Westminster. From Flint Castle Richard II was taken to London and held in the Tower to await the decision of the lords and commons. To enhance his claim to the English throne Henry quickly formed a new government of his allies and exacted few reprisals against the former council to maintain the peace. Before the parliament assembled the two cousins met in the Tower where, after several heated conferences, Richard II, deserted by all but a few close friends, finally agreed to abdicate and on September 30, 1399, in Westminster, he formally renounced his crown in favor of Henry IV.

Following his dethronement Richard II continued to be held in the Tower as the new Lancaster council decided his destiny, knowing that he would serve as a potential threat to the legitimacy and survival of the newly usurped administration while he was still alive. In late October he was taken to the Lancaster fortress of Pontefract to be held in close captivity. While Richard II remained isolated, a small faction of Plantagenet supporters began to plot the overthrow of Henry IV and the restoration of the former regime. However, their conspiracy was discovered and the Lancaster king escaped capture. The failed attack now sealed the fate of Richard II and on February 14, 1400, it was announced that he had died. No official word was given for the cause of his death. However, it was widely speculated that the last direct Plantagenet king had died from the harsh conditions of his imprisonment.

Part Two
Gothic Kings of Scotland

Genealogical Charts

Chart 5
House of Canmore,
1058–1290

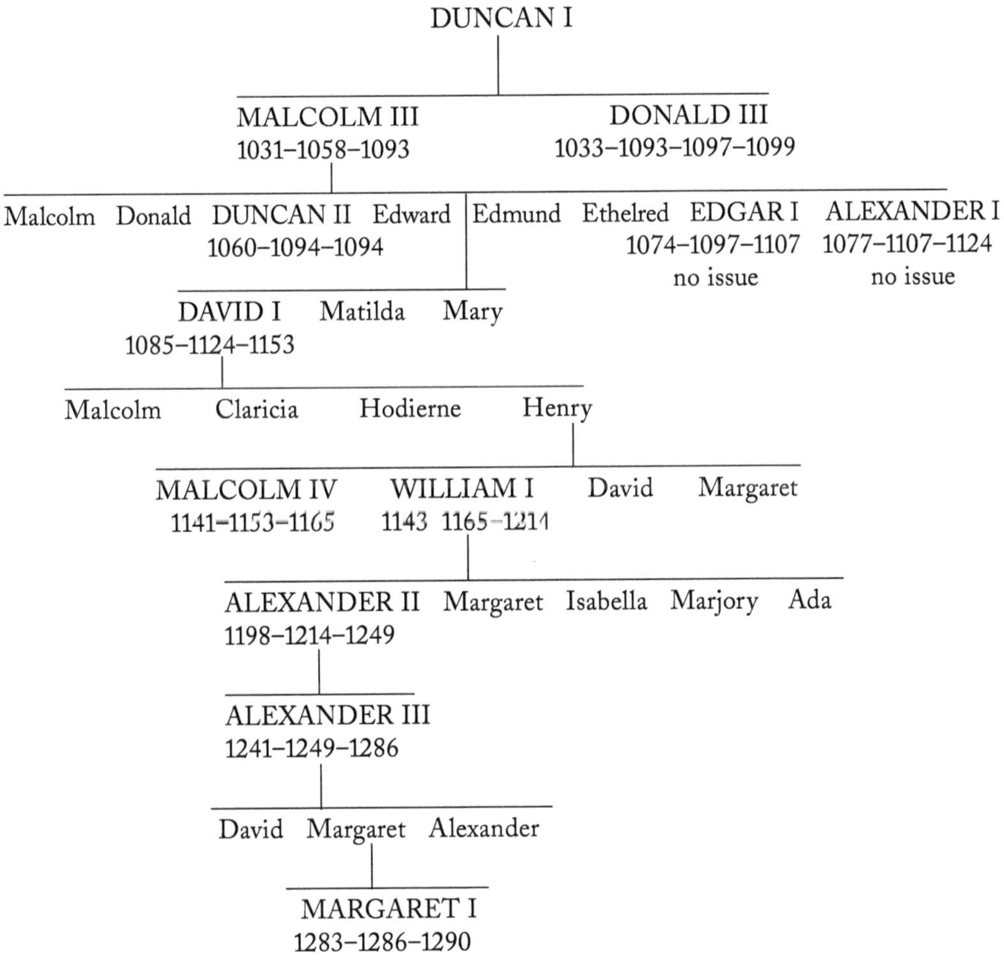

```
                            DUNCAN I
                               |
         ┌─────────────────────┴─────────────────────┐
      MALCOLM III                                DONALD III
     1031–1058–1093                          1033–1093–1097–1099
```

Malcolm Donald DUNCAN II Edward Edmund Ethelred EDGAR I ALEXANDER I
                 1060–1094–1094   1074–1097–1107 1077–1107–1124
                                                        no issue   no issue

DAVID I   Matilda   Mary
1085–1124–1153

Malcolm   Claricia   Hodierne   Henry

MALCOLM IV   WILLIAM I   David   Margaret
1141–1153–1165   1143 1165–1214

ALEXANDER II   Margaret   Isabella   Marjory   Ada
1198–1214–1249

ALEXANDER III
1241–1249–1286

David   Margaret   Alexander

MARGARET I
1283–1286–1290

Chart 6
House of Bruce,
1292–1371

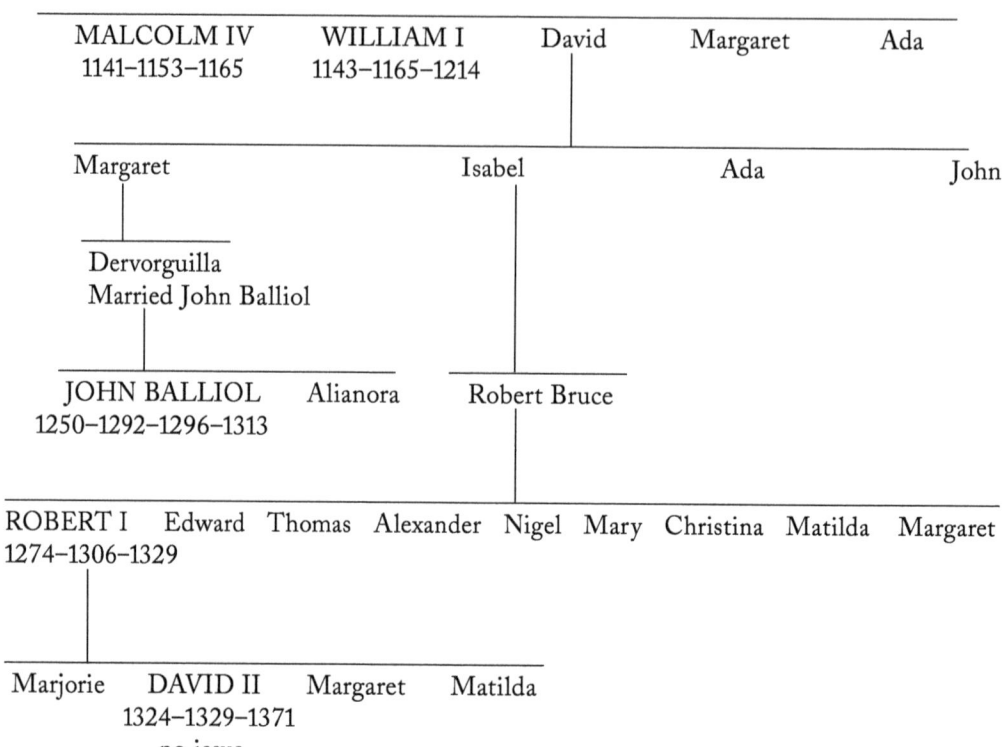

House of Canmore, 1058–1290

The lands that evolved into Scotland had been occupied by five independent tribes by the early ninth century. The conquest and amalgamation of an united kingdom was begun in 843 when Kenneth I MacAlpin seized the monarchy of the Picts and Scots to establish the genesis of a central governing authority. The House of Canmore became the dominant political force in Scotland at the death of the last MacAlpin overlord, Lulach I, and the resulting usurpation of the kingship by Malcolm III. The Canmore lineage reigned through eleven sovereigns, from 1058 until the death of Margaret I in 1290. After establishing a formidable power base in the Lowland fiefdoms, the early kings began the process of imposing the supremacy of the throne over the near independent northern clans. Through armed conquests, negotiated settlements and arranged marriages, they promoted the centralization of power and unification of Scotland. The Canmores encouraged the anglicization of their realm with English institutions, laws and customs by actively sponsoring the emigration of Saxon and Norman noble families. By advocating the theologies of the Holy See against the Celtic-based local associations, the Canmore House became an active patron of the Roman Church. Through a series of frontier wars against the repeated invasions of England, the kings energetically defended the independence of their territory. Under the regime of David I, who asserted his rule over the Highland warlords and expanded his southern borders into England, the monarchy attained its zenith, while the Canmores reached their depths with the death of Margaret I and the resulting civil war and English occupation.

MALCOLM III, 1031–1058–1093

The Canmore dynasty was founded by Malcolm III in 1058 when he usurped the Scottish kingdom from the House of MacAlpin by force of arms to establish a lineage that ruled for over two hundred years. The first Canmore king was born in 1031 and was the son of the Scottish overlord Duncan I and Sybilla, the sister of the earl of Northumbria. In 1034 Duncan I ascended to the throne and, by later annexing the fiefdom of Stratahclyde, reigned over a united Scotland, with the exception of the western territories, which had come under the domination of Norway. However, his succession was not without opposition when his ambitious and formidable cousin, Macbeth, actively challenged his right to the monarchy, marking the beginning of a bitter rivalry. Duncan I's political power base was centered in the Lowlands while Macbeth secured a large following among the Highland nobles and Church.

The ongoing struggle for control of the realm was further strained when, in defiance of historical practice, Duncan I appointed his young son, Malcolm, as his successor. Under the governing Tanist Law of Succession, Macbeth was the recognized heir to Scotland until the eldest male issue of the Canmore sovereign attained the age of majority. Following the naming of the minor Malcolm, the northern lord's inheritance claim to Scotland became questionable. As the result of his exclusion from the suzerainty, to enforce his birthright Macbeth began to plot against his cousin to seize the throne. In August 1040 Duncan I assembled his army, marching north to contend the growing insurgency movement. In the ensuing battle at Pitgaveny, his forces were defeated and the king killed, forcing Malcolm and his brother, Donald, to flee from Scotland.

Driven from his homeland the nine-year-old Malcolm found sanctuary at the court of the English king, Harthacnut. The Canmore lord soon settled in northern England at York in the household of his uncle, the earl of Northumbria, Siward. Under the influence of Siward the young prince was raised as an Anglo-Norse, receiving instruction in the weapons and battle tactics of a Viking warlord. He received little if any formal education but was routinely trained in the use of the sword, battle-axe and spear. The region surrounding York was predominately under the Scandinavian influence as Malcolm became exposed to their culture and society, as opposed to his native Celtic heritage and traditions.

While Malcolm remained in exile in England, the government of Macbeth was becoming increasingly unpopular. The high magnates of Scotland began to appear at the court of Siward to petition Malcolm to seize his rightful inheritance, pledging their financial and martial aid. The Canmore heir stayed in contact with his father's allies and vassals in the Lowland territories as his prestige among the nobles and clerics intensified. He continued to maintain friendly relations with the English monarchy, aggressively appealing to Edward III the Confessor for military forces for an invasion against Macbeth. Finally in 1054 the Saxons agreed to furnish troops and war provisions, allowing Malcolm, backed by his uncle and numerous dissident Scottish lords, to advance against Scotland. To counter the threat to his realm, Macbeth mobilized his friends and vassals, mounting a counter-assault against Malcolm's coalition. On July 27 the two rivals met at Dunsinnan, where the English army drove Macbeth from the battlefield however the victory was not decisive. With the partial triumph the Canmore warlord was only able to impose his authority over the south while the Scottish king fled to the center of his support in Moray. Over the next four years Malcolm consolidated his control over the Lowlands while pursuing his quest for the uncontested overlordship. By 1057 he had expanded his supremacy into the Highland lordships as the retainers of Macbeth increasingly abandoned his cause. In July the Canmores assembled their formidable militia to launch a major offensive initiative against the Scottish ruler, overwhelming and killing him at the battle of Lumphanan. Despite his success Malcolm still lacked the political power base in the northern and western lands to be recognized as monarch, allowing the stepson of the former overlord, Lulach I, to seize the crown. However, he ruled only until March 1058 when Malcolm again attacked Moray, vanquishing Lulach I at the battle of Strathbogie. With his conquest the Canmore prince was able to assume the throne and on April 25, 1058, he was proclaimed as the rightful king of Scotland.

Through his father's prestige and his successful campaigns against Macbeth, Malcolm III had received the homage of the southern magnates, Church and burghs, but his control over the Highland warlords remained only superficial. However, the opportunity to consolidate his dominance over the recalcitrant lords occurred with the death of the earl of Orkney, who died without a direct male successor. The Orkney earl, Thorfinn, was recognized as the overlord for a large region of the northern territories and his death created a power vacuum, allowing his vassals to establish separate autonomous fiefdoms. Malcolm III seized the growing chaos to solidify his rule by marrying Ingibiorg, the heir and daughter of Thorfinn. The political union brought the Canmore throne authority, influence and allies among the Highland noble families, enabling the king to establish a central governing council to impose his supremacy. The personal relationship that developed between Malcolm III and the queen is not known, though the marriage did result in three sons, Malcolm, Duncan and Donald.

While the Scottish monarch was occupied with the consolidation of his realm, he initiated a diplomatic policy that fostered friendly relations with Edward III of England. In 1055 the earl of Northumbria died and the Saxon crown appointed Tostig Godwinson as his successor. The new earl's reign became harsh and unpopular among the local lords and clerics and by 1061 the region was in open rebellion. With the Canmore throne in firm control of the kingdom, Malcolm III was anxious to enlarge his domain to the south, seizing the opportunity of unrest and instability in the northern English earldom to launch an invasion of conquest. However, the Northumbrian warlords rallied to Tostig, thwarting the encroachment, resulting in only the pillaging and sacking of the towns and countryside. The incursion was the first of five major campaigns directed against the border counties with the primary objective of expanding the territory under Canmore rule.

In January 1066 Edward III died without a direct heir. He had earlier appointed Harold Godwinson, the elder brother of the earl of Northumbria, as his successor but Tostig disputed his claim to the kingship. The dissident earl began negotiations for a military alliance with the Norwegian overlord, Harald III Hardrada, agreeing in September to openly challenge Harold II. Malcolm III actively supported and encouraged the rebellion, hoping to aggrandize English lands during the resulting civil war. As the Saxon army marched to York in September to confront the attempted usurpation of Tostig and the Vikings, in the south William, duke of Normandy, who also had a valid claim to the monarchy, crossed the English Channel in an attempt to seize the crown. Harold II quickly defeated the Viking forces at Stamford Bridge, moving south to defend his throne against the Norman invasion. At the battle of Hastings in October the English were defeated and, by the end of the year, William I had been anointed sovereign. While the Normans consolidated their rule in the London region, the political stability of northern England was thrown into disarray with the lack of a central governing authority.

As William I's army swept across England many royal Saxon families were compelled to flee to the safety of Scotland. Among the emigrants were Edgar Atheling, who had been declared king after the death of Harold II, and his two sisters, Christina and Margaret. Malcolm III welcomed the Saxon refugees to his court, allowing them to settle in his realm. Over the following months he remained in close association with the outlawed family, developing a deep affection and devotion to Margaret. His first wife, Ingibiorg, had died several years earlier, creating the prospects for an alliance through marriage to the sister of the Saxon claimant to the English crown. The Canmore governing council negotiated a marriage treaty with Edgar, who was popular among the northern warlords, creating a potential strong base of political support for Malcolm III's ambitions in England. Margaret was a princess of great beauty, grace and royal bearing who had been born in exile in Hungary. She had been educated in the arts and letters by tutors from the Catholic Church, developing from her religious instructors a strong pious character. Malcolm III and Margaret were married in 1070 at the royal residence in Dunfermline. The union resulted in the birth of six sons and two daughters. Three of their sons, Edgar, Alexander and David, reigned as monarchs of Scotland while the eldest, Edward, was killed with his father in battle at

Alnwick. The second son, Edmund, revolted against his family, forming a coalition with his usurper uncle, Donald III, in an attempt to seize the throne. He was captured in battle defending his lands, later dying in prison. To secure the loyalty of the strategic and powerful earldom of Dunkeld, Malcolm III granted the region to his third son, Ethelred, who administered the fiefdom as a vassal of the Canmore court until his death. The eldest daughter, Matilda, married the Norman sovereign, Henry I, becoming queen of England, while the youngest, Mary, became the countess of Boulogne.

Margaret was highly intelligent and energetic, exerting a strong influence on the direction of her husband's policy. Under her guidance the Scottish court was made less Celtic by adopting an orientation toward a more English and western European style society and culture. She took a special interest in transforming the Scottish Church from its predominately Celtic heritage to a more Romanized doctrine. The queen fostered the building of new churches, chapels and monasteries, while inviting the Benedictine monks of Canterbury to establish a priory. The Order was established at Dunfermline, where a small church was built and the monks introduced a new spiritual presence into the life of the Scottish population. At the queen's direction the cult of Saint Andrew was renewed and encouraged. Margaret lived a life devoted to charity and piety, initiating the first measures toward the integration of Scotland into the medieval European community.

While the Canmore court continued to impose its domination over the Scottish realm, the conquest of the northern English counties remained the principal foreign policy goal throughout Malcolm III's kingship. Scotland lacked the military might and financial resources to directly challenge the more powerful English but attempted to establish a presence in Northumbria and Cumbria during the political upheaval, resulting from the Norman overthrow of the recognized Saxon regime. As William I consolidated his authority over England, the barons of Northumbria fiercely resisted the alien usurpation of the crown, while the Normans responded by pillaging and ravaging their lands. In 1070, with the English northern region in turmoil, to support the claim to the Saxon throne of his brother-in-law, Edgar, and to further his aggrandizement ambitions, Malcolm III invaded the frontier countships. However, the second incursion ended in only limited success, as the area had been so severely desolated by the Normans that the Canmore king could not maintain his army in the border lordships due to the lack of shelter and food, forcing his return to Scotland.

By 1072 William I had secured his control over southern England, allowing him to march his formidable army to the north to counter the Scottish aggression of 1070 and assert his sovereignty over the rebellious marchland lordships. Malcolm III lacked the military power necessary to actively contend the campaign, withdrawing without giving battle. William I realized no settlement by force of arms would be possible, offering to negotiate a resolution to the border conflict. Under the resulting Treaty of Abernathy the Norman court agreed to recognize Malcolm III's rights to Northumbria and Cumbria while the Scots pledged homage for the demesne to the English, giving the king's eldest son, Duncan, as hostage to ensure their fealty.

With peace once again restored between Scotland and England, the Canmore king and queen initiated a series of reforms to bring the Scottish Church into closer conformity with the dogma of Rome. There were also measures taken to improve trade by inviting foreign merchants and craftsmen to settle in Scotland. The coming of the Benedictine monks brought education to the Scots, improved agriculture techniques and the introduction of new crops. Malcolm III continued his policy of encouraging emigrant Saxon and Norman families to settle in his kingdom. Through the throne's influence the Lowland regions of Scotland became more anglicized, with a new spirit and energy, while the northern and western districts retained their traditional Celtic traditions and ways. By the granting of lands to the refugees the Canmore regime introduced the continental feudal system to Scotland, which radically altered the structure of local government with new institutions, cultural, judicial and economic fabric.

While Malcolm III was pressing his reform programs in Scotland, he continued to support the quest of Edgar Atheling to the English monarchy while maneuvering to expand his supremacy beyond his Norman counties of Cumbria and Northumbria by initiating a series of sporadic raids against the local Norman lords. Finally in 1079, with William I increasingly occupied and distracted in Normandy defending his lands against the French regime and their allies, the Canmore king disregarded the Treaty of Abernathy, launching a third invasion in an attempt to aggrandize new cross-border lordships. The incursion resulted in the harrying of the countryside however no decisive battle occurred and, with the lack of a decisive victory, the Scots were again frustrated in their ambition to seize additional territories.

In the following year William I responded to the Scottish raid with a show of force, sending his eldest son, Robert Curthose, on a punitive campaign against Malcolm III's kingdom. The Scottish king refused to give battle against the formidable Norman army, withdrawing into the interior while offering to negotiate a settlement. He met the English envoys at Falkirk, agreeing to renew the terms of the Abernathy treaty and to respect the boundaries of the border between the two realms. Before returning to his father's court Robert began the construction of a stronghold at Newcastle to buttress the defenses of northern England as an additional safeguard against future Scottish attacks.

Following the Falkirk settlement the border counties largely remained pacified as the Normans imposed their sovereignty over the local warlords, establishing a strong military presence. However, in 1087 the stable and peaceful political environment in England was shattered by the death of William I, resulting in the eruption of civil war between his heirs. Seeking to exploit the developing impotency and uncertainty in the English power structure, Malcolm III broke his pledges of peace, invading northern England in 1091 while the new Norman king, William II Rufus, was occupied with the rebellion of his brother, Robert II Curthose, in Normandy. In anticipation of a renewal in the Scottish attacks, the English had significantly fortified their defenses by increasing the size of the garrison troops and reinforcing the walls and towers of their castles. As the Canmore army advanced into the marchlands on its fourth campaign, the Norman barons withdrew to the security of their strongholds, offering a spirited and determined resistance. Lacking siege engines and adequate military supplies, Malcolm III was forced to again abandon his incursion with no conquest of land.

After subduing his recalcitrant brother in Normandy, William II Rufus was determined to initiate a punitive campaign against Malcolm III in retaliation for his recent invasion into the English domain. He marched north, capturing several Scottish strongholds and occupying parts of southern Cumbria. He also ordered the construction of a formidable castle at Carlisle, which secured his new acquisitions in Cumbria. With his recent gains protected, William II offered to negotiate an end to the ongoing conflict with the Scots. The two kings met personally, with Malcolm III agreeing to give homage for his English borderlands while William II consented to return parts of his recent conquests. Nevertheless, despite their recent treaty, relations between the realms continued to deteriorate as the Norman crown refused to honor the terms of the agreement. In August 1093, under safe passage guaranteed by hostages, the Canmore monarch traveled to the English court at Gloucester to discuss a peaceful resolution. However, William II Rufus defiantly demanded that Malcolm

III acknowledge and give fealty to him as overlord for the whole of Scotland. In prior years homage had been pledged for only the English lordships of Northumbria and Cumbria and Malcolm III quickly refused to give his oath. With no resolution possible, he withdrew to begin preparations for war.

Malcolm III returned to his homeland to assemble a large invasion force comprised largely of spearmen from the various parts of his realm. The Scots renewed the conflict by advancing unopposed into northern England to begin siege operations against the Norman garrison at Alnwick. While the Canmore troops were enforcing the blockade, the local English earl mobilized his militia to contend the encroachment, attacking the besieging Scots on November 13, 1093. In the ensuing battle Malcolm III, along with his eldest son and heir, Edward, was killed, plunging the succession of the Scottish monarchy into turmoil. Malcolm III Canmore was sixty-two years old at his death and had held the kingship for thirty-five years. As the founder of the Canmore dynasty he had successfully seized the throne of Scotland, consolidated his rule over the whole of the realm with the exception of the western isles and began the process of integrating the kingdom into the European orbit. His descendents reigned for the next 232 years.

DONALD III, 1033–1093–1097–1099

Donald was the second son of the Scottish king, Duncan I, and Sybilla of Northumbria and was born in 1033. His early years were spent in the Celtic-dominated court of his father in southwestern Scotland. At age seven he was forced to flee his homeland when Duncan I was killed in battle, resulting in the usurpation of the realm by the northern warlord, Macbeth. While his older brother, Malcolm, escaped to safety with his mother's relatives in England, Donald found sanctuary with his father's family in the western maritime isles. The Canmore lord grew up in a region which did not acknowledge the sovereignty of the Scottish throne but was claimed by Norway. The emigrant prince became a part of the local nobility, receiving training as a Viking warrior while embracing the Norse-Celtic culture. Through his family's relationships many of the local magnates supported Donald's political ambitions, enabling him to develop a significant following among the western and northern earldoms. While remaining in the maritime territories Donald was married and was known to have had one daughter whose descendents later unsuccessfully challenged the Scottish kingship.

In 1058 Malcolm, backed by an English army and numerous rogue Scottish magnates, overthrew Macbeth seizing the monarchy of his homeland. Donald did not actively support his brother's political faction or invasion and was excluded from the new ruling council and court. He continued to live in exile in relative obscurity, spending a period of his life in the Hebrides Isles and Ireland. By 1060 Donald had settled in the fiefdom of Gowria, assuming the title of earl while maintaining little contact with the Scottish regime. Under the laws of Tanistry, as the brother of Malcolm III, the earl of Gowria was the recognized heir apparent. However, he did not pursue his birthright in the royal household, remaining in the Viking-Celtic-dominated North, rejecting the increasing anglicization orientation of the reigning Canmore administration. As the Norman influence accelerated in the southern lordships, Donald grew increasingly popular among the predominately conservative local population taking no part in Malcolm III's domestic or foreign policies.

The political status quo of Scotland was shattered when the Canmore king and his designated heir, Edward, were killed in battle in 1093 during an unsuccessful invasion into northern England. In the resulting power vacuum the Scottish realm erupted into civil war as hostile factions formed to contest the sovereignty. A party of magnates and clerics in the western and northern earldoms was soon organized around Donald as the rightful heir. As their strength grew the Highland supporters of the Gowria earl assembled an army to oppose the competing Canmore family who was actively advancing Malcolm III's second son, Edgar, for the monarchy. Late in the year the formidable military forces of Donald attacked the Lowland fiefdoms, driving the royal troops into their stronghold at Edinburgh. The might and energy of the Highlanders' initiative forced the Canmores to acknowledge defeat and go into exile. Following their ouster the sons of Malcolm III fled to England for sanctuary, enabling Donald to complete his seizure of the throne of Scotland.

With the banishment of Malcolm III's family Donald III was acknowledged as overlord by the earls, Church and burghs and on November 13, 1093, was invested with the monarchy of Scotland at the historical site of enthronement at Scone. As he began to establish his reign he maintained his popularity in the northern and western earldoms but his usurpation of power had resulted in rebellion among the southern lords and Church. In an attempt to consolidate his rule and to prevent a rival hostile faction from forming around the Canmore claimant, Donald III initiated a policy of expelling the English and Norman emigrants who had been permitted by his brother to settle in Scotland. He had never supported Malcolm III's anglicization program, quickly enacting measures to restore the Scottish Church and local society to the traditional Celtic values. While the restructuring was welcomed by the Highland lordships, the regime was unable to reestablish peace in the Lowland fiefdoms as many of the nobles and clerics remained recalcitrant and unsubmissive, actively resisting the Celtic revival.

The Norman-Scottish border conflict remained unresolved after the death of Malcolm III and the seizure of the monarchy by his brother, as the Lowland warlords continued to raid into northern England with impunity. To secure peaceful relations with his northern neighbor, William II Rufus of England initiated a policy directed at achieving the overthrow of Donald III and the placement of a client vassal on the Scottish throne. He entered into negotiations with Duncan, the eldest son of Malcolm III and his first wife Ingibiorg, to command an invasion army to depose his uncle. Under the ensuing treaty Duncan was granted Norman troops and money for the seizure of the Scottish kingdom for his pledge of fealty. In the spring of 1094 the Canmore lord marched north at the head of a formidable expeditionary force of Normans and dissident Scots, declaring by right of birth to be the legitimate Scottish king. To counter his nephew's attempted usurpation Donald III assembled his local allies and retainers, maneuvering to give battle in defense of his sovereignty. In June the two armies met in battle, resulting in the Scottish regime's infantry being overwhelmed and driven back in defeat by the military might of the English. Despite the allies' victory Donald III managed to escape withdrawing to the base of his Highlands support. Duncan II was soon invested with the kingship of Scotland at Scone, however, his authority was not broadly recognized as his uncle continued to actively resist the loss of his power.

As the new Canmore ruler attempted to solidify his government, the presence of the English army grew increasingly unpopular among the Scottish magnates and clerics, igniting the danger of rebellion, compelling Duncan II to return the foreign soldiers to William II. Without Norman military might to support his monarchy, many of the warlords abandoned the throne as Donald III energetically renewed his campaign against his nephew by rebuilding his armed forces while negotiating new alliances. The deposed sovereign was able to gain the support of many of the southern lords by forging a coalition with Edmund, the third son of Malcolm III and Margaret. With his troop strength greatly enhanced Donald

III renewed the attacks against the regime. After a series of sporadic, inconclusive raids, finally, at the decisive battle of Mondyres on November 12, 1094, the Canmore army was defeated and the king killed, enabling Donald III to once again assert his kingship over Scotland.

In order to consolidate his reign and maintain control over the Lowland nobles and prelates, the king appointed his nephew and ally, Edmund, as the earl of Lothian and Cumbria. Donald III had no acknowledged heir and, to further solidify his sovereignty, Edmund was named as the successor designate. However, despite these measures his political strength remained centered only in the area of Moray and the surrounding northern fiefdoms. To effectively govern the southern earldoms he was compelled to appoint Edmund to rule the region as co-king.

Following the overthrow of Duncan II relations between Scotland and England increasingly deteriorated as Donald III continued to support various rebel Norman magnates from the border counties in their ongoing disputes with their English overlord. While Donald III had succeeded in regaining sovereignty, the Norman court refused to acknowledge the legality of his regime, remaining determined to replace him with its vassal client-king. In 1095 the English ruling council formally recognized Edgar, the second son of Malcolm III and Margaret, as the rightful successor to the disputed monarchy. Over the next three years Donald III retained control over his kingdom as his government instituted measures to return Scotland to the historic Celtic culture and institutions. However, in 1097 Edgar finalized an agreement with William II Rufus for military support for the conquest of the Scottish throne in return for his pledge of fealty. A large army of English and exiled Scottish troops was assembled and in October the second son of Malcolm III invaded his homeland, determined to seize power. The Scottish government countered the threat to its reign by mobilizing its local retainers, marching to give battle. In the resulting encounter the forces of Donald III were decisively defeated and he was captured, along with his nephew, Edmund. The deposed king was imprisoned in Forfarshire Castle in eastern Scotland, where he was blinded to prevent any future conspiracy from rallying around him. He died three years later and was buried at Dunkeld. Donald III's body was later removed and re-interred on the island of Iona, the traditional burial site of the Celtic monarchs of Scotland. Donald III died at age sixty-six and with a combined reign of less than four years.

DUNCAN II, 1060–1094–1094

In 1094 Duncan commanded an army of Norman troops and exiled Scottish emigrants, invading his native Scotland, overthrowing Donald III to seize the monarchy. The Canmore lord was the eldest son of the Scottish King Malcolm III and his first wife Ingibiorg, the daughter of the earl of Orkney, and was born in 1060. His early years were spent in the coarse and uncultivated environment of his father's Norse-dominated court, where he received little formal education but was trained as a Scottish warlord. He became skilled in the use of various feudal weapons including the battle-axe, sword and spear. Duncan spent long hours hunting in the abundant northern forests, practicing his martial prowess.

In 1072 at the age of twelve the Canmore prince joined his father's army to defend Scotland against the English invasion led by William I. Lacking adequate military resources Malcolm III was compelled to negotiate the Treaty of Abernathy to resolve the conflict, pledging his oath of peace and giving Duncan as a hostage to ensure his compliance. The Scottish lord was taken to England and raised as part of the English court, growing up with the advantages of Norman culture, education and institutions. He attended the schools of the royal household and was trained as a Norman knight, actively campaigning with the forces of William I in his wars in France and against rogue English warlords.

Duncan remained under the direct control of the Norman crown until the death of William I in 1087 and his release by the successor William II Rufus. After over fifteen years in England, the Scottish prince had developed a firm relationship with the royal household, coming under the influence of Norman society and institutions, choosing to stay with his adoptive court after gaining his liberty. His decision was further prompted by Malcolm III's designation of Edward, the oldest son of his father's second marriage, as the heir apparent, forcing Duncan to find better opportunities for glory and wealth in the south. He became a part of William II's council, serving as a warrior knight in Normandy and later in the northern border counties.

During his service to the Norman military and governing council, Duncan married Octreda, the daughter of the earl of Northumbria. The marriage was a political arrangement, which gave the Scottish emigrant an alliance with a powerful warlord in the northern English marchland counties, enhancing his prestige at the English court and among the local magnates. The marriage resulted in the birth of one son, William.

In 1093 Malcolm III was killed in battle at Alnwick, resulting in the seizure of the Scottish kingship by his brother, Donald III. The usurper was unable to effectively consolidate his domination over the whole of the realm as a large segment of the Lowland magnates and Church refused to give homage, retaining their loyal to the family of Malcolm III. As the eldest son of the first Canmore ruler, Duncan had a claim to the Scottish monarchy and, while remaining in England, grew increasingly ambitious to seize the kingship of his homeland. He began to form a series of coalitions by negotiating with various recalcitrant Scottish lords and clerics to gain their military and financial backing for his arrogation initiative. To further his cause a treaty of alliance was signed with the English court, resulting in the pledge of a Norman army for the planned invasion while the Canmore warrior-prince swore an oath of fealty to William II Rufus. To augment his levies Duncan was granted permission to raise additional troops in England from the local barons and towns. With the promise of estates and titles, by 1094 a sizable force of mercenary knights, infantry and Northumbrian soldiers from his wife's father had been recruited. To broaden the campaign's political base the favor of the Scottish Church was actively sought with the gifts of land and offers of privileges. In the early summer the invasion coalition was assembled and the war of usurpation was launched as Duncan marched into Scotland. To counter the threat of his nephew, Donald III mobilized his vassals and friends, maneuvering to give battle. In the ensuing encounter in June, with the military might of the English behind him, Duncan was able to defeat the Scottish king, compelling him to abandon the regime and withdraw to the center of his strength in the Highlands. With the victory Duncan II claimed the suzerainty and was invested with the throne of Scotland at Scone. However, he had little popular support among the local warlords and bishops as his authority was not widely recognized. Duncan II was only able to retain supremacy with the threat of the Norman army.

During the summer months the reign of the king grew increasingly unpopular as the presence of a large foreign occupation army was greatly resented. Having spent the past twenty years in England, he was considered an outsider with an alien government. As the foreign influence continued the magnates and prelates rose in revolt, attacking and defeating the Normans in a series of ongoing sporadic raids. Duncan II only remained in power by negotiating peace with the opposition faction by agreeing to send his English forces back to William II.

With the departure of his base of power to England, the royal court's control over Scotland grew increasingly precarious while the popularity of the deposed Donald III was revived. The granting of large Lowland fiefdoms to the half-brothers of the king had also generated widespread resentment. After his defeat in June Donald III had withdrawn to his strength in the northern earldoms to begin rebuilding his army and political support. By November the dethroned monarch had sufficiently reformed his coalition among the Scottish magnates and Church to initiate a campaign of re-conquest against his nephew. On November 12, 1094, Duncan II was ambushed as he advanced against the attempted coup and was killed in the resulting battle. Duncan II had ruled for less than seven months and was thirty-four years old at the time of his death.

EDGAR I, 1074–1097–1107

In 1093 the reigning Scottish king, Malcolm III, was killed in battle at Alnwick, resulting in the usurpation of his throne by Donald III. In the aftermath of the defeat and loss of power, the surviving members of the Canmore House were compelled to abandon Scotland, seeking safety in the Norman court. The family was returned to supremacy three years later when Edgar overwhelmed the usurper sovereign, seizing the monarchy. Edgar was the fourth son of Malcolm III and his second wife Margaret and was born in 1074. He grew up in the royal household where his childhood came under the domination of his devout mother. It was through Queen Margaret that the young Scottish lord developed a deep pious nature and devotion to the Church, which remained a prominent part of his character. He was educated at the Canmore court, which was now under the influence of Norman culture and institutions. His formal education was provided by his mother, who arranged for church tutors to instruct her son in the basics of reading and writing, along with Latin and religion. With his older brothers Edgar was trained as a feudal warlord, receiving instruction in various weapons, along with the equestrian skills of a knight.

By age nineteen Edgar was actively participating in the military campaigns of the Scottish army as a feudal warrior, accompanying his father on his last invasion into the northern English counties in 1093. He was present at the battle of Alnwick where his elder brother, Edward, and Malcolm III were killed. As the direct result of the death of the king and his designated heir, the political stability of Scotland was thrown into disarray as civil war erupted among competing factions for control of the realm. Emerging from the unrest, Malcolm III's younger brother, Donald, succeeded in unifying the northern warlords, usurping the Scottish throne and forcing the Canmore family to flee to sanctuary in England.

Edgar and his brothers were welcomed at the royal court of William II Rufus where they were reunited with their half-brother, Duncan, who had been earlier given as a hostage to William I and had been raised in his household. From his many years in England Duncan had established a firm relationship with the Norman crown and with Scotland in rebellion began negotiations to reclaim the sovereignty for himself. Edgar energetically backed his half-brother's claim to the throne, participating in the formation of military alliances with rogue Scottish warlords and prelates for their support in deposing Donald III, while initiating preparations for the invasion from England. For his pledge of homage Duncan was granted an English army and, as he began his campaign in the north, Edgar joined the advancing troops. In June 1094 the usurper Donald III was defeated, allowing Duncan II to assume the Scottish monarchy. Edgar had been actively involved in the conquest of the kingdom, becoming a part of his brother's government and court. However, the Canmore king was unable to successfully consolidate his authority and was overthrown and killed seven months later by a powerful faction loyal to Donald III. Edgar again was forced to flee from his homeland, returning to the protection of William II Rufus.

In England Edgar became an active member of the Norman household, where he became the acknowledged rightful heir to the Scottish realm. With the death of Duncan II the exiled Canmore prince assumed the leadership of the dissident party, initiating measures to assume the Scottish throne. To secure his succession he began to intrigue with southern Scottish magnates and clerics for their military and political support while remaining involved in local English affairs. In early 1095 Edgar signed a treaty with the English court, giving his oath of fealty while the Norman king pledged to provide an army for the seizure of Scotland from Donald III. However, William II Rufus was soon involved with revolts in Wales and Northumbria and was unable to provide the promised troops. With the lack of Norman military might the attempted usurpation had to be delayed. Forced to stay in England, to further build a base of power for his return to Scotland, Edgar began to form a series of political alliances with the exiled Scots while staying in contact with numerous friendly warlords in his homeland. Later in the year he participated in the English campaign against the rebellious earl of Northumbria, Robert of Mowbray, while continuing to press his cause for Scotland with the Normans. For his successful military actions in the north William II granted the Canmore lord the county of Lothian, which Edgar had captured from the allies of Robert. Finally, in the late summer of 1097, the Normans had resolved their internal conflicts and Edgar was invested with an invasion force.

In October of 1097 an army of Norman and emigrant Scottish knights and infantry began the march north to Scotland. As the allies advanced into the Lowlands the troops of the Canmore prince were joined by contingents of local soldiers. King Donald III had remained popular among the Highland earldoms, assembling his retainers to counter the assault against his realm. The reinforced forces of Edgar launched their attack and, in a fierce confrontation, the Canmore levies defeated and captured the ruling sovereign, seizing the throne of Scotland. After his usurpation of power Edgar I was formally invested with the monarchy at Scone.

With the elimination of the usurper king, in the following months Edgar I was able to consolidate his supremacy over Scotland, establishing his government with the enthusiastic support of the Lowland nobles and clerics. To prevent the growth of anti–Canmore hostilities, which had caused the downfall of Duncan II, the Norman army was quickly returned to England. Edgar I maintained his loyalty to William II Rufus, initiating a pro–English foreign strategy, which fostered friendly relations with the Norman court. The Scottish monarch refused to reintroduce his father's program of territorial expansion along the border counties, staying at peace with his overlord. However, the prior policy of encouraging Saxon and Norman emigrates to settle in Scotland was re-introduced. He granted the new noble families lands, titles and positions of influence in his administration. The English brought new institutions, laws and the introduction of the feudal system into Edgar I's kingdom. The Canmore king continued his mother's policy of favoring the Church of Rome and its integration into the local religious doctrine. The Benedictine Order, which had been expelled during the reign of Donald III, was invited to return to its priory at Dunfermline. The regime sponsored the restoration and construction of new churches and monasteries and granted additional estates to various orders of monks to encourage their expansion. Edgar I remained a patron of the Scottish Church and engaged in numerous acts of piety to the poor and sick. His kingship favored a pro–Anglo-Norman orientation, which served to integrate the Scottish organizations into the mainstream of medieval European society. His reign was one of internal peace as he successfully solidified his authority, imposing his will over the southern and northern lordships.

While Edgar I maintained order on his southern border with England in 1098, he was compelled to counter an invasion against the Scottish western coast and the Isle of Orkney. The Norwegian king, Magnus Bareleg, sailed south with a large fleet, aggressively attacking the vassals of the Scottish throne seizing their fiefdoms. The local warlords could not contain the overwhelming military might of the Norse, appealing to the royal government for support. However, the regime lacked the finances and troops to send aid while it was still consolidating its power over the magnates and bishops. Magnus deposed the western earls to assert his authority over the Isle of Orkney and the maritime coast. Edgar I was forced to acknowledge the conquest of the Norwegian crown while agreeing to a settlement, ceding the territories in return for a pledge of peace.

In August 1100 William II Rufus died and, to maintain his friendly ties with England, the Scottish monarch traveled to London to renew his vassal relationship with the new regime of Henry I. The earlier treaties signed with William II Rufus were reinstated and, to foster a closer alliance, Edgar I negotiated the marriage of his sister, Matilda, to the new Norman overlord. Throughout his reign it remained the policy of the Canmore court to preserve the friendship of the kings of England and the marriage of Matilda facilitated this cause.

Edgar I had never married and had no direct legitimate successor. To ensure the continued sovereignty of the House of Canmore he appointed his brother, Alexander, as the heir apparent, associating him with his reign. He granted the earldom of Gowrie to his brother to establish a local Canmore presence and foster better relations with the northern noble families and clerics, with Alexander administering the fiefdom as a loyal vassal imposing the throne's will and justice.

Edgar I ruled Scotland for nine years before his death at Edinburgh Castle on January 8, 1107, from unknown causes at age thirty-two. His reign had brought peace and stability to Scotland after years of internal strife and wars. He was buried in the church at Dunfermline alongside his father and mother.

ALEXANDER I, 1077–1107–1124

In 1107 the Scottish king Edgar I died without a direct heir and was succeeded by his younger brother, Alexander, who had earlier been appointed as the heir designate. Alexander was the fifth son of the founder of the House of Canmore, Malcolm III, and his Saxon queen, Margaret. The young Scottish prince was raised in the royal court, which was increasingly anglicized at the direction of Margaret, exposing him to Norman culture and society. His education was under the direction of his mother, who provided church tutors for the instruction of her children. The Canmore lord was taught the basics of reading and writing along with Latin and religion. Under the influence of the queen, Alexander became devoted to the Church of Rome, developing a deep sense of piety. At the age of seven he began his training as a feudal warlord, becoming skilled in the use of the sword, battle-axe and spear, developing into a formidable warrior and military captain.

In 1093 Alexander's father was killed in battle during a raid against northern England. The king's death, along with that of the designated heir, Edward, resulted in a Scottish civil war as the northern earls and clerics rose in revolt, favoring the succession to the throne of the younger brother of Malcolm III as opposed to the direct Canmore line. The usurper army marched against the ruling family, forcing Alexander and his brothers to flee to sanctuary in England. The emigrants were welcomed at the court of William II Rufus, where Alexander became directly exposed to Norman organizations, government and culture, which greatly influenced his future reign.

While in exile the Canmore family continued to remain active in Scottish politics, retaining a large base of support among the Lowland nobles and Church. As the regime of the usurper king grew increasingly unpopular and unstable, the parties favoring the restoration of the Canmores intensified their resistance and intrigues. Factions of rogue Scottish magnates and bishops began to appear at the English court, appealing to the deposed dynasty for its intervention. In 1095 the English council recognized Edgar, the elder brother of Alexander, as the acknowledged successor to the Scottish throne. With the backing of Norman revenue and military might the Canmore heir began his preparations for an invasion to seize the realm of Scotland with the aid of Alexander, who became a part of his inner circle of advisors.

In September 1097, largely supported by an English army, Edgar initiated his campaign of conquest to regain the kingship for the Canmore family. Alexander had energetically championed his brother's usurpation movement and was a member of the expeditionary force as it began the march north. In October the invading troops defeated and deposed Donald III, allowing Edgar I to successfully establish his reign.

At the time of his accession to the monarchy Edgar I was unmarried and without a designated heir. Soon after seizing the Scottish regime he appointed his brother, Alexander, as the acknowledged successor to provide for the uninterrupted continuance of the Canmore dynasty and to prevent the danger of internal revolt erupting over the future succession. The ruling court appointed Alexander as the earl of Gowrie to reinforce his position as the next in line to the throne, sending him to the northern fiefdom to impose the authority of the Canmore administration over the recalcitrant noble families and clerics. The Scottish prince enthusiastically pursued his duties and by the force of his personality grew in prominence and popularity among the Scots. In the north Alexander advanced the kingship of his brother while creating a strong presence in Scottish affairs for himself.

In January 1107 the Scottish king died without issue and Alexander I readily assumed the throne with his power widely recognized. As the earl of Gowrie he had previously established a broad-based political party and drew on the support of the Highland nobles and Church to solidify his regime. After a brief period of consolidation he reinstituted the anglicization policies of his brother and noble Anglo-Norman families were once again encouraged to settle in Scotland with grants of land, titles and positions as advisors and officials in his government. The programs to advance the doctrines of the Scottish Church into greater conformity with the teachings of Rome were continued and expanded. Alexander I energetically sponsored the construction and restoration of numerous churches and monasteries while promoting the growth of the Benedictine priory and bishoprics. The royal court invited the Order of Augustinian monks to establish a presence at Scone, which later was expanded to other locations. New initiatives were introduced to secure the independence of the local Church from the dominance and interference of the Canterbury and York bishops, which resulted in the investiture of the king's bishop at Saint Andrews as the spiritual head of the realm. Throughout his reign Alexander I exhibited a pious nature toward the Church and its works, providing for the needs of the sick and poor.

At the time of his death Edgar I had designated his younger brother, David, as the earl of the southern lordships of Lothian and Strathclyde but the new regime refused to honor the appointment. David had spent most of his life in close association with the Norman court, appealing to the English crown for support to secure his inheritance. Despite his friendly relationship with the young Scottish prince, Henry I was involved with rebellions in Normandy and Wales and it was not until 1113 that he could provide adequate military forces to enforce David's claim. Under the threat of invasion Alexander I finally agreed to cede the two fiefdoms to his brother. The grants of Lothian and Strathclyde allowed David to assert his authority over much of Lowland Scotland, weakening the supremacy of the throne and forcing the king to move the seat of his government to the north, establishing a royal presence at Stirling and Scone.

In the aftermath of the threatened English invasion of 1113 the ongoing friendly relationship between the Scottish and Norman governments had been weakened. In the following year Alexander I traveled to England to personally meet with Henry I to repair their damaged alliance. While he remained with the royal court a Welsh insurgency under the leadership of the prince of Gwynedd, Gruffydd ap Cynan, rose in revolt against the Norman occupation of their demesne. The English army was quickly mobilized to reassert royal authority and, as a vassal of Henry I, the Scottish king was appointed to command a division of the invading troops. The campaign of subjugation afforded Alexander I the opportunity to regain the goodwill of his overlord through his bravery and diplomatic skills. With the advance of the Anglo-Norman cavalry and infantry into Gwynedd, Alexander I initiated contacts with the opposition forces to begin negotiations with Gruffydd to find a peaceful resolution. After meetings with the rebel leaders a treaty was arranged, with the insurgents agreeing to end their uprising with their pledges of peace. Alexander I stayed with the English regime, reestablishing his bonds and close association with the administration. His success in ending the Welsh rebellion coupled to his renewed oaths of fealty won the favor of Henry I, allowing the Scottish monarch to return home with the Norman-Scottish détente once again restored.

With the loss of influence and domination in the Lowland fiefdoms, Alexander I had been compelled to shift the political center of his ruling council to the northern earldoms. As the Scottish court increasingly enforced its government, the power of royal authority and ongoing anlicization reform measures were more heavily felt among the Highland lords and Church. As these initiatives intensified the magnates of Moray revolted in defense of their conservative Celtic values, forcing the Canmore throne to counter the rebellion by launching a punitive campaign to reassert its control. The army was mobilized, with Alexander I mounting a massive assault against the growing insurgency movement, which completely destroyed the ongoing uprising. To discourage any future dissension a formidable castle was constructed at Stirling in a display of royal supremacy, while other strongholds in the region were enlarged and fortified to solidify the regime's presence.

As part of the ongoing policy of expanding the Anglo-Norman institutions into his kingdom, Alexander I began a modest attempt to reform his civil ruling authority. To enforce his will and justice, the office of sheriff was introduced into the various earldoms as a royal agent. The administration of the Canmore court was brought into closer conformity with the Norman style of government with the establishment of the offices of constable and chancellor as chief advisors and the creation of a ministry of the treasury. The economic system was modernized while trade was facilitated with the introduction of legal coins as a means of commerce. The king's programs fostered the growth of the industrial and commercial sectors while the adoption of improved farming methods, along with new crops, expanded the agricultural output.

Through the family of Queen Margaret, the House of Canmore had long established cordial relations with the sovereigns of England. Upon assuming the Scottish monarchy in

1107 Alexander I remained a loyal vassal to Henry I and throughout his reign maintained order on his southern borders. He continued to honor the terms of his brother's treaty with Magnus Bareleg to retain friendship with the Norwegian court. His consistent foreign policies of non-intervention produced a sustained period of peace for the Scottish kingdom, resulting in an opportunity for the local economy to recover from years of civil war and external conflicts.

Alexander I succeeded to the throne at age thirty, initiating a sovereignty of law and order combined with a policy that fostered the consolidation of his authority over the whole of the realm. His ruling council continued the anglicization programs of the Scottish Church, society and institutions, integrating Scotland closer to the established pattern of European kingship. Alexander I died on April 25, 1124, without a direct heir at Stirling Castle of unknown causes at age forty-seven and with a reign of fourteen years. The fifth Canmore king was buried at Dunfermline Abbey, the traditional place of interment for the reigning house.

DAVID I, 1084–1124–1153

In 1124 the Scottish monarch Alexander I died without a direct heir, resulting in the acknowledgement of his younger brother, David, as the successor to the throne. David was the sixth son of Malcolm III and Margaret, the sister of the Saxon claimant to the English crown. His youth was spent in the Canmore household, where he was raised under the guidance of the queen. Under her direction various Church tutors were provided for the formal education of the seignior, where he was taught the basics of reading, writing, and Latin while being introduced to religious studies, along with the social graces of music and dancing. From his mother David developed a pious nature, becoming devoted to the teachings of the Church and the dogma of Rome. Along with his older brothers the Canmore lord began military training as a feudal warrior, receiving routine instruction under the guidance of renowned masters of arms in the use of the sword, lance and battle-axe, along with the equestrian skills of a knight.

In 1093, when David was nine his father was killed in battle at Alnwick, throwing the Scottish kingdom into turmoil over the issue of the succession. His uncle, Donald III, seized the throne by force of arms, compelling the surviving Canmore family to flee into exile in England. At the court of William II Rufus the young Scottish emigrant's education was continued at the royal household schools, where he came directly under the influence of the Anglo-Norman political, social and cultural institutions. His instruction as a warlord was renewed as he began training as a Norman knight. The Canmore lord was described physically as being unusually handsome, possessing a natural friendliness. With his charismatic personality he quickly became a favorite of the king's court, which gave him direct access to English patronage.

In 1097 William II invested David's eldest surviving brother, Edgar, with an army of Norman cavalry, foot soldiers and exiled Scottish magnates, enabling him to launch an invasion of conquest into his homeland. Augmented with the support of the Lowland lords and clerics, the Canmore levies defeated the usurper king to once again seize the throne. David was a participant in the attacking forces, accompanying his brothers into Scotland. However, as Edgar I consolidated and established his monarchy, his youngest brother was excluded from any position in the new court or government, compelling him to return to the household of the English king.

As the youngest of the three surviving sons of Malcolm III, David had little prospects for acquiring lands or titles in his homeland, devoting himself to promotion in the employment of William II Rufus. His family's relationship to the Scottish throne, coupled to his charismatic nature, attracted royal favor as he soon advanced his presence at the court. His position in the royal household was greatly enhanced in 1100 when his sister, Matilda, married the new English monarch, Henry I. As the brother of the queen, the Scottish lord rose in the royal hierarchy, receiving the personal protection and tutelage of the crown. With direct access to Henry I and his inner circle, his potential for appointments to offices, titles and lands was ameliorated and he was being educated to serve as an advisor to the king. While becoming involved with his self-aggrandizement with the Normans, the Scottish exile had little contact with his homeland, becoming increasingly drawn to service and enrichment within the regime.

Remaining in England David's future changed dramatically in 1107 when the sovereign of Scotland, Edgar I, died without issue. The throne passed to his second brother, Alexander, who was also without a direct heir, propelling David into the role of successor. The Canmore lord's stature among the Scottish nobility was further enhanced with his appointment as overlord for Lothian and Strathclyde, which gave him control over the major fiefdoms in southern Scotland. However, the new king ignored the bequeathal, refusing to transfer the demesne to his brother. To secure his rightful inheritance David was compelled to petition the Norman ruling council for military intervention. In 1107 Henry I was burdened with the revolt of his brother, Robert II Curthose, for supremacy of Normandy, spending much of the next six years resolving the rebellion, along with numerous internal conflicts. The exiled prince was forced to wait until the summer of 1113 before finally being invested with a Norman army to secure his birthright. With the threat of English might against him, Alexander I reluctantly agreed to honor the grants of Lothian and Strathclyde.

During the interim period before his acquisition of the Lowland princedoms, David had stayed in England in the employment of his patron to advance his cause. As Henry I sailed for Normandy to subdue the insurgency of Robert II, the Scottish emigrant served as a knight with the invasion army. He remained in the rebellious duchy, participating in the pacification campaign until a resolution was finalized. In recognition of his faithful service the king granted David territories in Normandy and in the English Midlands. His wealth and repute were further enhanced through the intervention of his sister who influenced her husband to arrange David's marriage to Matilda, the widow of the earl of Huntingdon and Northampton. She was directly related to the Norman dynasty, which greatly enhanced David's personal prestige and relationship with the royal court. The political agreement brought the acquisition of valuable and strategically located lands in the English north, along with the title of earl.

By 1114, through his marriage and the patronage of the Norman throne, David had become a wealthy, powerful and influential magnate with estates in England, Normandy and Scotland. The Canmore warlord settled in his Scottish lordships to actively manage his lands and consolidate his supremacy. The earl continued his relationship with the inner circle of the English regime while traveling extensively throughout his territories, enforcing his will and imposing his justice. To closely align his government with Norman institutions, a series of social, economic and religious reforms became the focus of his local rule. Under the guidance of his mother, Queen Margaret, he had developed a sense of piety and began to refashion the ecclesiastic system to the doctrines of the Roman Church. From his military employment in Normandy the Scottish lord had become a sponsor of the Tironensian religious order, soon inviting its monks to establish a monastery in his demesne. He aggressively defended his feudal prerogatives in spiritual affairs against the intriguing of the bishopric of York, retaining control of the Church under his personal authority. From his many years of service to the English crown David had acquired a large following of lesser noble houses and clerics. Many of these families were invited and encouraged to settle in his fiefdoms with grants of honors, lands and appointments as court officials. The Anglo-Normans brought with them English organizations along with new economic and political systems, which the earl readily employed to restructure his earldom.

The marriage to Matilda in 1113 was a political arrangement instituted to enhance the wealth, court standing and social position of David. As earl and later king he became totally devoted to his wife and, after her death in 1130, never considered a second marriage, which was counter to common practice among his contemporaries. Unlike many of the princes of the day he remained faithful and had no illegitimate children. Matilda was described as a patron of the Church and monasteries, living a life of piety and devotion to Christian values. Together David and Matilda had four children, two sons and two daughters. Neither of David's sons succeeded to the monarchy, as the first son, Malcolm, died in infancy and the second, Henry, died in 1152.

As the lord of southern Scotland and earl of Huntingdon, David occupied his time between administering his various princedoms while honoring his responsibilities as a prominent vassal to Henry I in England. By 1122 his brother, Alexander I, still had no direct heir to the throne as David's standing among the local Scottish magnates and clerics grew increasingly more important. The prospects of Alexander I producing an offspring were greatly diminished in July when his wife died, prompting Henry I to exert external pressure on the Scottish court to formally appoint David as the successor designate. In the autumn of 1122 the Norman king marched to the Scottish border with a powerful army in a show of force, threatening to intercede in favor of David's recognition as heir. While the Canmore prince continued his challenge for acknowledgement, a counter-campaign was initiated by William fitz Duncan, the son of the deposed Duncan II, who possessed a similar claim to the monarchy. However, by the end of the year fitz Duncan had been politically outmaneuvered, as David became the accepted successor to Alexander I.

After his designation as heir, in the following year David spent long periods of time away from his fiefdoms. In the spring of 1123 he was with the Norman court in southern England when Normandy again erupted into rebellion in support of the quest for the usurpation of the duchy by William Clito, the son of Robert II Curthose. As a powerful vassal of Henry I, the Canmore prince was summoned by his overlord to perform obligatory military service against the insurrection. David spent the campaigning season in western France subduing the revolt of the English king's nephew, where he remained until the spring of 1124.

Upon returning to England from his prolonged absence, David traveled north to continue with the personal administration of his lands, where in April 1124 he was informed of the unexpected death of Alexander I. As the accepted heir to his brother's realm and a formidable and wealthy warlord with a close relationship to the English crown, David easily overcame the challenge to the monarchy from his nephew, William fitz Duncan, who had forged a faction in opposition. On April 25 David I was invested with the throne at Scone without dissent. However, Scotland, its people and institutions were alien to the new king who had spent the vast majority of his life in the Anglo-Norman society. In establishing his royal household and government the majority of the newly appointed advisors and officials were trusted Normans and friends from England, while he excluded most of the prominent and influential native lords and prelates from his administration. To attract and retain a qualified court from his English allies, David I offered grants of estates and titles in Scotland in exchange for service as a vassal.

While the Canmore king had succeeded to the throne, his reign was not unopposed. David I was considered an outsider with an alien court and institutions, giving cause to opposition factions who began to rally around the earl of Moray, Malcolm, the illegitimate son of Alexander I. The conspiracy favoring William fitz Duncan had been earlier defeated. However, Malcolm possessed a broader base of political and military support among the conservative Celtic magnates and clerics. The earl of Moray utilized his local popularity to muster an army of northern barons, launching a series of assaults in a campaign to seize the realm. The rebellion was easily suppressed by the overwhelming military might of the regime, but the earl continued to plot against the monarchy, remaining a potential source of future insurrection. The earldoms in the Highlands largely maintained their loyalty to Malcolm, as David I's authority was only marginally acknowledged.

After suppressing Malcolm's rebellion the Scottish king established his political center at Roxburgh Castle to begin the process of consolidating his regime. As a regional warlord, he had previously successfully defended the ecclesiastic independence of his southern princedoms against the interference of the archbishop of York and as ruler began a campaign to free the Church of Scotland from the dominance of English jurisdiction. As dissention with the York prelate escalated in early 1125, Pope Honorius II sent his personal legate to Scotland to settle the issue of the throne's right to establish an autonomous archdiocese. All attempts at compromise failed as David I continued to demand freedom of action for his Church. In the following year the pope issued an edict reaffirming the supremacy of the York archbishopric. David I was not willing to accept foreign intervention into his religious affairs and in the autumn personally traveled to England to seek the aid of Henry I. The Norman crown agreed to intercede against the archbishop and to pressure the See of Rome into a more favorable settlement. By the following summer a reconciliation had been forged, which permitted the consecration of the Scottish bishops without a pledge of obedience to York. However, no unfettered archbishopric was authorized for Scotland. David I was dedicated to the principal of self-determination in Scottish affairs, fighting throughout his reign to maintain the autonomy of his kingdom against all alien encroachments.

With the issue of ecclesiastic freedom at least temporarily resolved, David I continued to reform the local Church with numerous initiatives to more closely align the bishoprics and their religious teachings toward the dogma of Rome and away from the Celtic traditions. The anglicization programs introduced earlier in Lothian and Strathclyde were extended over all of southern Scotland as Anglo-Norman social, political and cultural institutions were increasingly implemented. To encourage the growth of trade and commerce, measures were taken to designate selected strategic towns as special economic centers receiving royal tax exemptions and favors. To further stimulate the economy the minting of coins was standardized while weights and measures were made uniform. The focus of the king's government was in the south as he traveled throughout the region, personally administering his justice and law. David I remained a loyal vassal of Henry I, retaining his earlier practice of spending considerable periods of time at the English court.

In 1130 David I traveled south from his royal domains and was once again in the Norman household in the performance of his feudal responsibilities to Henry I. Seeking to seize upon his prolonged absence, the king's rogue nephew and northern warlord, Malcolm, forged an alliance with Oengus of Moray in an attempt to usurp the monarchy. The coalition drew widespread support among the conservative Celtic lords and clerics, uniting two formidable regional insurgent armies, which launched a potent military force against the throne.

Prior to his departure for England David I had entrusted the defenses of southern Scotland to his cousin and constable, Edward of Siward. As the rebels advanced into the Lowlands Edward mobilized the administration's allies and vassals, marching to give battle. In the resulting encounter the northern allies were shattered and Oengus killed, but during the course of the attack Malcolm again escaped to his Highland sanctuary. However, the strength and extent of the revolt finally convinced David I of the seriousness of the threat to his reign and the need to fully impose his will over the recalcitrant northern earls and prelates.

To end the danger of continued defiance among the Highland earldoms, David I began military preparations for a prolonged expedition against the strongholds of the insurgency movement in Moray. A powerful army was assembled and in late 1130 the pacification campaign was launched. Malcolm was widely recognized as the leader of the resistance, waging a spirited and energetic defense from his base of support. However, while the throne was attempting to assert its supremacy over Moray, David I was forced to counter the mounting aggression of the western kingdom of Argyll, resulting in a diversion of his resources away from the Highlands war effort.

While the campaigns of David I in 1130 were directed at the subjugation of Malcolm in Moray, the autonomous king of the western maritime kingdom of Argyll, Gillebrigte, had invaded and annexed numerous Canmore lands. He strengthened his military and political position by negotiating an alliance with the earl of Moray, which was ratified with the marriage of his daughter to Malcolm. The ruler of Argyll, along with his ambitious and powerful son, Somairle, had previously extended their realm from its western power base into the neighboring fiefdoms of the rulers of the Isle of Man and Norway and were now eager to extend their authority farther to the south into Scotland. Gillebrigte was also resisting the expansion of Anglo-Norman feudalism represented by the Lowland Scots while protecting his traditional Celtic values. Sharing a common enemy in David I the coalition between the magnates and clerics of Moray and the Argyll regime presented a formidable obstacle to Scottish ambitions for the domination of the north.

As the Canmore king was personally engaged with the rebellion in the Moray earldom, in 1130 he sent a second formidable invasion army to counter the Argyll encroachments. Over the next four years a relentless military campaign was waged against Gillebrigte and Somairle to break their alliance with Moray and force their recognition of David I as overlord. In 1134 the defeat and capture of Malcolm resulted in the reluctant submission of the Argyll regime and the acceptance of David I as feudal suzerain. The rebellious warlords were permitted to retain their titles and lands while Gillebrigte maintained his throne as a vassal of the Scottish court. With the subjugation of the western kingdom, David I had broadened his sphere of influence and authority by gaining a powerful ally and base of operations for future territorial ambitions.

The conquest and annexation of the Highland earldom brought a substantial conquest directly under the Canmore regime's supremacy. To bind the new territory securely to his realm, David I began a colonization campaign using the grants of the fiefdom's lands, towns and offices to encourage the Church and loyal vassals to establish a permanent presence. The monks from the abbey at Dunfermline were given large estates at Urquhart while a new priory was established which served as a symbol of royal power and authority. Under the government's patronage new monasteries and churches were constructed and the Cistercian Order was invited to settle at Kinloss. The religious institutions advanced the Canmore cause by bringing an impetus to the local economy with the introduction of new agriculture and industrial innovations. The Church served as a center for learning while providing the throne with many capable officials and advisors. Under David I's direction the Highland ecclesiastical system was reorganized and several regional bishoprics were established, giving the Canmore court a greater suzerainty and control over the districts.

While David I actively encouraged the Church to settle in the Highlands, he also initiated a policy directed at inducing his nobles to locate in the new territories. After his defeat in 1124 the king's nephew, William fitz Duncan, had been won to David I's cause and had strongly supported the seizure of the northern counties. After the destruction of the insurgent army in 1134, the Scottish governing council negotiated the marriage of William to the widow of Oengus of Moray, giving the Canmore court an increased presence with the rogue clerics and magnates. Seeking to exploit William's new position of prestige and stature in the earldom, he was appointed as the lord of the recently conquered lands to govern in the king's name. While fitz Duncan enhanced the throne's authority and standing among the warlords, he acted only as a figurehead with the actual administration remaining under royal officials. To expand the Canmore influence numerous English knights and friends were granted Upland estates and these families imported Anglo-Norman culture, law and organizations to the princedom. The Scottish ruler's reign was further secured by the construction of a formidable network of strategic castles, which enhanced his power and supremacy while serving as the centers of his justice and economic reforms. The Canmore family had many long-standing historical ties among the northern magnates and churchmen, which David I drew upon to solidify his regime.

As a part of his diplomatic policy to further consolidate his control over the recent Highland conquests, David I launched a political initiative to bind his kingdom closer to the autonomous earl of Orkney and Caithness. In 1134 he negotiated the marriage of his vassal, Maddad, earl of Atholl, to Margaret, the daughter of the overlord of Orkney, gaining the Scots greater stature and influence in the maritime lordship. While enhancing Canmore presence, the treaty secured the military might of the earldom against future revolt by the Moray magnates and prelates, strengthening the king's jurisdiction over the fiefdoms. At the death of the earl of Orkney in 1139, David I used his relationship with Maddad to plot in the ensuing internal power struggle over the suzerainty of the region to gain half of the earldom for his retainer's son. The intervention added to the king's prestige and power in northern affairs, drawing the Orkney principality more directly under Scottish dominion. David I continued to administer Moray by maintaining the alliances with the family of William fitz Duncan and the earls of Orkney until 1147 when he annexed the territories directly under royal authority.

In December 1135 Henry I died and his nephew, Stephen, seized the English crown, usurping the claims of the king's daughter, Matilda. The new monarch's hold on the throne was precarious as his cousin mounted a challenge to attain her rightful inheritance. Seeking to exploit the developing civil war with its internal distractions as an opportunity for the aggrandizement of English lands, in late December David I launched a hastily prepared invasion in an attempt to conquer southern Northumbria. Initially the surprise attack quickly captured many of the campaign's objectives, emboldening the Scottish troops in February 1136 to advance farther south to assault the stronghold of Durham. However, Stephen, supported by a formidable Anglo-Norman army, marched to the city to counter David I's initiative. Rather than risk the outcome of a pitched battle, the two rivals agreed to negotiate a settlement. In the resulting Treaty of Durham Stephen ceded large sections of his borderlands to the Canmores while releasing them from all feudal obligations for Scotland in return for David I's pledge of peace.

The Northumbrian territorial aspirations of David I were largely unresolved by the Durham agreement and over the following year relations between the two realms grew increasingly strained. Tensions were further escalated by the re-emergence of the claim from the archbishop of York for ecclesiastical jurisdiction over all Scottish affairs, which had continued to lay dormant under Henry I. The mounting conflict was further inflamed when the political factions of Empress Matilda intensified their appeals to David I, demanding his pledge of support for her rights of inheritance. Nevertheless, the primary cause for the breach with the Norman government remained the thwarted regional ambitions of the Scots. In the spring of 1137 with Stephen occupied against the Angevin rebellion in Normandy, the Canmores again attacked into Northumbria. However, the local Norman magnates rallied to their king's defense, compelling David I to agree to a six-month truce. In November the Scottish court demanded the whole of Northumbria as the price for peace on the border and Stephen refused to cede the lands.

As the time period for the truce began to expire the Canmore throne began to make military preparations for an invasion to seize the northern English lordships. In January 1138 the offensive was initiated with a siege against the fortification at Wark-on-Tweed, where the local lords refused to give battle, withdrawing to the defenses of the stronghold, forcing the king into a prolonged investment. After leaving troops to maintain the blockade, David I advanced deeper into Northumbria, where his army brutally harried the towns and countryside. However, the Scots were unable to impose their will as the English barons and clerics maintained their loyalty to Stephen. In the following month he personally responded to the attacks against his demesne by mounting a plundering counter-raid into Scotland, compelling David I to abandon his campaign again with no territorial gains, retreating to his realm to defend his borders.

After returning to Scotland the king became resolved to force a decisive battle with the English, mobilizing a formidable army of his allies and retainers from the whole of his realm, with the objective of attacking deep into the heart of Stephen's kingdom. In April 1138 as David I's troops marched south, they again pillaged and devastated the local population. The Norman crown countered the Scots' invasion by placing its defenses under the command of Thurstan, archbishop of York. The patriarch summoned the loyal Northumbrian barons, assembling a powerful fighting force, which was dispatched to the north. The opposing armies clashed at Cowton Moor on August 23, 1138, in what came to be known as the Battle of the Standards for the numerous religious flags sent by the prelate of York. In the ensuing encounter the Scots were driven from the battlefield by the overwhelming military might and discipline of the Norman knights against David I's light infantry. The Scottish were compelled to withdraw from the immediate region, though still maintaining control over much of Northumbria and Cumbria. Hard pressed by his ongoing struggles against Empress Matilda, Stephen utilized his victory to seek a resolution to the conflict, sending a delegation to negotiate with the Scots. The deliberations continued through the year until April 1139 when a final settlement was ratified. Under the terms of the revised Treaty of Durham, David I's son, Henry, received the earldom of Northumbria as a vassal of the English and authority over Huntingdon, Carlisle and Cumbria, while the Scots pledged their peace and fealty to Stephen in his war against Matilda.

The Treaty of Durham had largely provided the Scottish court with the additional lands it had demanded. To secure Canmore authority over the new lordships, a castle was constructed at Carlisle, which became the political and economic center of the southern principalities. However, David I's hold on the territory became threatened in February 1141 when Stephen was defeated and captured by Matilda. In the resulting turmoil the Canmore throne occupied additional towns and castles in northern England to ensure its recent gains. To enhance his cause and protect the acquisitions, the Scottish king initiated a diplomatic campaign to gain greater influence in English affairs by abandoning the pledges of fealty to Stephen, declaring support for the empress and seeking to join her inner council of advisors. In early June David I was in London for the coronation of Matilda when the city rose in revolt in favor of the deposed sovereign, forcing the empress's political faction to flee to Oxford. Over the summer months, in southern England the strength of Stephen's army steadily solidified while the usurper was deserted by many of her warlords and bishops. In September her forces were attacked at Winchester and quickly overwhelmed, compelling a withdrawal to safety in the west while David I returned to the security of Durham and the consolidation of his recent conquest.

The political stability in northern England was again in turmoil in November 1141 when Stephen was freed from captivity in exchange for Robert of Gloucester, the half-brother of the empress. However, the Norman king's authority and popularity among the Northumbrian population had been tarnished by his defeat and David I actively negotiated with the local barons and prelates to gain their support. The Canmore ruler succeeded in attracting a strong faction of vassals to his allegiance, which significantly strengthened his hold over the region. As the civil war between Matilda and Stephen was renewed in the south, the Northumbria earldom was largely ignored, which enabled the Scots to solidify their presence and power. The ongoing turmoil in England allowed David I to finally break his feudal bonds for the Norman fiefdoms by annexing the area directly into his kingdom without fear of intervention. To firmly unite and integrate the conquest directly under Scottish authority, an effective administration and judicial and economic system was established as the Scot's rule ushered in an era of peace and prosperity. He appointed his son and successor, Henry, as his personal representative in the lordships to administer the throne's justice and laws and win the friendship of the Church and magnates. In May 1149 David I secured an additional safeguard for his recent territorial gains by forging an alliance with his great-nephew, Henry Plantagenet. In the ensuing treaty the young son of Matilda and heir to the English crown formally recognized the Canmores' rightful possession of the northern provinces.

With his southern borders finally secured and extended, in 1150 David I again turned his initiatives to the north and the embellishment of his defenses and authority. To protect his realm against an external attack and local rebellion, a line of strategic castles was built and heavily garrisoned with royal troops, which enhanced the king's presence and power over the local magnates. In the following year in the earldom of Orkney, the king of Norway, Inge I, seized the loyal vassal of the Canmore throne, forcing him to pledge his fealty and abandon the Scots. David I responded to his loss of sovereignty by appointing a second earl, igniting an ongoing struggle for control of the northernmost district, which was to last for several generations.

David I had earlier designated his only surviving son, Henry, as his heir, but in June 1152 the Scottish earl suddenly died. To ensure the peaceful assumption of the House of Canmore, the king had his eldest grandson, Malcolm, recognized as successor, associating the eleven-year-old prince with his government. To unite him to the kingdom he was sent on an extended tour of his demesne receiving the acknowledgement and homage of the lordships. To safeguard the southern fiefdoms, the second grandson, William, was named earl and established in Northumbria as its overlord.

In 1153 David I was 69 years old and had become physically exhausted by over 29 years of kingship. During the spring months his health steadily deteriorated and on May 29 he died in the Lowlands at Carlisle Castle. David I was buried alongside his father, mother and brothers in the abbey at Dunfermline.

Malcolm IV, 1141–1153–1165

The potential for political instability and fragmentation in Scotland resulted from the sudden death of David I's only surviving son and successor, Henry, in 1152 and the resulting advancement of his eleven-year-old grandson, Malcolm, as the next in line for the throne. As the heir designate, Henry had been associated with his father's government from an early age, playing a major role in the conquest of northern England. The Canmore lord was recognized as the earl of Northumbria and Cumbria by the English crown, spending considerable effort in establishing a firm relationship with the local barons and bishops. He had proven to be an energetic and skilled administrator and military captain. His early death and the succession of his young son, Malcolm, as heir created a vacuum in the court's power structure, reducing the authority and stature of the monarchy.

Malcolm was born on March 20, 1141, and was the eldest of the three sons of Earl Henry and Ada of Surrey. Through the family of his mother, the Canmore prince was directly related to the Norman kings of England and the Capetian dynasty of France, which added to his prestige and social standing among the European courts. At an early age Malcolm's mother exerted a dominating influence on his religious and cultural orientation. From her the Scottish lord acquired a sense of piety and devotion to the doctrines of the Church while becoming drawn to Norman institutions and society. Physically he was described as fair and slim, possessing a frail health.

The future king's childhood was spent in the Scottish court at Roxburgh under the increasingly anglicized royal household. The Canmore lord's formal education was entrusted to tutors provided from the Church, who instructed him in the basics of reading, writing, Latin and religion. Beginning around age seven he received training as a knight, becoming accomplished in the use of the lance, poleax, and sword along with the equestrian skills of a mounted warrior. From his military instruction he became dedicated to the ideals and grandeur of Norman chivalry.

Malcolm's father died in 1152 and, as the eldest son of the heir, he was readily recognized as the successor designate by his grandfather, David I. Prior to his death, the king made preparations for the reign of Malcolm by appointing the powerful and influential Duncan, earl of Fife, as regent to govern the realm until the young prince reached the age of majority. To more closely unite Malcolm with his future allies and vassals, the Church and burghs, he was sent on an extended tour of the kingdom. He was associated with the throne's administration, attending council meetings to gain experience in diplomacy and the machinations of government.

In May 1153 David I died and his grandson was readily acknowledged as successor at age twelve. Malcolm IV was taken to the historical and traditional enthronement site at Scone for the formal ceremony shortly following the death of his grandfather. The administration of the kingdom was entrusted to a formidable regency council under the leadership of Duncan of Fife. Assuming control of the regime the royal counsels were able to successfully enforce the rule of Malcolm IV over the Lowland fiefdoms but, in 1154, the earl of Argyll, Somerled, challenged the overlordship of the new sovereign. Seeking to exploit the period of transition and uncertainty under the Duncan guardianship, the Celtic-Norse warlord rebelled, mounting a military campaign to secure the autonomy of his earldom. The throne's allies and vassals were sent north to enforce Canmore supremacy and, by the end of the year, the revolt had been suppressed, with Somerled fleeing to the sanctuary of his relatives in the western isles. Following the loss of his earldom, the recalcitrant Argyll magnate was soon involved in local political intrigues, rallying a powerful faction of western lords and bishops to his quest for a separate realm by waging war against the ruler of the Isle of Man, Godred. By 1158 Somerled had defeated Godred, establishing a kingdom for himself by claiming the coastal isles. The western king governed with the old Celtic traditions and values, greatly resenting the extension of the anglicization policies of Malcolm IV into his maritime lands. As the Canmore government continued to expand its influence into the northern lordships, in 1164 Somerled launched an attack against the Scottish army near Glasgow in defense of his independence. To counter the invasion the royal garrison mounted a spirited resistance, advancing against the rebel forces. In the ensuing battle the overlord of the Isles was killed and his troops overwhelmed. His three surviving sons soon divided their father's territories among themselves, remaining at peace with Scotland from their autonomous princedoms.

The Plantagenet king Henry II ended the ongoing English civil war in 1154, succeeding unchallenged to the throne. The overlord of the Angevin Empire had earlier inherited his father's demesne in Normandy and Anjou and with his marriage to Eleanor had gained control over the powerful and wealthy duchy of Aquitaine. With the addition of England, Henry II ruled the most formidable empire in Europe and disputed the Scottish sovereignty rights to his northern counties of Cumbria and Northumbria. Ignoring his prior pledge to David I to honor Canmore dominance over the border region, in 1157 he met with Malcolm IV, who had assumed independent authority of his kingdom, at Chester to reclaim the earldoms. The balance of power had shifted heavily to Henry II's favor and, with unrest still persistent in the realm, the Canmore court was compelled to acknowledge the loss of the territories. As compensation Malcolm IV was granted the lordship of Huntingdon as a vassal of the English crown. The loss of Northumbria and Cumbria and the acceptance of Plantagenet suzerainty for Huntingdon were greatly resented by the Scottish earls and bishops, laying the foundation for future rebellion among the conservative Celtic Highland warlords.

Malcolm IV had been forced to accept the harsh conditions of the Treaty of Chester to preserve the peace with his powerful southern neighbor at a time when his kingship had not yet been firmly established. The accord resulted in a loss of authority and prestige among his nobles and clerics, which was magnified by his vassal service to Henry II in France in 1159. Through his marriage to Eleanor of Aquitaine, the Plantagenet king had a rightful claim to the French county of Toulouse. After securing his Scottish borders he launched a military campaign against the local count to enforce his homage. As a liege retainer of Henry II, the Scottish sovereign was summoned to perform his fealty obligation. Together with a company of knights and infantry, he crossed the Channel in June, joining the English army at Poitiers. Following the Plantagenet capture of several towns and strongholds, Malcolm IV was knighted by his overlord in recognition of services performed. With most of the countship in his possession, Henry II mounted an attack against the city of Toulouse with Malcolm IV and his Scots forming a contingent of the assault troops. However, the garrison defenders refused to surrender, compelling the English to initiate siege operations. The French king, Louis VII, had been engaged in a sporadic war with the Angevin Empire and, to prevent the expansion of Plantagenet power, personally commanded a relief force to the city. With the castle reinforced and with the approach of winter, the investment had to be abandoned. Henry II withdrew his troops to Normandy to continue his offensive against the French court, taking Malcolm IV and his Scottish men-at-arms with him. The Canmores spent several additional months campaigning with the English, capturing numerous border fortifications while pillaging the region before a truce was negotiated. With the end of hostilities in early 1160, Malcolm IV returned to Scotland to face the wrath of his rebellious northern warlords and bishops.

The close personal association which developed between the Scottish king and Henry

II, coupled to his liege obligation associated with the earldom of Huntingdon, gave cause for revolt among Malcolm IV's northern Celtic population. An alliance of six earls under the leadership of Fergus of Galloway was forged, marching their armies against the Canmore court at Perth Castle to seize the throne. The attack of the rebels was thwarted by loyal levies of Malcolm IV as the attempted coup ended in failure. However, in the assault against Perth, Fergus escaped and his nobles and clerics continued to resist the authority of the ruling council. Malcolm IV, with the support of his English allies and Scottish vassals, was compelled to launch three invasions into the region before Fergus was finally subdued and forced to accept royal sovereignty.

The devotion to the dogma of the Roman Church, which Malcolm IV had acquired as a youth, was enthusiastically applied to his kingship. Assuming the realm, he became a pious supporter of the clergy and, under his sponsorship, many new churches and monasteries were constructed throughout his lands. New religious orders were brought into the kingdom, endowed with estates and royal patronage. The anglicization policies of his grandfather were continued and expanded with the active recruitment of emigrants from France and Flanders. Through its many associations with England, the royal court of Malcolm IV had a pronounced English flavor which served to further alienate the native conservative-oriented northern warlords and clerics.

By 1161 the king still had not married and, responding to the urgings of his mother and court, negotiations were begun with the duke of Brittany for marriage to his daughter, Constance. However, despite the mounting concerns for the perpetuation of the House of Canmore, the deliberations ended in failure and Malcolm IV never married.

Malcolm IV had asserted his supremacy over the southern Scottish earldoms, but his reign continued to be only marginally acknowledged among the Highland warlords. The ongoing threat of rebellion in the north compelled his foreign policy to be directed at the maintenance of peace with the powerful Plantagenet crown. Henry II ruled over the expansive Angevin Empire, stretching from the Scottish border to the Pyrenees, which accorded him vast financial resources and military might. In 1163 the Canmore sovereign traveled to the court of his overlord to render his pledge of homage for Huntingdon and renew the border security agreements. Malcolm IV actively courted the friendship of the English throne, avoiding any perception of hostile actions throughout his kingship to recover the lost territories of Cumbria and Northumbria.

In 1163 the health of the Scottish king began to seriously deteriorate from unknown causes. He partially recovered from the initial illness, though, never fully regaining his strength. Malcolm IV was able to return to the government of his realm, but over the following two years, the ailment grew more severe as his brother, William, assumed more control over the kingdom. On December 9, 1165, Malcolm IV died at Jedburgh Castle at age twenty-four and with a reign of twelve years to be succeeded by his brother, William I. By the end of Malcolm IV's rule the first seven Canmore sovereigns had strongly bound the Lowland fiefdoms to their monarchy and had begun the total subjugation of the Celtic-dominated northern earldoms with the introduction of new Anglo-Norman emigrants and religious orders. A series of defensive castles had been constructed and strongly garrisoned with loyal southern troops to enforce the royal dominion over the local warlords, bishops and population. The strongholds served as centers for imposing the throne's will and justice while developing into sites of economic activity. The regime's authority had been introduced into the northernmost regions of Orkney and the western maritime islands but many of the more mountainous areas still openly defied the Canmore court, clinging to their native cultures and traditions.

WILLIAM I, 1143–1165–1214

At the age of twenty-two William I assumed the throne of Scotland at the death of his brother, King Malcolm IV. William was born in 1143 and was the second son of Henry, earl of Northumbria, and Ada, the daughter of the earl of Surrey. His father was the only surviving son of David I and the recognized heir designate, while his mother had been raised and educated in the French manner at the Anglo-Norman court. The young Canmore prince grew up in the Scottish royal household with his older brother, Malcolm, where their mother dominated their early lives. She appointed tutors from the Church to provide for their welfare and education. William received instruction in reading, writing, Latin, and religious doctrine and was introduced to the social graces of dancing, music and etiquette. From his mother he acquired a devotion to the teachings of Roman Catholicism, developing a pious nature while later becoming a patron and protector of the Church. As a part of the court William was exposed to Norman society and culture, as opposed to the native Celtic values. While his formal education was continued, the majority of his instruction was dedicated to military training as a feudal warrior. The Scottish lord was taught the equestrian skills of a knight, becoming proficient in the use of the Norman lance, sword and poleax under the tutelage of experienced masters of arms. Away from his formal education William spent long hours in the abundant forests hunting and hawking, sharpening his martial prowess. It was through his training for knighthood that he acquired a dedication and zeal for the ideals and glory of French feudal chivalry.

In 1152 the recognized heir to the Scottish throne, Henry, died and William's older brother, Malcolm, was named as successor. While his brother inherited the whole of Scotland, the younger Canmore was granted the strategic English fiefdom of Northumbria. To associate his grandson with his new domain, David I personally escorted William to the earldom for his investiture as overlord. Henry had spent considerable time and effort in the northern English counties winning the acceptance and respect of the local nobles, clerics and towns. The strong allegiance and loyalty generated by his father was willingly transferred to William as he was readily acknowledged as the new earl. However, in 1157 after the death of David I and the ascension of his grandson, Malcolm IV, the new king was compelled to cede his brother's birthright under threat of force by arms to the powerful Henry II of England. William was later partially compensated by the English court for the loss by the gift of Tynesdale as a liege vassal to the Norman crown.

With the loss of his earldom William returned at his brother's court, becoming associated with the regime's council and government as the acknowledged heir apparent. He stayed in Scotland until 1159, when Henry II summoned his Scottish vassals to appear in France to perform their fealty obligation by participating in the invasion of Toulouse. As the overlord of the Angevin Empire and duke of Aquitaine, the Plantagenet ruler had a claim to the rebellious countship. He began to amass his allies and retainers to enforce his rights to the lordship, launching a campaign of conquest against the rogue count, Raymond V. In June William and his brother, Malcolm IV, assembled a company of knights and foot soldiers, crossing the English Channel to join the army of Henry II at Poitiers. A formidable military force had been mobilized from the various princedoms of the Angevin Empire, which quickly captured the majority of Raymond V's demesne. With most of the county occupied, Henry II began the final phase of his war by advancing with the Scottish troops to initiate siege operations against the major stronghold at the capital city of Toulouse. The castle's garrison refused to surrender and, when the French monarch, Louis VII, reinforced the defenders, the Angevins were compelled to abandon the investment. William and the Scottish king remained with the Angevin army, continuing to serve Henry II in the ongoing conflict against the French crown. A new offensive was mounted against Louis VII's border defenses in Normandy, with the Scottish contingent participating in the capture of several castles. With the approach of winter a truce was arranged and in early 1160 the Canmores sailed to Scotland.

The Scottish king and his brother had been occupied in France for over six months and during their absence a powerful faction of northern warlords had forged an alliance in opposition to the Canmores' loss of Northumbria and the resulting subjugation of Scottish rights and independence to England. Under the command of Fergus of Galloway, the regional militia launched an assault against the regime at Perth, which was easily thwarted by Malcolm IV and his brother. Following the defeat of the insurgents' attack against Perth, William remained with the army and government, participating in the suppression campaigns against Galloway, winning respect and prestige for his skills as a soldier and administrator. The rebellion continued to rage in Galloway compelling the Canmore throne to invade three times before the earldom again came under royal supremacy.

In 1163 the Scottish sovereign began to display signs of a serious illness, increasingly withdrawing from active participation in his government. Malcolm IV had remained unmarried and as the heir apparent William became more closely associated with the administration of the regime, assuming a major role in the ruling of the kingdom. On December 9, 1165, Malcolm IV died at Jedburgh Castle and his brother readily became the acknowledged successor. On December 24 William I was inaugurated at Scone Abbey as the new king of Scotland.

At the time of William I's succession to the throne, the Scottish realm was stable and at peace. The renegade Highland warlords had been subdued and his brother's appeasement initiative of fostering friendship and cooperation with the formidable Henry II had guaranteed the security of the southern borders. With his kingship secured William I redirected the prior policy of accommodation with the English in a more bellicose direction with the objective of re-acquiring the forfeited counties of Northumbria and Cumbria, where he had previously established a loyal power base during his reign as earl. In the spring of 1166 he traveled south, meeting with Henry II at Windsor to re-affirm the outstanding treaties, offer homage for his English lands and negotiate the return of the northern English lordships. The Plantagenet refused all offers of compromise, soon sailing for Normandy to subdue the rebellion of his vassals in Maine and Brittany. Determined to recover his usurped territories, William I seized the opportunity for foreign adventure in his overlord's army, departing with Henry II. The military campaign provided the possibility of gaining additional favor with the English court and the chance to personally press his claims for Northumbria and Cumbria. In France Henry II's forces first subdued the insurrection in Maine and by late August the conquest of Brittany had been completed. The war was largely a series of sieges, with the Scottish king energetically participating in the battles, winning a reputation as a chivalrous knight. In France he became active in the new sport of jousting, enhancing his martial repute among the warrior elite. By the late autumn the conflict had been resolved and William I departed to his homeland but without re-acquiring the northern earldoms.

In Scotland William I quickly re-established his court with his domination widely accepted among the magnates and clerics. He traveled extensively throughout the kingdom, personally imposing his laws and justice and ensuring for the economic prosperity of the burghs and population. While he was able to maintain peace within the realm, events were beginning to unfold to the south which soon re-ignited the war with the Plantagenets over the return of Northumbria and Cumbria.

In 1170 Henry II crossed the Channel to England, summoning his local vassals to renew their pledges of fealty and to witness the coronation of his eldest son, Henry the Younger, as co-king. William I and his brother, David, met with their overlord at Windsor, giving homage and again pressing the claim for the northern earldoms. The Plantagenet crown refused to mediate the transfer of the territory, forcing the Scots to return home, again rebuked but more determined to acquire the fiefdoms. While the direct talks with Henry II proved fruitless, diplomatic negotiations were begun with the court of the French sovereign, Louis VII, seeking a military alliance. William I offered a Scottish army in the service of the French against his English overlord in exchange for his former possessions. However, the Capetian throne rejected the proposal and William I was compelled to temporarily abandon the quest of the lordships.

Over the following three years Scotland remained at peace as Henry II continued to be occupied with events on the continent and William I found no cause to renew his quest for northern England. However, by April 1173 the sons of the Plantagenet king were in open rebellion against their father forging an alliance with Louis VII. To broaden and strengthen their cause the rebels offered the throne of Scotland, the earldom of Northumbria and the surrounding fiefdoms for its participation in their revolt. A final attempt was made to peacefully acquire the lands by sending royal agents to the Norman court, offering the use of a Scottish army in exchange for the ceding of the earldoms. When the envoys returned to Scotland with Henry II's defiant rejection, William I became determined to forcibly seize his rightful possessions, agreeing to join the French war coalition.

In late 1173 the Scots launched their first raids into the English border counties in support of the rebellion against Henry II, but little success was achieved. Advancing into Northumbria the king attacked the castle at Wark. However, the garrison was heavily reinforced and attempts to take the defenses by storm had to be abandoned. Several additional strongholds were assaulted but, lacking siege engines to batter the walls, the Scots were unable to force the defenders' surrender. With his initiatives thwarted William I marched farther south, where he pillaged the countryside, seizing the small fortification at Warkworth. Further attempts to take the castles at Carlisle and Prudhoe failed and, as the English warlord, Richard de Lacy, approached with a strong relief army, William I was compelled to end his incursion, retreating to the safety of Roxburgh. With the end of the campaigning season, the bishop of Durham negotiated a truce, which lasted until March 1174, allowing William I the opportunity to use the winter months to better prepare for the renewal of the conflict.

In the spring the Scottish throne again summoned its allies and vassals to mobilize for the coming assault against the border castles in support of the French alliance and the return of Northumbria and Cumbria. A formidable force of men-at-arms and infantry was assembled from all regions of the kingdom with the campaign launched against the heavily fortified Wark Castle. The defensive system had been strengthened during the truce and the garrison successfully thwarted all attempts to storm the walls. William I was compelled to again abandon the investment and after holding a council of war his cavalry and levies were sent against the fortifications at Carlisle. Prior to attacking the defenses the Scots first attempted to bribe the garrison's commander however he refused to surrender resulting in the fortress being placed under siege. Leaving a contingent of his troops to force the defenders into submission the king personally led the remainder of his retainers on a pillaging raid destroying numerous towns and devastating the population. In July after failing to capture Prudhoe he marched the royal army north to Alnwick where the stronghold was placed under investment. William I again sent part of his knights and foot soldiers to harry the countryside while he commanded the blockade. As the Scots settled into the daily routine of siege operations the northern English barons assembled their militias in Yorkshire advancing to counter the invaders. In the early morning of July 13 the vanguard of the Plantagenets surprised the besiegers at Alnwick capturing William I and scattering his soldiers.

The king of the Scots was first taken in chains to Newcastle and later was transferred to Henry II's court in Normandy at Falaise. The two rivals did not meet until December when William I was forced to accept the humiliating Treaty of Falaise to gain his freedom. Under the terms of the agreement the Canmore monarch, his descendents and vassals were compelled to offer homage for the whole of Scotland to the Plantagenets while his Church was to come under the jurisdiction of the English diocese. The strategic castles and economic centers of Edinburgh, Stirling, Roxburgh, Jedburgh and Berwick were to be garrisoned with English troops at Scottish expense while the sovereign's brother, David, was to be given as hostage. On December 11, 1174 the treaty was ratified and William I soon departed for his kingdom. The peace was secured in August of 1175 when William I, his lords and prelates gave fealty to England at York.

With much of his southern region under English occupation, William I moved his court north establishing his government at Perth where he soon had to counter the aftereffects of the disastrous Treaty of Falaise. The warlords and clerics of Galloway had only partially come under royal sovereignty and the king's capture and homage to the Plantagenet crown had given cause to rebellion under the leadership of Gilbert, lord of Galloway. Gilbert brutally attacked and murdered the English and French emigrants in his earldom while pillaging their estates. The royal castles in Galloway were methodically destroyed and the garrisons killed. In late 1176 William I moved to counter the initiatives against his demesne and supremacy by advancing against the revolt with a large army. Gilbert and his rebel faction were soon defeated, with Galloway again subdued. The dissident leader was taken to the Plantagenet court for justice, where he was pardoned for his pledge of loyalty, returning to his earldom where he continued to be a source of ongoing insurgency against his Scottish overlord.

With the uprisings in his northern lordships settled, William I directed his initiatives away from any further foreign adventurism and toward securing his kingship. The Scottish Church continued to receive royal patronage while new chapels and monasteries were sponsored under the regime's direction, including the great abbey at Arbroath. Additional religious orders were introduced into the Highlands, which served to enhance the royal presence and power. Under William I's orders reforms were directed at encouraging economic growth with the granting of special trading privileges and concessions to the regional commercial centers. The flow of commerce was facilitated with the greater use of coins promoting the creation of a money-based economy. All challenges against the supremacy of the Canmores were met by an immediate response. To enforce his sovereignty the king mounted a military campaign to subdue rebellion in Ross, bringing the area more tightly under his control. A line of castles was constructed and garrisoned with loyal southern troops to secure the throne's authority over the fiefdom. While William I advanced his domestic affairs, as a vassal of the Plantagenet crown he attended court with his overlord, performing his fealty duties, and was frequently absent from his kingdom.

The ongoing ecclesiastic discord over the rightful jurisdiction of the Scottish Church had remained dormant since the reign of David I. In 1178 the dispute was renewed when the Priory of Saint Andrews elected its own bishop in defiance of William I, who immediately appointed a counter-prelate. The diocese petitioned the papacy for support, which Pope Alexander III confirmed by issuing a decree approving the actions of the Priory. The royal court ignored the order seeking the intervention of Henry II. Meeting with his overlord in Normandy, a compromise was arranged however the settlement was rejected by the Holy See and William I again refused to recognize the papal nomination. To enforce his ruling Pope Alexander III issued an excommunication bull against the Scottish king, placing his realm under an interdictment. The conflict again was temporarily resolved in March 1182 with the death of the pope and the lifting of his declarations against Scotland by the new pontiff, Lucius III. With the victory William I regained his rights and dominion over Scottish ecclesiastic affairs. His prerogative was confirmed in 1189 with his successful appointment of his cousin, Roger, as the new bishop of Saint Andrews.

In 1184 William I was forty-one years old and still had not married, leaving the question of his future succession in doubt. With the consent of Henry II the Scottish court began negotiations for the marriage of the king to the daughter of the duke of Saxony. However, for reasons of consanguinity the papacy denied the petition, forcing William I to wait two additional years before finding a queen. In May 1186 Henry II gave his permission for his vassal to marry Ermengarde, the daughter of the count of Maine. The Plantagenet council favored the political union as it offered no material gains for Scotland while retaining the balance of power. The ceremony was held at Oxford on September 5 amid a great celebration attended by many Scottish lords and bishops. The queen was described as a princess of intelligence, well educated and possessing a pious nature. Ermengarde became a trusted advisor to her husband, assuming some of his duties. The marriage resulted in the birth of four children, including the heir designate, Alexander, born in 1198.

After the prolonged stay in England for the marriage ceremony, William I returned to Scotland where he was soon compelled to resolve the ongoing rebellion against his authority in the earldom of Moray. The local earl, Donald MacWilliam, had first attacked and ravaged his overlord's lands in 1182, driving the Canmore troops and governmental officials from the region to seize autonomous control. His aggression and defiance of the throne's supremacy had gone unchallenged, however, early in 1187 William I assembled a large army of his retainers determined to re-impose his kingship over the recalcitrant warlord. Advancing into the fiefdom Donald was hunted down and killed, with his severed head presented to the king, while his lands were occupied with royal vassals. With the triumph William I was once again able to claim the territory as a part of his realm.

In July 1189 William I's relationship with his powerful southern neighbor became more favorable with the death of the elder Plantagenet. Henry II's French demesne and the kingdom of England were inherited by his son, Richard I, who had spent the majority of his life on the continent, exhibiting little interest in cross–Channel affairs. While establishing his supremacy over his French lands, the new Plantagenet monarch became absorbed with his participation in a new Crusade. In October 1187 the Saracen warlord, Saladin, had captured Jerusalem and systematically destroyed the Christian Kingdom in the Holy Land, compelling Pope Gregory VIII to issue a summons for the princes of Europe to reclaim the lost region. While the petition was largely ignored by the Scottish lords, Richard I became an enthusiastic supporter in search of personal glory and adventure. In 1189 he assembled his English and Scottish vassals to renew their oaths of obedience and to raise gold for his expedition. William I traveled south to the English court to pledge his fealty, where Richard I offered to abrogate the terms of the Treaty of Falaise in exchange for a large cash payment. The Canmore readily accepted the proposal, known as the Quitclaim Deed of Canterbury, which returned Scotland to its former independence, free of all feudal homage to England.

With the English king occupied in distant lands, William I continued the process of consolidating his supremacy over his demesne and Church. A series of marriages of his illegitimate children was arranged with various northern English earls, enhancing his influence and presence in an area where he still held territorial ambitions. With Richard I's prolonged absence from England, his brother, John Lackland, began to conspire to gain control over the kingdom. However, the Scots remained loyal to their suzerain for their northern English fiefdoms. In April 1193 the Plantagenet monarch returned to re-establish his authority over the realm summoning his Scottish retainers to court to renew their homage. Traveling to England William I was well received by Richard I as a faithful and respected vassal. However, all attempts to regain the marchland counties of Northumbria and Cumbria were rejected.

After ensuring the peace with his southern neighbor, William I returned to his court and the administration of his lands. He continued to travel extensively throughout his realm, asserting his justice and will. Under the king's direction his sovereignty slowly became more firmly accepted among the native Celtic lords and clerics, while he maintained a firm hold over the Lowland region. Nevertheless, in 1196 Harald, earl of the northernmost princedom of Orkney, who had only marginally recognized the monarchy of William I, openly defied his overlord, pillaging his estates and population. The regime aggressively responded to the rebellion and sacking of its lordship, sending the royal army into Orkney, attacking and capturing the earl. Harald was permitted to retain his fiefdom in return for his pledge of loyalty. Despite his oath of fealty, in 1202 Harald of Orkney again revolted, forcing William I to send troops north to impose his supremacy. He was soon defeated and compelled to accept the harsh royal council's terms of surrender. By his decisive and timely response to the uprising, William I demonstrated to his vassals that he possessed the will and military might to enforce his sovereignty.

In April 1199 the Scottish court's relationship with England was once again thrust into a state of uncertainty and confusion with the death of Richard I during siege operations against a rebel warlord. The Plantagenet king had no direct heir but, before his death, his brother, John, had been appointed as successor to the Angevin Empire. However, his accession was disputed as a rebellious faction of French and English barons and bishops soon rallied to the cause of his nephew, Arthur. In the resulting political upheaval, William I again pressed his birthright to Northumbria and Cumbria, threatening to invade the northern demesne. John Lackland largely ignored relations with Scotland as he continued to be involved with asserting his sovereignty over his rogue French retainers and the ongoing war against Philip II of France. It was not until November 1200 that he turned to English affairs, summoning his Scottish vassal to court at Lincoln. William I traveled south, meeting with his overlord, pledging his fealty while utilizing the opportunity to demand the restoration of the disputed border counties. John refused to give an immediate decision, leaving for the continent, compelling the Canmore king to return home again with no resolution.

In France Philip II increasingly gained the military advantage over John Lackland and by early 1204 had driven him from his lands to assert Capet sovereignty. The deposed Plantagenet was forced to abandon all pretensions to the Angevin Empire and concentrate his initiatives at retaining control over his English possessions and keeping the territorial ambitions of the Scots in check. However, the Scottish king was largely confined to internal activities within his realm and, lacking the military means to forcibly seize Northumbria and Cumbria, realized no advantage from John's downfall on the continent. What association William I had with English affairs was mainly through his brother, David, who spent long periods of time at the Plantagenet court. During the next few years the Canmore council held several meetings with John to discuss the disposition of the northern counties but no satisfaction was given.

By 1208 with his authority over England secured, John Lackland began to initiate a more hostile posture against his northern vassal by strengthening his defensive system at the strategic stronghold of Tweedmouth. The Scots perceived the bellicose actions as a prelude to attack and a direct threat to their security, beginning to prepare for war. In April of the following year, the two courts met near Alnwick to resolve the growing dispute but no accord was reached. William I withdrew to Stirling Castle where on May 24 a council of war was convened with the leading prelates and magnates. As a result of the talks envoys were dispatched to the Plantagenet regime, seeking a peaceful reconciliation of the escalating conflict. However, John refused to negotiate, ordering his army to march north. As the English troops approached the Scottish border, William I realized the necessity of finding a peaceful solution, lacking the financial and military means to resist the imminent assault, and was forced to agree to the humiliating terms of his overlord. The two kings met at Norham, where the Scots were required to end their cross-border raids, pay a huge indemnity, provide hostages and give the two daughters of William I to John to arrange their marriages. The Treaty of Norham effectively ended all Scottish aspirations of ever regaining the lost earldoms of Cumbria and Northumbria.

The acceptance of the harsh terms of the Norham Treaty was greatly resented by the Scottish magnates and clerics, especially in the Celtic-dominated Highlands. In 1211 the warlord of Ross, Guthred MacWilliam, revolted against the authority of William I. Despite his advancing years and steadily declining health, during the summer the king personally mounted an aggressive campaign of conquest against the northern insurgents. Several bloody skirmishes were fought but no decisive battle resulted and with the approach of winter the royal army was withdrawn, with Guthred remaining in defiance of his overlord.

With the conflict in Ross still unsettled, in January 1212 William I arranged to meet with John Lackland at Norham to request English troops for the coming campaigning season against the northern uprising. A treaty was signed, with John pledging to send a small military force to aid in the subjugation of Guthred. To further bind the two realms in friendship, the negotiations resulted in the marriage agreement between the Scottish heir, Alexander, and an English princess of Johns choosing. In the summer the king's reinforced army marched north to end the insurrection. The earl of Ross was soon captured and later executed for his treasonous activities as the royal jurisdiction of the Canmore throne was again fully imposed.

The aging king spent the remaining two years of his reign engaged in generally routine domestic affairs, with his queen and son increasingly playing larger roles. In May 1214 William I traveled north to Moray to invest the new earl in his fiefdom and receive his homage. On the return journey his health declined rapidly and he died at Stirling Castle on December 4. At his death William I was 71 and had reigned for nearly a half-century. Six days later he was buried at his great abbey at Arbroath to be succeeded by his son, Alexander II.

ALEXANDER II, 1198–1214–1249

At the end of the long reign of King William I in 1214, the throne of Scotland was assumed by the successor designate, Alexander II. The Canmore heir was born on August 24, 1198, at Haddington and was the only son of William I and Queen Ermengarde, the daughter of the French count of Maine. His early childhood was spent in the royal household under the dominance of his mother. Various Church tutors were provided for his formal education and he was taught reading, writing, Latin, French and religious doctrine.

However, the focus of his training was directed at preparations for knighthood. The Scottish prince was instructed in the equestrian skills of a feudal warlord, becoming accomplished in the use of the Norman lance, poleax and sword, along with mastering archery. While continuing his military education, he received instruction in the cultural graces of dancing, music and court etiquette. Alexander was physically described as small in height and attractive in features, with red hair and a pronounced royal bearing.

In October 1201 William I assembled the leading Scottish magnates and prelates to give their pledges of fealty to his son to ensure Alexander's peaceful succession. The Canmore heir was associated with the administration around the age of twelve, participating in the king's council meetings. In 1212 he accompanied his father to the English court at Norham to be presented to the sovereign of England, John. While William I traveled back to Scotland the fourteen-year-old Alexander remained in the Plantagenet household, continuing his martial training and where he was later knighted. While he was preparing to return to Scotland, the ongoing rebellion against his father's authority in Ross was renewed. The English crown agreed to send an army to aid the subjugation campaign in the Highlands, with Alexander readily joining the advancing troops, anxious to earn his spurs as a recently consecrated knight. However, he experienced little combat as the revolt was quickly subdued with the capture and execution of the rebel leader.

After the defeat of the Ross uprising Alexander returned to his father's court, becoming increasingly associated with the administration of the government with the steadily declining health of the monarch. On December 4, 1214, William I died and his son was readily recognized as his rightful successor. Two days later Alexander II was escorted to the historical and traditional site of enthronement at Scone, where, before the great nobles and bishops of Scotland, he assumed the kingship at the age of sixteen.

The Canmore kings had established an unchallenged hold over the Lowland fiefdoms. However, among the Celtic northern earldoms, their sovereignty continued to be openly opposed. Soon after Alexander II's assumption of the throne, Donald MacWilliam, son of the rebellious earl of Ross, crossed the Irish Sea from his base of power in Ulster to raise an army in revolt to assert his territorial rights and independence. The governing council countered the threat to its authority by mounting an assault against MacWilliam under the local commander. The insurgency movement had found little favor among the Ross warlords and the rogue leader was quickly captured and executed. With the defeat of Donald's uprising the Canmore court's control over the Highland magnates and bishops was generally respected, with only the western islands and Orkney remaining outside the perimeter of its supremacy.

While Alexander II was occupied with the consolidation of his kingship and the suppression of Donald MacWilliam, to the south the political stability of England was again in turmoil. A powerful faction of barons and prelates had risen in rebellion against the tyrannical rule of King John. In June 1215 the English crown was forced to sign the Magna Carta, relinquishing a portion of its absolute powers to the rebels. As the insurgency continued to escalate and with John's control over his realm steadily diminishing, Alexander II seized upon the internal crisis to mount a challenge for the northern counties of Northumbria and Cumbria. The Canmore monarch had been raised at his father's court in an atmosphere where the possession of the region had been a primary goal and he was equally determined to reacquire the earldoms. In the summer he mounted a diplomatic initiative to gain the political and military support of the dissident northern English earls and clerics while preparing his army for war.

In October 1215, with England escalating into civil war, Alexander II mobilized his armed forces, crossing the border into Northumbria. The earldom's warlords and bishops quickly rallied to the Scottish flag, giving their homage. By the end of the month most of the countryside was under Alexander II's control, though the large fortified cities remained loyal to John. In January 1216, using its remaining strongholds as a military staging area, the English crown launched its army against Alexander II's soldiers and his renegade northern vassals in an attempt to reassert its sovereignty. After first skirmishing with the Scottish occupation troops, the English campaign was advanced across the frontier into Scotland, where the local population was pillaged and murdered. While the Plantagenets were sacking his kingdom, Alexander II responded by mounting a counter-raid deep into England. As the Scottish levies marched south, many of the northern English barons rallied to the Canmore cause. With Alexander II's invasion force reinforced with the household retainers of the Northumbrian magnates, the fortification at Carlisle was stormed and the local towns and population ravaged. Carlisle Castle became the center of the Scottish administration for the newly acquired lands as Alexander II began to consolidate his conquest and establish his personal government. The Canmore king continued down the coast to Dover, where he met the heir to the French throne, Louis Capet.

The leading English rebel barons and bishops had earlier traveled to France, meeting with Prince Louis in Paris offering him their support and homage for his seizure of the Plantagenet throne. The Capetian heir accepted their petition, crossing the Channel in May 1216 and landing in Dover with an army of French cavalry and infantry. Soon after his arrival the southern English nobles, Church and towns rallied to his cause, enabling Louis to quickly claim the whole of eastern England. As John's authority steadily collapsed throughout his kingdom and he was increasingly abandoned by his vassals, Alexander II pledged his fealty to Louis in exchange for the earldoms of Cumbria and Northumbria. The agreement gave the Scots a firm legal basis to annex the territories directly to Scotland. However, Alexander II's easy victory was transitory. On October 18, 1216, John Lackland suddenly died at Newark Castle. The English magnates and prelates readily deserted Louis, ending their rebellion, rallying to the monarchy of the new king, Henry III, the eldest son of John. Alexander II continued to defiantly hold the northern conquered lands until late 1217 when his local support collapsed as he became threatened by a newly united England. To exert additional political pressure on Alexander II, the English sought the intervention of the See of Rome, which placed an interdiction against Scotland to force its withdrawal from the disputed demesne. The Canmore council began negotiations with Henry III's court, reaching a final resolution in June 1220. Under the terms of the settlement the Scottish monarch gave his oath of homage for the English county of Huntingdon and agreed to abandon his claims to Cumbria and Northumbria, while the Plantagenet crown recognized Scotland's separate sovereignty. To further bind the two realms in peace and foster a spirit of goodwill, Alexander II agreed to marry Joan, the eldest daughter of John.

The marriage ceremony between the Scottish monarch and Joan was held at York on June 9, 1221. The political union with the sister of the English sovereign brought increased prestige to the Scottish realm among the European courts while serving to strengthen the recent reconciliation with the Plantagenets. The marriage proved to be unhappy, with the couple ill-suited to each other. The king lived a largely separate life from his wife, taking numerous mistresses. The queen played only a marginal role in throne affairs, having little influence over Alexander II and his council. Joan died childless in 1238 while visiting her brother in London.

The treaty of 1220 secured peace with England on the southern Scottish border, permitting Alexander II to direct his government's initiatives toward domestic issues. He became the first Canmore to mount a diplomatic effort to gain papal approval for the consecration and anointment of Scottish kings by the Church. Under present practice the investiture ceremony was purely secular, with no acknowledgement of the monarch from the local bishops. Seeking to put the Scottish throne on equal status with other European powers and to gain the formal association with the Church, Alexander II petitioned Pope Honorius III to sanction the ecclesiastic observance. However, it was in the best interest of the English to keep the Scots in an inferior position and Henry III's court used its considerable influence with the papacy to thwart the request. Several additional attempts were made but no formal recognition was given. Nevertheless, the ordination of the monarchy remained a policy goal of Alexander II.

As the king continued to negotiate with the Holy See, initiatives were undertaken to firmly secure the loyalty of the rogue Highland warlords and bishops and to extend full royal sovereignty into the recalcitrant western isles. In 1221 Alexander II mobilized a militia of his southern allies and vassals, sailing to Argyll to assert his kingship over the local magnates, Alan of Galloway and Duncan of Carrick. The army of Arygll was quickly defeated and the earls deposed. To impose the throne's will the earldoms were dissolved and the region placed under the direct control of the Canmore court, while several castles were constructed and garrisoned with Lowland troops to ensure the peace. The western earldoms were later re-created under loyal exiled Anglo-Norman retainers appointed by Alexander II, while the Argyll lords and clerics remained subservient to the power of the monarchy.

While the northern earldoms had largely been subdued, there continued to be isolated acts of defiance against the Canmore throne. In late 1222 Alexander II was again compelled to assemble his army to intervene against the Highland fiefdom of Caithness to assert his supremacy. The local warlords had risen in revolt against the authority of the royal bailiff, openly challenging the king's supremacy. The Canmore regime's military launched a devastating campaign against the rebels and by the aggressive destruction of their estates Alexander II demonstrated that his will would be uncontested.

By the aggressive enforcement of his feudal rights as overlord over the Scottish mainland, Alexander II had imposed the acceptance of the monarchy beyond the limits achieved by any of his predecessors. However, the lands in the northwest had continued to remain outside the perimeter of Scottish dominion and in 1230 the ruling council began to direct its initiatives toward securing the autonomous region. The western isles centered in the Hebrides had been under the marginal authority of the crown of Norway but, under the energetic and aggressive King Hakon IV, a new campaign had been mounted to reestablish Scandinavian sovereignty. The Norwegian offensive was focused on the Hebrides, successfully reasserting the power of Hakon IV as suzerain. To counter the growing influence of the Scandinavians over a region where the Scottish court had ambitions, Alexander II empowered the deposed Alan of Galloway to thwart the efforts of the Northmen. The lord of Galloway attacked and plundered the western isles, succeeding in limiting the effectiveness of the Norwegian subjugation incursion at little expense to the Canmore throne.

Alexander II's kingship had succeeded in firmly establishing his supremacy over much of Scotland and, with his realm secured, in 1234 the royal court again turned its policy south and the unfulfilled ambition of re-acquiring Northumbria and Cumbria. The Canmore government issued a demand to Henry III for the return of the usurped earldoms, paired with the threat of armed invasion. The two rivals agreed to open negotiations and in September 1237 a final settlement was achieved. Under the Treaty of York the Scots pledged to abandon all claims for the northern territories in exchange for the grant of the English counties of Tynedale and Penrith. The accord set the boundary between the two kingdoms on a line from the Tweed River in the east to the Solway Firth in the west, which has virtually remained unchanged to this day.

While Alexander II was solidifying and expanding his monarchy he also continued the Canmore practice of royal patronage and support to the Church. During his reign many new churches and monasteries were built, while many existing structures were enlarged and richly enhanced. New religious orders were introduced and priories were expanded into new regions. The Dominicans were invited to establish a presence in Edinburgh while the Vallis Caulium Order was founded in the upper Highlands. The king took a personal interest in all appointments to the Church hierarchy, naming many of his allies and friends to high positions within the bishoprics. Under the direct sponsorship of the court, numerous clerical councils and diocese conferences were held to enact new Church laws unifying the Roman and Celtic dogma. There was a movement toward a national ecclesiastic tribunal, which fostered the centralization of all religious authority. The bond between the throne and Church was further promoted with the selection of many clerics and bishops as Canmore advisors and officials. To enhance the functioning and efficiency of his government in the earldoms, the power of his bailiffs and sheriffs was expanded and made directly responsible to the ruling council. The growth of commerce was encouraged and under Alexander II's reign Scotland experienced a sustained period of expanding economic growth.

In 1238 Queen Joan died childless, leaving the Canmore succession to the throne of Scotland in doubt. The following year Alexander II turned his search for a wife and a future heir to the kingdom of France. After securing the approval of the Capetian monarchy, a treaty was soon negotiated for the marriage of the king to Marie of Coucy, the daughter of the duke of Picardy. The ceremony was held at Roxburgh Castle on May 15, 1239, establishing a bond between the French crown and Scotland. The new queen was from a wealthy and powerful family with a strong affiliation with the court of Louis IX. The marriage also served to strengthen the independence and prestige of Alexander II's realm as an equal member of the European community while raising concerns in England of a possible future Franco-Scottish military league. Marie was described as possessing beauty, refinement and grace, readily adapting to Scottish customs and playing a more dominant role in council policy and politics than Joan. The future of the Canmore lineage was secured in 1241 when she gave birth to the future Alexander III.

In the aftermath of the Treaty of York, relations between Scotland and England had remained peaceful but strained. However, in 1242 Henry III began to regularly infringe in Scottish domestic issues by offering support to rogue Lowland warlords in defiance of the justice of Alexander II. As cross-border tensions mounted, to protect the marchland counties against the threat of invasion, the Scots began construction of two castles, which the English perceived as an act of war. Henry III mobilized a formidable army and began to advance north, compelling Alexander II to summon his vassals and allies. A battle was only averted by a hastily arranged conference between the two rivals where the peace was renewed under the provisions of the Treaty of York and a marriage agreement was signed between the infant Alexander and the young Margaret, daughter of Henry III. The English court pledged to respect the sovereignty and independence of Scotland while refraining from interference in Scottish internal affairs.

By 1242 the policies of Alexander II had secured his border with England and his active intervention in Arygll and the northern earldoms had effectively established Scottish supremacy over the magnates, clerics and population. However, the region to the northwest, centered on the Hebrides Islands, remained largely autonomous with feudal obligations to Norway and in 1244 the Scots began negotiations to acquire the Isles. The Norwegians had partially reasserted their overlordship in the Western Isles in 1230 but in recent years the local warlords had regained much of their authority. Envoys were dispatched to the Norwegian king, Hakon IV, offering to purchase the disputed area. The proposals were repeatedly rejected and, finding no peaceful resolution, Alexander II began to prepare for war. In Arygll several castles and burghs were fortified while their garrisons were strengthened to be used as a base of operations for the planned invasion. The royal council initiated a series of alliances with the nobles, assuring their loyalty and support against Hakon IV. As the Scots mobilized for war the Norwegians responded to the growing militancy by forging a counter-coalition with the powerful and ambitious warrior, Ewan Macdougall of Argyll, to strengthen his coastal defenses. In the spring of 1249 Alexander II assembled a formidable army and fleet, launching his naval expedition to conquer the Western Isles. Under the court's battle plan the first objective was to eliminate the Macdougall faction in Argyll and impose its sovereignty over the rebellious area. With the major base of Hakon IV's military power subdued with the seizure of Argyll, the naval force was to sail north, capturing the Hebrides. However, as his ships lay in anchor in Kerrera Sound, Alexander II became seriously ill with a fever, dying on July 8, 1249, before the campaign could be initiated. The ninth Canmore sovereign was nearly fifty-one and had ruled Scotland for thirty-five years. At his death he was succeeded by his seven-year-old son, Alexander III.

ALEXANDER III, 1241–1249–1286

In the summer of 1249 the Scottish king, Alexander II, mounted an ambitious military campaign to seize the Hebrides Islands from Hakon IV of Norway. However, as the Scots prepared to launch their sea-borne operation, on July 8 the monarch unexpectedly died from the effects of a high fever and was succeeded by his only issue, Alexander III.

Alexander was born on September 4, 1241, and was the son of Alexander II and Marie of Coucy, the daughter of a powerful French duke with strong family ties to the ruling Capetian dynasty. The sovereign took a personal interest in the education of the heir apparent, appointing scholars from the Church as tutors. The young Canmore prince received instruction in reading, writing, languages to include French, Latin and Flemish, religion and history. Around the age of seven he began military preparations for knighthood, receiving regular training in the use of weapons and equestrianship. Away from his formal studies he spent time hunting and hawking while participating in various field sports and games with the children of other noble families.

In July 1249 Alexander II died unexpectedly and his seven-year-old son ascended the monarchy of Scotland as Alexander III. On July 13 he was formally invested at the traditional site of enthronement in the Scone Abbey. The ceremony was attended by the foremost earls and prelates of the realm, who pledged their fealty to the young king. With the succession of a minor a regency council was quickly appointed by the parliament to govern Scotland in the name of Alexander III. Soon after the establishment of the new administration, two rival political parties began to contend for the leadership of the kingdom and the minority years of the Canmore sovereign were dominated by the supremacy struggle between the Durward and Comyn noble houses.

The Durward family was headed by Alan of Scotia, who had earlier acquired the royal office of chancellor while the leadership of the Comyns was centered on Walter, earl of Menteith. Initially Alan Durward was able to forge an alliance with powerful warlords and bishops, securing control of Alexander III and the kingdom. As the chief judicial official of the court, Durward used his position of influence and authority to advance the members of his family and friends with key offices and patronage. As the ruling faction consolidated its dominance over the government, the earl of Menteith was actively engaged in forming a counter political league with the earl of Mar, William, and other magnate and prelates in the northern and southwestern lordships. As the power struggle between the two rival parties intensified, Walter of Menteith and William began secret negotiations with Henry III of England to gain his support in the overthrow of the Durwards.

During the minority years of Alexander III with its resulting political uncertainty and insecurity, the maintenance of peaceful relations with the English throne was the focal point of the regency administration's foreign policy. To promote the continuance of friendship, in 1251 the Scottish government began negotiations with Henry III for the marriage of his daughter, Margaret, to the Canmore monarch. By the summer an agreement had been finalized and in December Alexander III traveled south with his court to York for the official ceremony. On Christmas Day Henry III knighted the boy-king and on the following day Alexander III was formally married to the English princess. Following the royal celebrations Henry III reopened the dormant issue of Plantagenet overlordship with the Canmore council by demanding homage for the whole of Scotland, which was refused by the ten-year-old Alexander III after discussions with his regents. However, the event marked the beginning of a series of intrigues by the Plantagenet crown to revive its claims of sovereignty.

At the time of the wedding ceremony, the king and his new wife were only ten years old, occupying separate households during the early period of their marriage. Margaret spent her initial years as queen at the Scottish court in isolation and despair. Nevertheless, despite the unhappy beginning, Alexander III and Margaret through the coming years developed a happy and loving relationship. She was described as a princess of poise, beauty and piety, becoming a close advisor to her husband. The queen had a great influence on both her father and brother, the future Edward I, facilitating a closer cooperation between the two realms. The marriage resulted in two sons, Alexander and David, neither of whom succeeded their father, and one daughter, Margaret.

While Alexander III and the Scottish court remained in England following the wedding ceremony, after his rebuke of fealty from the Canmore throne, Henry III finalized his ongoing secret negotiations with William of Mar and Walter Comyn for their assumption of the Scottish regime. With the financial and military support of the English, a formidable coalition was formed, which moved immediately against the governing faction in York, forcing the Durward regents from power. The earl of Mar was named as chamberlain, using his high offices to replace the Durward officials with members of his alliance. When Alexander III and his new queen returned to Scotland in late January, the Plantagenet king sent secret agents with his daughter to promote his interest and influence within the new ruling council. The usurpation of the realm was later confirmed by the Scottish Parliament as Earl William and Walter of Menteith successfully consolidated their seizure of the monarchy.

The Comyn family remained in authority over the next three years but their administration grew steadily unpopular among the magnates, clerics and burghs as abuses of power and government grew more severe. The political alliance forged between the earls of Mar and Menteith with Henry III slowly collapsed as the English crown became increasingly involved and distracted with the revolt of its French duchy of Gascony and the Comyns acted independently of any foreign influences. As the regents lost the support of the Scottish fiefdoms, Alan Durward began to conspire to regain control of the kingdom. In 1254 Durward traveled to the court of Henry III and was soon serving with the English military forces in Gascony in an attempt to secure the patronage of the English regime. The following year the Gascon rebels were subdued allowing the Plantagenet expeditionary army along with their Scottish allies to return to England.

During his service in France Alan Durward had used his close association with Henry III to gain his favor and the agreement for military support in the toppling of the Comyns. After finalizing his alliance with the English court, the Scotia lord returned to Scotland to initiate his insurrection campaign. During the summer of 1255 a Plantagenet army moved north to aid the coup, while the Durward family negotiated a league of local warlords in an attempt to seize the king and his ruling council. In August the newly formed coalition marched against the Comyns and Alexander III at Edinburgh Castle, quickly forcing the garrison to surrender. With Scotland in political disarray and with no central authority in power, Henry III used the threat of his military might to impose his puppet Durward's regime on the realm. However, the new administration received little backing from the nobles and high clerics, struggling to rule effectively. After two years of increasing division the pro-Plantagenet regency opened talks to include the dissident Comyn family in a new unity council, but all attempts at reconciliation failed. The escalating crisis was only resolved in October 1257 when Walter of Menteith kidnapped Alexander III and, with control of the symbolic figurehead of Scotland, reestablished the Comyn government. However, the regency of Walter Comyn remained in supremacy last less than a year as the Canmore king began to openly and aggressively assert his royal sovereignty, slowly imposing his will. By the time Alexander III reached the age of eighteen in 1260, he had assumed full dominance over his kingdom and was acknowledged as overlord.

Upon claiming control of his realm Alexander III energetically formed a series of political alliances to consolidate his reign by negotiating a reconciliation with the militant warlords. A policy of toleration, inclusion and patronage was begun as members of the warring parties were made a part of the royal court with important positions of high office and authority. The king utilized the Comyn faction as the center of his administration to assert his dominion in the northern lordships through their retainers. In the western earldoms the ambitious Stewart family actively supported the regime and through their leadership the region remained loyal to the throne. Throughout Scotland the magnates, clerics and burghs rallied to the monarchy of Alexander III, ending the fragmentation that had divided and threatened the kingdom during the minority years.

Through his political alliances Alexander III was able to end the internal turmoil to unite the realm under his authority. With Scotland secure he began negotiations with the Plantagenet regime to solidify friendly relations. In 1260 the Canmore ruler with Queen Margaret traveled to the Plantagenet court to renew Scotland's bonds of détente with Henry III. The English king was occupied with ongoing problems in France while facing growing rebellion at home and needed to ensure peace in his northern border counties. With both governments desiring a reconciliation of outstanding differences, an accord was quickly reached, allowing Alexander III to return to Scotland assured that his southern marchland was secure from invasion.

As Alexander III asserted his independent rule, in 1260 the Scottish economy was struggling from the ongoing effects of famine, poor harvests and misgovernment. To revive commercial activities and improve agricultural output, the royal court instituted a series of reforms. As a result of the initiatives the towns were able to increase their level of exports based largely on wool and leather trade with France and Flanders. With better weather and new growing techniques, farm production steadily improved while the overall economy grew at a modest rate. In ecclesiastic affairs the Canmore council took a special interest in the appointments of new clerics to Church offices to ensure that the royal prerogative would be enforced. The sovereign was an active sponsor of the Scottish Church, favoring the prelates with his patronage. Alexander III supported the restoration and building of new churches and abbeys along with the continued expansion of the monastic orders. The Scottish throne regularly drew on the Church as a major source of advisors, envoys and high court officials. During the king's reign parliaments were summoned on a regular basis and measures were enacted to enlarge and enhance the legal system with new sheriffdoms and law courts. Scotland under Alexander III experienced its first golden era, characterized by a growing prosperity, stable and responsive government and an expanding international presence.

Alexander III's first two years of kingship had resulted in an accommodation with his magnates, ending the years of political strife, and had reestablished amiable relations with England, which enabled Scotland to pursue an aggressive foreign policy in the north. The Scottish kings had steadily advanced their sovereignty into the Highlands and had begun to contend for control of the Western Isles as early as the late eleventh century during the reign of Edgar I. The maritime fiefdoms consisted of a chain of islands and the northernmost coastline of the Sea of the Hebrides and formed a part of the seaborne empire of Norway. In 1261 Alexander III revived his father's plan for northern expansion, dispatching envoys to the Scandinavian court of Hakon IV in an attempt to purchase the Isles. While the ongoing negotiations evolved the Scottish regime began to make arrangements for war by buttressing its defenses along the maritime coast. The royal castles were strengthened and the garrisons reinforced with additional troops. As Alexander III traveled through the kingdom to rally the warlords to his cause, he ordered the regional earls to mobilize their local military forces while war provisions were stockpiled and a small number of mercenary soldiers hired.

In the spring of 1262 the Scottish negotiators returned home with Hakin IV's formal rejection of the proposed fiefdom purchase. As relations between the two realms deteriorated, Alexander III renewed his claims to the Isles, ordering the earl of Ross to mount a pillaging raid against the Norwegian-held island of Skye. With hostilities intensifying the Norwegian court began to assemble its navy and military forces, preparing to depart for the Western Isles to defend its demesne. In July the Norse squadron of over forty vessels sailed for the Shetlands and down the Scottish coast where they were joined by ships from their allies in the Isles and the Isle of Man, which swelled the fleet to over two hundred. In September Hakon IV sent emissaries to Alexander III with an offer of peace if the Scots would agree to respect Norwegian sovereignty over the Western Isles. The negotiations dragged on into late September while the Highlanders rallied to Alexander III in defense of their kingdom against a foreign incursion. While the Canmore throne massed its militia, the Norse navy was anchored off Largs in the Firth of Clyde on September 30, where during the night a strong gale blew many of the ships against the shore. In the morning the Norwegian king personally led a landing party of over one thousand soldiers ashore to rescue the stranded troops when the Scots mounted their attack. The Norsemen were steadily driven back while Hakon IV managed to escape with a small band of his army. The combined losses from the battle and storm compelled the Norwegians to abandon their invasion campaign, sailing north to Orkney. Due to the lateness of the season, with the increased risk of severe storms, Hakon IV was forced to spend the winter on the island. With much of the Norse fleet still intact, Scotland continued to face the danger of an encroachment but the balance of power shifted in Alexander III's favor in December when Hakin IV died.

The Scandinavian navy remained a serious threat to Scotland, but the new king, Magnus VI, was beset with unrest in his realm, sending envoys to Alexander III to mediate a settlement. Delaying the talks the Scots seized the initiative by invading the Hebrides, occupying much of the Norse fiefdom. When negotiations began anew in 1265 Magnus VI had lost the military advantage and was forced to agree to the harsh terms of the Treaty of Perth dictated by Alexander III. Under the accord the Inner and Outer Hebrides were annexed to Scotland along with the Isle of Man for a cash payment. While the battle of Largs had been inconclusive, its aftermath was decisive for the Scottish kingdom, securing the regime's power base in the northwestern territories.

With his lands safe from foreign invasion and with the high magnates pacified, the Canmore king devoted his policies toward the enhancement of his government with a reign of peace and justice. In November 1272 Henry III of England died and was succeeded by his ambitious and charismatic son, Edward I. In August of the following year Alexander III and Margaret along with many high Scottish lords and clerics traveled to London for the coronation of the new sovereign. The occasion presented the opportunity to renew the bonds of friendship between the two kingdoms and resolve various outstanding border disputes.

While Alexander III's administration ushered in an era of good government and economic prosperity, in August 1275 Godfrey Magnusson, the illegitimate son of the deposed king of Man, attempted to restore the old Isle of Man kingdom by forming an alliance with the local warlords, seizing control of the island and overthrowing the Scottish governor. Alexander III countered the threat to his sovereignty by ordering troops from Galloway to suppress the revolt. In October the throne's army attacked the forces of Magnusson, brutally subjugating the rebels to reimpose the Canmore's authority. The rebellion of the Manx nobles was the last organized opposition to the rule of the monarch and he was able to govern in peace for the remainder of his reign.

With the submission of the Manx lords Alexander III's regime was at peace until 1276 when a serious border dispute erupted between the Canmores and Edward I over royal property rights along the Tweed River. Angry letters were exchanged between the two courts, with conditions threatening to escalate into open hostilities. However, in the summer the English ruling council became occupied with war in Wales and with the Scottish king's offer to negotiate a resolution in person the prospects for armed conflict became diminished. In October Alexander III traveled south to London, offering homage for his English estates while successfully arranging a settlement to the Tweed River disagreement. The bonds of friendship were revived and the monarch returned to his realm once again assured of peace on his southern borders.

In the aftermath of the Treaty of Perth, relations between the Scottish court and Norway had remained peaceful but strained. However, the status quo changed in 1280 when the Norwegian king, Magnus VI, died and was succeeded by his minor son, Erik II. With the kingdom governed by a weak regency council, Norway desired to maintain friendly relations with its neighbors. Envoys were sent to Alexander III proposing the marriage of Erik II to the sovereign's only daughter, Margaret, as a means to reinforce the terms of the Perth accord. The Scottish throne accepted the offer and in September 1281 the Canmore princess sailed to Bergen to her new household. The Norwegian marriage was followed in the next year by the wedding of Alexander III's only surviving son and heir to the daughter of the count of Flanders. The unions with two powerful and esteemed European princedoms signaled Scotland as a rising realm, bringing prestige and stature.

At the death of Queen Margaret in 1275 Alexander III had expressed no desire to remarry. However, in January 1284 the heir designate died and with the deaths of the Norwegian queen the year prior and the youngest son, David, in 1280, the future succession of the Canmore family came into question. The sole survivor of the ruling house was Margaret, the one-year-old Norwegian granddaughter of Alexander III. In February the Scottish Parliament was assembled by the royal court and the representatives of the nobles, clerics and burghs designated the young Margaret as the successor to secure the continuance of the Canmore dynasty.

With the infant Canmore princess a ward of a foreign court, it became essential that the monarch marry a second time and produce a Scottish heir. In February 1285 the regime dispatched envoys to France in the search for a new wife, reaching an agreement with the count of Dreux for marriage to his daughter, Yolande. The official ceremony was held on October 14 amid a grand celebration at Jedburgh Castle. However, the marriage ended after only five months with the accidental death of Alexander III and, tragically for Scotland, with no direct successor.

On March 18, 1286, the ruling council met at Edinburgh Castle to consider numerous petitions and routine court affairs. The day had turned stormy, with snow blowing in from the sea as Alexander III left Edinburgh to travel the few miles to his castle at Kinghorn. During the course of the journey his horse stumbled in the darkness, throwing Alexander III to his death and plunging the kingdom into a succession crisis. At the time of his death the tenth Canmore king was 44 years old and had ruled Scotland for 38 years.

MARGARET I, 1283–1286–1290

Margaret was born in April 1283 and was the daughter of the Norwegian king Erik II and Margaret of Scotland. With the death of her mother shortly after her birth and the deaths of the Scottish monarch's only two sons, Margaret became the sole surviving member in the line of succession to the Canmore dynasty. On February 5, 1284, the Scottish Parliament formally acknowledged her as the heir apparent, though no preparations were made to bring the princess to her grandfather's kingdom. Margaret spent her first years in the Norwegian court under the control of her father's government. In March 1286 Alexander III unexpectedly died and Margaret became the recognized successor to the throne. An interim council of six Guardians was appointed by the parliament to govern the regime and keep the peace as rival families began to openly contend for the monarchy. To bring political stability to the realm, the regency counselors began negotiations with the Norwegian court to acquire custody of the new queen.

As the threat of disorder and civil war mounted, Edward I of England began to conspire to gain dominion over Scotland. To impose its will the English ruling council began deliberations with both the Guardians and Norway, resulting in the July 1290 Treaty of Birgham. Under the central provisions of the accord, Margaret was to marry the son of the Plantagenet king, the future Edward II, with guarantees provided for a separate and independent Scottish realm. The agreement would have effectively given the English supremacy over their northern neighbors. In September 1290 Margaret sailed from Bergen in a Norwegian ship bound for her new kingdom. However, she never reached Scotland, dying during the voyage. The death of the last Canmore at age seven thrust Scotland into a dangerous succession crisis that was only resolved by the bloody and prolonged Wars of Independence and the emergence of Robert the Bruce and the Stewart dynasty.

House of Bruce, 1292–1371

The political stability of Scotland was plunged into turmoil with the threat of civil war at the death of the last Canmore monarch in 1290. As various warring factions prepared for war, the six parliamentary-elected Guardians of the kingdom petitioned Edward I of England to intervene to appoint the next ruler. In the ensuing parliament John Balliol was acknowledged as the dominant magnate and with the full support of England was appointed as the new king. However, Balliol lacked the political and military might to enforce his independence from the English and soon the realm was in revolt against Plantagenet subjugation and occupation. In 1296 Scotland was invaded by Edward I and Balliol deposed. In the resulting Wars of Independence the charismatic Robert Bruce emerged from the internal anarchy and foreign invasions as the preeminent warlord, establishing a dynasty that reigned for over four hundred years. However, during the rule of the second Bruce king, David II, the autonomy of the Scottish throne was once again lost to England and was not fully regained until 1337 when the Plantagenet crown became distracted by the Hundred Years War with France. Initially the Bruce authority was firmly recognized in only the Lowlands, however through a series of alliances, marriages and armed encroachments, full sovereignty was eventually imposed over the whole of Scotland.

JOHN BALLIOL, 1250–1292–1296–1313

With the death of Margaret I, the last surviving member of the direct Canmore dynasty, the succession to the monarchy of Scotland was thrust into uncertainty and turmoil. As the threat of civil war mounted, six Guardians were elected by the Scottish Parliament to administer the government and resolve the devolution crisis. The custodian council recognized the hereditary claims of thirteen competitors who came forward to claim the kingship. Three of the claimants soon emerged as possessing the superior right of inheritance as direct descendants of David, earl of Huntingdon and younger brother of King William I. However, the Guardians were unable to reach a final decision as the competitors began to mobilize their allies and armies, moving the kingdom closer to warfare. To prevent the armed usurpation of the throne, Edward I of England was invited to arbitrate the disputed succession. He offered to decide the issue on condition that the domain's major castles be placed under English control while each claimant acknowledge English overlordship for Scotland. With the realm quickly evolving closer to rebellion, the Guardians were compelled to accept the provisions.

In May 1291 each of the claimants was required to appear before Edward I at Norham Castle to pledge their homage. John Balliol and his faction had earlier begun to maneuver for the throne by aggressively initiating a political campaign to win the favor of the Scottish warlords and clerics with the promise of titles, court positions and lands. Many of the influential and powerful magnates and prelates openly supported his candidacy, petitioning the English king for his appointment as the rightful heir. However, to decide the succession Edward I elected to convene a parliament of 104 representatives, with forty electors to be appointed by each of the two leading contenders, John Balliol and Robert the Bruce, and the final twenty-four to be chosen by the English court. Over the next eighteen months a series of legal hearings was held to determine the successor with each candidate arguing for his rights to the kingship. Finally under the dictates of Edward I the assembly voted on November 6, 1292, to recognize the hereditary claims of John Balliol as the superior. On November 30 at Scone he was invested with the monarchy of Scotland in an enthronement ceremony that was dominated by a strong English presence.

John Balliol was born in 1250 in England and was the third son of John Balliol of Barnard and Dervorguilla, the daughter of the Scottish earl, Alan of Galloway, who was a direct descendant of King David I. The Balliols were an influential and wealthy family, holding extensive lands in England and Picardy, while John's mother was the direct heir to the Scottish earldom of Galloway. His father held positions of prestige and importance in the English court and was a trusted advisor to Henry III. As the youngest issue John was not expected to play a major role in the administration of the family's affairs, beginning preparations for a life in the Church at an early age. Tutors were provided for his formal education and he was instructed in reading, writing, Latin and religious doctrine. However, by 1278 both his father and elder brothers had died, leaving John as the sole inheritor of the Balliols' English and French estates. As the lord of Barnard, he controlled great wealth and commanded respect and repute among the Picardy and northern English nobles and clerics.

In 1281 John was married to Isabella of Surrey, the daughter of the local English earl. The political union with the powerful magnate increased Balliol's personal esteem while offering increased access to the English court. The marriage resulted in the birth of two sons and several daughters. The eldest son, Edward, later challenged unsuccessfully for the throne of Scotland.

Following the death of his father, John Balliol continued to occupy his life with the administration of his demesne, playing no part in the politics of Scotland. However, in 1286 with the death of King Alexander III and the assumption of the realm by his Norwegian granddaughter, Margaret, the lord of Barnard became the heir apparent. As the son of a direct descendant of Earl David of Huntingdon, John now held the superior claim to the monarchy, second only to his cousin Margaret. His position among the Scottish magnates and bishops was further expanded in 1290 with the death of his mother, leaving him the vast Scottish earldom of Galloway in the southwest. A strong political party began to form around the new earl as he began to intrigue in Scottish court affairs to advance his standing and authority. His power among the local fiefdoms was greatly enhanced by the marriage of his sister, Eleanor, to the formidable and influential John Comyn, lord of Badenoch. With the added prestige and military might of his brother-in-law, John actively began to conspire for control of the kingdom after the death of Margaret I in August 1290, bringing him into direct conflict with the rival Bruce family.

The Scottish monarchy remained vacant over the next two years as the two main political factions maneuvered against each other to gain the favor of the magnates and prelates.

However, as the succession crisis deteriorated and civil war threatened, neither the Balliol or Bruce alliance possessed the necessary supremacy to seize the government, resulting in the invited intervention of the English court in November 1292. After eighteen months of formal hearings John Balliol was finally declared king of Scotland. Nevertheless, his accession had been compromised by the pledge of fealty for his lands to Edward I as overlord. At Newcastle in January 1293 John was again forced to give homage to the English crown and to release the Plantagenet regime from any prior guarantees of Scottish independence. The act effectively ended the local autonomy of the kingdom, placing Scotland under the direct domination of England.

After his succession John Balliol began the difficult process of consolidating his reign and asserting his monarchy over a deeply divided realm. His regime was readily accepted in the earldom of Galloway and the northwestern territories of his brother-in-law, John Comyn. However, the lands of the Bruce alliance remained hostile, continuing to conspire against the throne and refusing to give homage. While his government was recognized in the western lordships, large parts of Scotland regarded John as a foreigner, only reluctantly acknowledging his authority. With only a limited power base he lacked the personal charisma and strength of personality necessary to impose his rights over the recalcitrant earldoms.

Under the Balliol court's direction modest attempts were made to re-introduce the policy initiatives of Alexander III by expanding the royal justice and prerogative into the west. Parliaments continued to be regularly summoned but little legislation was enacted. John was able to maintain peace throughout his realm under the increasing influence of the Comyn faction as the threat of open rebellion gradually subsided. However, his independent authority was severely compromised and his rule undermined by his dependency on John Comyn for support and the plottings of the Bruce family.

As John struggled to retain the throne and the internal peace, his relationship with Edward I grew increasingly contentious over the issue of his right to maintain an autonomous judicial system. In defiance of the Scottish monarchy, the English crown began to offer a Parliament of Appeals to disgruntled nobles. The direct assault against Balliol's royal prerogative served to further weaken his power and prestige among the magnates and clerics. In an attempt to reassert his kingship, Balliol largely ignored the rulings of the English court, however, Edward I escalated the discord by demanding that he personally attend every appeal hearing. John defended his independence by refusing to travel to the November 1293 Westminster Parliament. For his act of dissent, he was quickly found in contempt and threatened with the seizure of Scottish burghs and castles. Facing forfeiture of his demesne John reluctantly agreed to recognize the jurisdiction of the English. Edward I's continued thwarting of Balliol's local authority resulted in a serious breach in the confidence and trust among the Scottish king's supporters, dangerously weakening his hold on the realm.

Edward I's subjugation of Scotland continued in 1295 when he claimed military service from Balliol as his feudal overlord. When the Plantagenet king inherited the throne of England, he also assumed the duchy of Gascony as a vassal of the French court. In 1293 Philip IV ordered Edward I to Paris under penalty of forfeiture of lands to answer charges of rebellion along the Franco-Gascony frontier. When the petition was ignored the French invaded the duchy, quickly occupying many of the border towns and strongholds. In early 1296 Edward I began military preparations for a large cross-Channel invasion army to defend his territory, summoning John Balliol and the leading Scottish magnates to honor their fealty as retainers. John refused to comply with the demands, initiating negotiations with the French ruling council to forge a counter-alliance of mutual support. By February the terms of the treaty were ratified as the Scots began to prepare for war.

In response to the Scottish defiance of his feudal rights, Edward I directed his formidable army north with the intent of invading and subduing his rebellious vassals. The Wars of Scottish Independence were begun with a preemptive assault by Balliol's earls against the English castle at Carlisle. The Scots failed to capture the stronghold but the surrounding towns and countryside were pillaged and burned. In late March the Plantagenet forces crossed the border into Scotland, attacking Berwick Castle. The defenders offered little resistance, soon surrendering. However in a display of anger over the Scottish uprising and the ravaging of his demesne, Edward I allowed his troops to brutally sack the city. After garrisoning the fortification the English king advanced north along the coast to Dunbar, where siege operations were undertaken. After a brief blockade and with no relief army responding to their plight, the stronghold submitted. The lack of any counter-measures by the Balliol court effectively ended all organized resistance and in short order the key fortresses were under English control. Edward I marched unopposed through the kingdom, receiving the homage of the local warlords and clerics. As sovereign, John Balliol, had failed to rally Scotland to his cause, quickly losing the trust of the realm. In less than three weeks the English had conquered all of Scotland.

With the whole of his kingdom under English control, John Balliol submitted to Edward I on July 10 at Montrose, renouncing his kingship. In an additional act of humiliation he was ceremoniously stripped of his ranks of office and taken to England to be held as a prisoner in the Tower of London. The crown jewels and royal records of the government along with the symbol of Scottish enthronement, the Stone of Destiny, were sent to England. Scotland was occupied with English troops while deputies of Edward I were appointed to administer the institutions and Church as a Plantagenet fiefdom.

John Balliol was confined to the Tower of London until 1299, when he was paroled into local papal custody. Royal envoys from the French court and Scotland lobbied Pope Boniface VIII to intercede in the defense of the deposed king. Finally, under the mounting pressure of a papal rebuke, in July Edward I exiled John to France. In the summer of 1301 he was released from the control of the Holy See and permitted to settle permanently on his estates in Picardy. The emigrant sovereign spent the rest of his life withdrawn from Scottish political concerns, administering his personal affairs and lands. However, in Scotland his supporters remained active while the kingdom continued to be governed in his name. There were several attempts to restore Balliol to the monarchy, but Edward I rejected all the petitions. In April 1313 John Balliol died in France at Chateau Gaillard at the age of sixty-three and with a turbulent reign of less than four years on the Scottish throne.

ROBERT I, 1274–1306–1329

Robert, the seventh earl of Bruce, was born on July 11, 1274, on his father's southwestern Scottish estates at Turnberry Castle. He was the first of the five sons of Robert of Annandale and Marjorie, the daughter and heiress of the earl of Carrick. Through his father, Robert was a direct descendant of Adam the Bruce, who had sailed from Normandy in 1066 with the invasion army of William I and had been granted lands in northern England for his military successes. Succeeding generations of the family had acquired additional estates, titles and wealth through marriage and military and diplomatic service to the kings of England and Scotland. The Bruce faction commanded prestige and a large following among both the Plantagenet and Scottish warlords and clerics.

Robert spent his youth in the household of his father where his formal education was provided by tutors from the local Church. Under the guidance of the scholar-monks he was taught reading, writing, and the languages of French, English and Latin, while receiving instruction in religious doctrines. While continuing his academic studies he was instructed in the social graces of music and dancing. However, the focus of his early years was the military preparations as a feudal warlord. At around the age of seven Robert began his martial training for knighthood under the direction of renowned masters of arms. The young lord became proficient in the use of the Norman lance, sword and poleax, developing into an accomplished equestrian. He spent many hours hunting boar and deer in the vast forest of the Bruce estates and practiced his military prowess in various jousting tournaments, where he acquired a reputation for his skills and chivalry.

In 1286 the Scottish king, Alexander III, died, leaving his Norwegian-born granddaughter, Margaret I, as his only surviving heir. She was recognized as the successor by the parliament, which appointed a regency council of six Guardians to administer the regime and keep the peace for the minor queen. However, Margaret I died in 1290 traveling from her native Norway to assume the Scottish sovereignty. With the right of succession in dispute, various militant parties began to assemble around the principal three claimants to the monarchy. The Bruce family offered a strong challenge to the throne as a direct descendant of David, the younger brother of the Canmore monarchs, Malcolm IV and William I, through a predominately male line. The young Robert was an active participant in the Bruce coalition as the allies and vassals of his aging grandfather mobilized for the coming conflict. With the kingdom rapidly moving toward civil war, the Scottish Parliament agreed to offer England's Edward I the right of intervention to arbitrate the growing crisis. The petition was accepted by the Plantagenet monarch with the provision that each claimant must acknowledge his overlordship for Scotland. With control of the realm increasingly escalating into open warfare, the Guardians were forced to agree to the terms. In November 1292 John Balliol was declared to possess the superior right of inheritance and was enthroned as the sovereign of Scotland upon the Stone of Destiny at Scone. The Bruce faction rejected the decision, defiantly refusing to offer fealty.

As the acknowledged overlord of Scotland Edward I increasingly created internal dissent among the local nobles and clerics by imposing his authority over the legal rights and independence of John Balliol's kingship in a series of demeaning demands. Finally in 1295, with the Scottish king's summons for military service from the Plantagenet regime, he rebelled against the English. During this period the Bruce faction had withdrawn from court affairs, refusing to give homage to Balliol, remaining largely on their estates in England and Scotland. Robert had been granted the Scottish earldom of Carrick by his father and the young lord continued to administer the extensive family lands in the north while Balliol struggled to assert his independence from England. The earl traveled widely throughout the region, expanding his power base by imposing his personal authority over the Bruce alliance's vassals and allies, securing a loyal following of warlords.

In 1295 Robert Bruce was married to Isabella, the daughter of the earl of Mar, uniting two formidable families with a long-standing close political and historical relationship. The marriage was brief ending with the premature death of Isabella two years later. Robert and Isabella had one child, Marjorie, whose descendents later established the Stewart dynasty. The earl of Carrick did not remarry again until 1302 when he married Elizabeth of Burgh, the daughter of the influential and powerful English earl of Ulster. The union was a political arrangement, giving the Bruce faction enhanced access to potential friends and allies in Ireland, and resulted in the birth of four children, including the future king David II.

In early 1296 John Balliol summoned the Scottish earls to assemble for war against the subjugation of Edward I. The Bruce faction had earlier refused to offer fealty to the throne, remaining loyal to the English king, and they ignored the petition to mobilize. The act of defiance resulted in the seizure of their Scottish estates by the court of Balliol. The War of Independence was initiated with the preemptive attack of the allies of John Balliol against the Plantagenet castle at Carlisle. Edward I countered the challenge to his overlordship by marching his powerful military forces into Scotland, sacking the important commercial center at Berwick. The English army continued north virtually unopposed as all support for the continued kingship of John Balliol vanished. On July 10, 1296, the Scottish sovereign submitted to Edward I at Montrose, where he was ceremoniously stripped of his royal rank and taken to England as a prisoner. The realm was occupied by foreign troops and the administration of the local institutions and Church was by appointees of the English regime. Scotland had been reduced to a virtual colonial possession of the Plantagenet crown.

The English army's triumphant advance through Scotland had ended the threat of any future organized resistance. However, Edward I was badly served by his appointed viceroy and officials, who initiated a policy of plunder and brutality against the Scottish population. By 1297 armed hostility slowly began to emerge against the occupiers under the leadership of the charismatic warrior lords William Wallace, Sir William Douglas and Andrew Moray. A successful series of small-scale attacks was launched against the English troops in the western territories as the insurrection gained momentum, with soldiers flocking to the banner of rebellion.

The Bruce family had not supported the Scottish in the war of 1296, remaining on their English estates, proclaiming loyalty to Edward I. In June 1297, as the resistance to foreign rule mounted the Plantagenet king ordered his vassal, Robert Bruce, to seize the lands and castle of the rebel leader, Sir William Douglas. As a direct descendant of the Canmore dynasty the twenty-two-year-old earl of Carrick still retained aspirations to the throne of Scotland, which had been earlier promised to his father by Edward I in return for his support and loyalty. He greatly resented the English usurpation of his homeland and the continued occupation with the humiliating loss of independence. As Robert approached the Douglas stronghold, he became convinced that the only avenue to his rightful inheritance was through the rebellion. The Bruce lord renounced his fealty to Edward I, marching his allies and retainers to join the growing army of the insurgency movement.

Soon after abandoning the English crown, Robert united his retainers with the Scottish army of James Stewart at Irvine. In response to the rising strength of the revolt, the Plantagenet viceroy offered to negotiate a settlement. While a faction of the dissidents agreed to honor the armistice agreement, including Robert Bruce, the remaining rebels under the command of William Wallace and Andrew Moray marched in September to confront the English as they advanced toward Stirling Bridge. In the ensuing battle the infantry of the Scots mounted a decisive attack against Edward I's army as his knights crossed the bridge. The triumph resulted in the renewal of the war against the occupation forces throughout the realm as Robert broke the truce, leading his vassals in revolt against the English to great effect in Carrick and Galloway. By the end of 1297 the foreign troops had been driven out of Scotland in all but the strongest castles while local officials once again administered the kingdom.

In March 1298 Robert Bruce met with the great magnates and bishops at Selkirk to formally establish the new government. William Wallace was appointed as Guardian with sole authority to rule in the name of the exiled John Balliol. While the Scots were reasserting their independence Edward I had returned to his kingdom from France determined to reimpose his sovereignty over the rogue northern lands. He summoned his vassals while hiring mercenary infantry and archers as a powerful invasion force was assembled at Roxburgh. In July the offensive was launched as the English marched north toward Edinburgh, where they encountered the entrenched foot soldiers of the Guardian Wallace at Falkirk. The Scots established a strong defensive position behind the wall of their shields. However, after repulsing numerous charges of the cavalry, their ranks were decimated by the Plantagenet archers. The Guardian managed to escape into the countryside with his reputation and prestige as the military commander of the conspiracy movement in shatters. As the Scots withdrew from the defeat, the remnants of their army burned and destroyed anything of use to the invading troops, compelling Edward I to retire to his supply base at Carlisle, effectively ending the campaigning season for 1298.

While the main focus of the rebellion had been with the Guardian's army, in the Carrick region Robert Bruce had mounted a successful series of sporadic attacks to drive out the English from his earldom, once again imposing his authority. As Edward I advanced his forces back to Carlisle, he became determined to reestablish his presence over the Scottish southwest by destroying the Bruce alliance. Despite his recent conquest of the earldom, at the approach of the formidable English military might, Bruce was compelled to abandon his demesne, withdrawing to the safety of the Highlands.

After William Wallace's decisive defeat at Falkirk, the great lords and prelates assembled again to appoint a new regency council. As the defender of Carrick and with the support of his powerful political faction, Robert Bruce was named as co-Guardian along with John Comyn, who represented the northern earldoms. Despite the victory at Falkirk the English still had not established their supremacy over the recalcitrant Scots as the local administration and institutions remained under the control of the Guardians in large parts of the realm.

To press the war against Edward I's occupation, in July 1299, at the direction of Robert Bruce and his co-Guardian, preparations were made and troops assembled for an assault against the great castle at Roxburgh. However, the stronghold was well garrisoned with seasoned soldiers and the siege had to be abandoned. Returning to the base camp at Selkirk, a council of war was held, which appointed Robert to command an expeditionary army into Annandale, while a second rebel contingent was sent to besiege Stirling Castle. While the Guardians launched their campaigns in November 1299, Edward I attempted to mobilize his military forces to relieve the fortification at Stirling. However, the Plantagenet king's summons to his nobles was largely ignored and no counterattack was initiated. With no possibility of relief, in December the defenders at Stirling surrendered.

After the victory at Stirling Castle dissension erupted between the Scottish warlords over the future focus of the war effort. The Bruce faction was determined to renew its campaign against the occupation forces in their ancestral home of Annandale, where they had achieved recent successes, while the co-Guardian, John Comyn, demanded an attack into the base of his power in the Galloway region. As the hostility escalated, Robert of Carrick resigned his position as regent, withdrawing with his allies and retainers to continue the war independently in the southwest.

While the Bruce army was initiating a series of sporadic raids against the English in its home region, Edward I attempted another invasion of Scotland to reclaim his supremacy. However, the incursion accomplished little as the English barons increasingly refused to support his campaign. As opposition to his war escalated, Pope Boniface VIII petitioned the Plantagenet king to withdraw from the occupation of Scotland. As internal and external pressures mounted against the renewal of the conflict, in late October 1300, through the intervention of the French king, a seven-month truce was arranged. However, Edward I remained defiantly resolved to seize Scotland, beginning military preparations for a new offensive for the summer of 1301.

Through the spring months the Plantagenet king mobilized his vassals, made arrangements for foreign mercenary troops and stockpiled war provisions. By July he had amassed two formidable military forces, launching the Scottish invasion by sending his son, Edward of Wales, up the west coast into Galloway, while the second wing attacked in the east from Berwick. To counter the prince of Wales's incursion, Robert Bruce, operating with a much smaller army, refused to give battle but constantly harassed the English flanks and lines of communications, compelling prince Edward to abandon the western campaign in September. With the failure of its initiative the English court again agreed to a truce, which lasted through the coming year of 1302.

Robert of Carrick had actively resisted the English subjugation campaign for over five years, which had resulted in the plundering and ravaging of his estates and territories. He remained unreconciled with the governing Scottish administration, which increasingly favored the northern earls and in particular John Comyn. In early 1302 the earl of Carrick's position deteriorated still further when preparations began for the restoration of the deposed king, John Balliol, which would eliminate Robert's claim to the throne and his Scottish fiefdoms. To protect his English estates and wealth, the earl entered into a negotiated appeasement settlement with Edward I in February 1302, withdrawing from the war effort and retiring to his lands.

During 1302 the English regime's international political problems eased dramatically with its reconciliation with Philip IV and the papacy. With peace restored after years of war in his French duchy of Gascony, Edward I could devote his full attention and resources to the Scottish war. In early 1303 new revenues were raised and in May a massive military force was assembled at Roxburgh. Again the army was divided into two wings with Edward, prince of Wales, commanding the western assault while the king led the campaign up the east coast. The Scottish resistance was completely overwhelmed by the might of the invaders' attack, compelling the Guardian, John Comyn, to surrender the kingdom. To govern the occupied realm Edward I garrisoned English troops in the major castles and towns while appointing a viceroy as the chief administrator with full dictatorial powers to totally subjugate his conquest. However, to give the appearance of local participation, a council of twenty Scottish magnates and prelates, including Robert Bruce, was appointed to advise the government.

Before his selection to the Scottish advisory body, Robert of Carrick had maintained generally friendly relations with the Plantagenet regime. He had been summoned several times to perform military service to his overlord, but his participation was delayed and diluted. Despite his expansive English estates and personal prestige at the Plantagenet court, Robert Bruce still remained a Scottish patriot, retaining a strong belief in his right of inheritance to the throne. To assert his rule, in June 1304 a secret conspiracy movement was formed between the earl and the chief prelate of the Scottish Church to begin preparations for rebellion. John Comyn, who represented the northern fiefdoms, was included in the opposition faction in the following year when he agreed to support the earl of Carrick's rights in exchange for additional lands and privileges. However, Comyn soon exposed the insurgency to Edward I, forcing Robert to flee from his English estates to refuge in Scotland. The treacherous disclosure was quickly discovered and, in a direct confrontation between the Carrick earl and Comyn, the Highlands warlord was killed. The success of the Bruce insurrection initiative was jeopardized by the possible defection of the upper half of the kingdom due to the murder of their leader, Comyn. However, the Scottish Church, which had steadfastly held to the independence of the realm, rallied to Carrick's defense as the only means of uniting the population and defeating the alien occupiers.

With the prelates openly backing Robert's usurpation movement, the magnates and commoners began to flock to his banner. A series of successful attacks was launched against the English-held castles and burghs, which eliminated the occupation in the western lordships. Following the triumphs, in an act of defiance against the Plantagenets' continuing occupation of Scotland, on March 25, 1306, Robert Bruce was enthroned as king at Scone. Despite his advancing years and increasingly frail health, Edward I was unrelenting in his determination to conquer the northern demesne. Upon learning of the rebellion he immediately ordered the Scottish viceroy, Aymer de Valence, earl of Pembroke, to assemble the Berwick army and reassert his sovereignty while Edward I marched from London with a hastily raised second invasion force. In May Pembroke mounted his attack into Scotland, quickly capturing the castle at Perth, encountering little resistance. Facing the loss of the strategic town Robert I advanced with his small army to recapture the stronghold. However, in a surprise sortie from the fortress, the superior English cavalry fell upon the unsuspecting rebels at Methven, resulting in their overwhelming defeat. The Scottish ruler narrowly avoided capture, escaping with only a small band of survivors into the safety of the dense forest. With the destruction of the kingdom's only organized military force, the cities and countryside were brutally harried and plundered by Edward I as his overlordship was brutally imposed.

After the defeat at Methven, Robert I of Bruce collected the remnants of the shattered army, marching to sanctuary in the western Argylls. As the Scots traveled through the territory of the supporters of the murdered John Comyn, they were ambushed at Dalry, managing to escape by withdrawing without their baggage train into the wilds of the forest before finally arriving at Dunaverty Castle in the western isles. However, the English and rival Scottish warlords soon learned of his location, forcing Bruce to abandon Scotland and sail to the eastern coast of Ireland. From this secure base of operations and with the continued backing of the earl of the Isles, the king dispatched envoys to Scotland to collect revenue and recruit soldiers while he traveled to the northern Highlands and the Isles to assert his authority. By early 1307 a small fleet and military force had been mobilized, enabling Robert I to begin the re-conquest of his kingdom.

In February the rebel-king landed on the Scottish coast in his native fiefdom of Carrick with a small army of men at arms and infantry. The region was heavily occupied by English soldiers, compelling the Scots to operate from the safety of the mountains of Carrick and Galloway, adopting a strategy of irregular style of warfare. Slowly Robert I began to rebuild his military by initiating a series of small-scale attacks, ambushes and marauding sorties against the occupation troops. As the news of the Scots' successes traveled throughout the kingdom and the English rule became harsher, many knights and pikemen began to flock to the uprising. In May 1307 the rebels ambushed a sizable English cavalry force commanded by Aymer de Valence of Pembroke at Loudoun Hill. The Scottish foot companies held firm against the repeated charges of the men-at-arms, forcing the earl of Pembroke to retire. The victory was a major triumph for the Scots against a vastly superior enemy. During the summer months Robert I continued to raid and harass the English garrisons and burghs as the size of his army grew steadily larger.

In 1307 the political outlook for the success of the Scottish rebellion was dramatically altered with the death of Edward I and the succession of the less dynamic and aggressive Edward II. The new English monarch did not share his father's determination and enthusiasm for the defeat of the Scots, resulting in a pronounced reduction in the strength of the

English war effort. Robert I Bruce utilized the lull to assert his kingship over the recalcitrant Scottish warlords in the northeast. In November he marched the army into the rogue earldom of Buchan to subdue the local lords. However, the campaign was delayed by the serious illness of the king and it was not until late December that he eliminated the earl's resistance. The region was ravaged and brought firmly under Robert I's authority. The submission of Buchan was followed by the subjugation of the northwestern earldom of Ross in 1308. Following these triumphs the war was pressed into the western theatre, where the Bruce throne won a notable victory over John of Lorne, who offered homage for Argyll, while the king's brother, Edward, invaded and conquered the fiefdom of Galloway. Since Robert I's landing in his native princedom of Carrick in February 1307 with a small band of supporters, in less than three years most of northern Scotland was under royal control.

As the size of the territory under Robert I's direct sovereignty expanded, a centralized government was established with the summons of his first parliament at Saint Andrews, where the great magnates and prelates gathered in mid–March 1309. The assembly issued a declaration re-affirming the independence of Scotland and Robert I's rightful assumption to power. The parliament reestablished diplomatic relations with the realm's historical ally, France, enabling envoys to be sent, seeking financial and military support along with the restoration of their traditional bonds of friendship. The parliament's actions gave a firm legal foundation and international recognition to the kingship of Robert I.

With the elimination of the internal Scottish resistance in the north and the formal establishment of his government Robert I was free to concentrate his military efforts on defeating the English in the south. In early 1309, at the intervention of Edward II's father-in-law, Philip IV of France, a series of peace conferences was held to resolve the ongoing English-Scottish war, but no final settlement of the outstanding issues could be found. Following the failure of the diplomatic initiative, Edward II was determined to forcibly impose his will on Scotland. In late autumn two formidable armies were assembled in Berwick and Carlisle. However, due to the lateness of the campaigning season and growing unrest among his English barons, a truce was arranged with the Scots, which was extended until June 1310. The break in the hostilities during 1309 allowed Robert I the opportunity to travel extensively throughout his realm, consolidating his authority and administration while setting in place royal officials to enforce his will and justice.

In September 1310, with the truce having expired, Edward II began his campaign of subjugation by advancing his powerful military force from the assembly point at Berwick to his northern castle in Roxburgh. The English launched their invasion from Roxburgh, however, their assault was frustrated by the Scots' refusal to give battle and by the constant harassing raids against their exposed long lines of communications. The Plantagenet troops were forced to march through abandoned and burnt lands, finding little food or shelter and were finally compelled to retire to Berwick in late October with the approach of winter. Edward II remained in his stronghold for the next six months while Bruce's small army continued its relentless offensive of ambushes and marauding attacks.

In the summer of 1311 the English sovereign returned to London to counter an uprising of his barons in parliament over their refusal to grant fresh revenues for the war effort. Robert I seized upon Edward II's absence to mount numerous brutal pillaging raids into northern England. The Scots harried and looted the towns and countryside, forcing the local population to pay a large indemnity to prevent additional attacks.

In the following year, as England was diverted by the increasing prospects of war between the crown and the rebellious barons, Robert I Bruce launched a large freebooting invasion into the district around Carlisle. The assault resulted in the destruction of the region and was extended to the east as far as Durham. The raiders were virtually unopposed, succeeding in collecting large sums of war spoils, capturing many prisoners for ransom and ravaging the local population. So great was the devastation that the northern towns sent a delegation to Robert I, offering to pay a huge levy to ensure a ten-month truce, which was later extended until the following September.

While Bruce was occupied in the north of England his regime began negotiations with the king of Norway, Hakon V, to reestablish formal relations, renew the favorable terms of the Treaty of Perth and reinstate peace on the border with Norwegian-controlled Shetland. On October 29, 1312, in the presence of the parliament at Inverness, Robert I ratified the final settlement with Hakon V's envoys restoring the friendship and bond between the two realms. The formal recognition by a foreign power added to the prestige and stature of the Scottish monarchy among the nobles while solidifying the legitimacy of his government among the European courts.

As the Bruce throne was imposing its control over the Scottish northern fiefdoms, in the south Edward II still maintained a formidable line of castles, which were a constant threat to the security of the kingdom. The English king had not been able to negotiate a settlement with his rogue lords, remaining in London, allowing the Scots the freedom to reclaim their demesne by first seizing the exposed fortification at Perth. The stronghold could not be captured by storm, compelling the Bruce regime to initiate investment operations in late November 1312. After six weeks of blockade the defenders showed little signs of surrender and, lacking siege engines Robert I was forced to revert to deception. A withdrawal of the army was feinted, but during the night after the guards were reduced the garrison was taken by surprise attack. While the Plantagenet crown stayed distracted with the barons' revolt, during the summer months additional English castles were captured and destroyed. The Scots succeeded in effectively clearing the invaders from the area north of Edinburgh with the exception of the great fortification at Stirling, which was now placed under investment. While maintaining the siege operations against Stirling, the salient castles at Roxburgh and Edinburgh were sieged by the stealth night assaults of Robert I's lieutenants, James Douglas and Thomas Randolph. By the end of spring 1314 the Scots had re-conquered the majority of their realm with the exception of Stirling and several formidable fortresses in the south.

Edward II had been forced to defend his monarchy in London, occupied with the rebellion of his barons, and had remained absent from Scotland for nearly three years. However, as the Scots increasingly drove out the English garrisons, the Plantagenet king became resolved to reimpose his sovereignty, arranging for a reconciliation with his warring lords. He utilized the spring months to mobilize a massive military force from all parts of his domain, including Ireland and Wales, while recruiting mercenary knights from the continent. In June 1314 the invasion army was assembled at Berwick Castle in northern England and the campaign was launched with over twenty-five thousand cavalry and foot soldiers, with his first objective the relief of the year-old siege at Stirling Castle. Robert I had earlier established his base of operations near the stronghold and at the approach of Edward II summoned the soldiers of Scotland to muster in defense of their kingdom. By June troops had come from all parts of the realm, numbering over eight thousand. The Scottish levies were formed into four large mobile schiltrons of pikemen to better utilize the skills of the infantry. Robert I chose his battlefield carefully to afford the maximum defensive advantages and awaited the English arrival at Bannockburn. In the afternoon of June 23 the Plantagenet cavalry began the battle by charging the Scots but was repeatedly repulsed by the solid defensive wall of pikes. The day ended with both rivals holding the field. During the night Edward II maneuvered his militia into open terrain to better employ the might of his knights.

However, upon learning of the new English position, Robert I countered the move by shifting his forces forward to severely restrict the size of the battlefield. In the morning the hostilities were renewed with the spirited advance of the schiltrons, which quickly came under attack by the English men-at-arms. Despite their many charges, the horsemen could not break the Scots' solid formation and were continually driven back in a bloody, brutal and close encounter. It was becoming clear to Edward II that the day was lost and, as he abandoned the battle, his army broke into a panicked retreat. With the victory won Robert I marched to Stirling Castle, securing its surrender.

After the triumph at Bannockburn the Scottish king held direct sovereignty over the whole of the realm with the exception of the area around Berwick. However, despite the loss of his presence in Scotland, Edward II rejected all overtures to find a settlement. To force the English to the peace table, the war was renewed in the autumn with the continuation of the large-scale raids into the northern border counties. The marauding attacks remained successful but they could not compel Edward II to negotiate.

In neighboring Ireland the strength and stability of the English control had steadily been eroded by the years of heavy taxation and steady demands for war supplies and soldiers. Buttressed by the Scots' victory at Bannockburn, the Irish population was poised for rebellion. To encourage the prevailing unrest—thereby creating additional pressure on Edward II—in early 1315 Bruce envoys were dispatched to Ulster to negotiate a mutual defense treaty. To secure Scottish military aid the Irish offered the crown of Ireland to Edward Bruce, the brother of the monarch. At a parliament held in April the proposal was accepted and in the following month a large expeditionary army was sent to Ulster. By May 1316 the English and their native allies had been defeated in the north of the kingdom and Edward Bruce was enthroned as the high-king of Ireland.

While his brother campaigned in Ireland, Robert I continued the war by again raiding into Plantagenet lands, pillaging and looting far to the south. In Ireland, by late 1316, the Ulster region had been brought under the control of the Bruce faction and the Scottish sovereign sailed with additional reinforcements to complete his brother's conquest. In February 1317 the army marched south, however, unlike the northern lordships, the local warlords refused to rally to Edward's cause and, lacking adequate supplies and troops to impose the Bruce will, the initiative had to be abandoned. In May Robert I returned to Scotland and the government of his kingdom as the war with England remained at a stalemate.

To force a resolution with the English government the Scottish king continued to raid and harass the northern counties with impunity, gaining a major success in April 1318 with the seizure of the great castle and commercial center at Berwick through the daring assault of Randolph and the Black Douglas. Following the victory a harrying incursion in force was mounted throughout the Yorkshire district as far south as York. However, despite the Scottish triumphs, the English regime still adamantly refused to negotiate a peace settlement.

While Robert I maintained his relentless campaign of raiding the English and pressing for the independence of his realm, he also attended to the administration of his kingdom. Parliaments were regularly summoned, enacting laws to encourage the growth of commerce and the restructuring of the military system. The issue of the future succession was resolved when the Assembly approved the appointment of Robert I's grandson, Robert Stewart, as heir apparent. Edward II had remained unreconciled with his high barons for several years. However, the loss of the important castle and commercial center at Berwick forced a union between the warring English factions. In September 1319 the Plantagenets again mobilized a formidable army, marching to invest Berwick by land and sea. Assaults were made against the garrison with scaling ladders and siege towers in conjunction with a seaborne attack; but the defenders managed to repel the English. Lacking adequate troops to relieve the siege, Robert I sent Randolph and Douglas on a devastating pillaging foray into Yorkshire, which destroyed numerous towns and ravaged the countryside. The extent of the destruction was so great that the English king was compelled to abandon the campaign, moving south to defend his demesne, leaving the castle at Berwick still under Scottish control.

In the aftermath of Robert I's relentless harassing of the northern counties and the negative political effects from the failed Berwick campaign, Edward II dispatched envoys to the Scottish court, seeking terms for a truce. The negotiations were held in late December, resulting in a two-year armistice lasting until the end of 1321. With the suspension of hostilities Pope John XXII sent papal legates to England and Scotland in an attempt to broker a final resolution. However, due to the inflexibility of Edward II over the issue of recognizing the independence of Scotland, no permanent peace was found.

At the end of the two-year truce, in January 1322 Robert I again sent a powerful plundering army into northern England, which was met with little resistance. While the Scots were pillaging his lands, Edward II and his high barons were once again at war. The English king finally became resolved to force a settlement over his rogue lords, advancing his loyal retainers against the insurrection, defeating the rebels and killing their leaders to end the internal conflict. With the elimination of the warring barons, Edward II could devote his full resources toward pursuing the Scottish conquest. A massive military force was assembled at Newcastle in August, including the crown's vassals and allies, along with mercenary troops from the continent. At the approach of the Plantagenet army Robert I Bruce, fresh from a raid, withdrew, refusing to give battle, ordering the region to be scorched and rendered useless to the invaders. The English could find little food or shelter and by September, with their provisions exhausted, Edward II was compelled to order a retreat to York. Following the failed invasion campaign the Scots counterattacked into the northern counties, barely missing the capture of Edward II however ravaging and burning a wide strip of his territory.

The north of England had endured over ten years of near-constant warfare from the Scottish raiding parties while the local lords' appeals to their king had been largely ignored. Finally, under the increasing pressure from his barons and Pope John XXII, who was anxious for a resolution to renew the crusade to Jerusalem, Edward II agreed to a thirteen-year truce, which was ratified at York on May 30, 1323.

With the extended period of peace Robert I could devote his full attention to the administration of his kingdom. The parliament was summoned into session on a regular basis and a government consisting of an advisory council was appointed, with a chamberlain for royal household affairs and chancellor for judicial matters. To impose the king's will and justice the system of sheriffs and bailiffs employed under Alexander III was re-introduced with trusted and loyal Bruce agents. New laws were passed, favoring the trading centers with grants of exceptions and privileges to encourage the revival of the economy, and a regular tax levy was enacted. The court regularly patronized the Scottish Church and its local abbeys and monasteries with financial gifts and special favors. While enacting domestic issues the Bruce regime negotiated a mutual defensive treaty with the French crown, ensuring Capet military aid in the event of an English invasion.

Despite his defeat of the barons' revolt in 1322, Edward II's autocratic style grew increasingly unpopular with his nobles and Church, resulting in his forced resignation on November 13, 1326, in a rebellion led by his queen, Isabella. With the abdication the truce between England and Scotland became invalid and the Scots quickly resumed border raids. In response to the resumption of the war, in June the English under the nominal command of the boy-king, Edward III, assembled a powerful military force at York for an invasion of Scotland. However, once again the Scots refused to give battle, drawing the English into an abandoned and barren land, using time and space as their greatest allies. After several weeks of Bruce's harassing attacks directed at their flanks and exposed lines of communications, the campaign had to be abandoned, compelling Edward III to return to York with his army decimated without ever having fought a battle. The Scottish success was followed by a massive plundering incursion deep into the northern counties, where the castles at Alnwick and Norham were ravaged. With the depletion of his troop strength and facing a revolt of the English Parliament, the government of Edward III offered to begin deliberations for a final peace accord. Negotiations lasted over five months before a final settlement was ratified, acknowledging the independence of Scotland on March 17, 1328. The Treaty of Edinburgh was to be guaranteed with the marriage of the Scottish king's infant son, David, and the sister of Edward III. The agreement also resulted in the lifting of the interdiction by the Holy See against Scotland and the recognition of Robert I as the lawful sovereign with the rights of anointment by the prelates of the Church.

Beginning in 1325 the Bruce king had begun to show signs of ill health, which grew increasingly more severe under the constant strains of campaigning against England and the consolidation of his rule. He began to spend more time away from court affairs, becoming largely confined to his bed by early 1329. Robert I died on June 7, 1329, after a reign of twenty-three years and at age fifty-five and was buried with the previous Scottish kings and queens at Dunfermline Abbey.

DAVID II, 1324–1329–1371

David was born on March 5, 1324, at Dunfermline Priory and was the only surviving son of Robert I and his second wife, Elizabeth of Burgh. Soon after his birth he was named earl of Carrick and a separate household was established for him at Turnberry Castle in southwestern Scotland. The young prince's early years were spent at Turnberry, where he had only a limited association with his father and the royal court. In 1329 Robert I died and his five-year-old son was acknowledged as the successor to the throne under a regency government headed by the earl of Moray, Thomas Randolph. The Bruce king spent the next five years principally at Dumbarton Castle with his two older sisters and the children of various magnates. Scholar monks were provided for his academic education and he was taught reading and writing along with languages and religious doctrine. However, the focus of his early instruction was military training as a feudal knight, which was initiated around the age of seven. In November 1331 David II was formally invested with the monarchy at Scone, where he became the first Scottish ruler to be anointed and officially recognized by the See of Rome in a lavish and grand ceremony designed to secure his succession at a time of escalating internal rebellion and threatening foreign invasion.

While David II remained at Dumbarton pursuing his education for kingship, the realm was ruled by Sir Thomas Randolph, who ably administered the throne's peace, taxes and laws. Periodic parliaments continued to be summoned by the regent under an effective governmental system that had been established by Robert I. Despite the occasional act of defiance in pursuit of greater local autonomy, the Scottish nobles maintained their loyalty to the Bruce crown.

The 1328 Treaty of Edinburgh had secured English recognition of Scotland's independence and with Edward III's government under the dominance of his mother, relations between the two rivals remained peaceful. However, by 1331 the English king began to increasingly assert his independent rule while maneuvering to renew the war with his northern neighbor. To establish a just cause he demanded Scotland return the seized estates of the expelled English barons under the provisions of the Edinburgh accord. While the Plantagenet regime continued its diplomatic initiatives against the Bruce throne, secret negotiations were begun with numerous rogue Scottish warlords who also controlled English lands to gain their support and loyalty. To further its campaign the English council permitted the exiled Edward Balliol, the heir of the deposed John Balliol, to return to court, using him as a rallying point for Scottish rebellion. As Edward III's intriguing for war escalated, in Scotland the kingdom was thrown into political turmoil in July 1332 with the death of Sir Thomas Randolph.

Following the death of the Guardian, in early August a Scottish Parliament was summoned to Perth to elect a new regency government. As the assembly gathered without the presence of Randolph, the Bruce faction lacked a strong and energetic leader as support for the young king began to wane, with many of the powerful magnates and bishops favoring the repatriation of the Balliol family. However, their campaign was thwarted when Donald of Mar rallied to David II's cause, forming a series of fragmented political alliances to force his acceptance as the new guardian. While the earl of Mar was attempting to establish his regency, on August 6 Edward Balliol, who had the unofficial backing of the English throne, landed in Fife with a small force of rogue Scots and mercenary troops in an attempt to seize the monarchy. To contend the invasion the regent struggled to mobilize his military forces as many warlords openly endorsed the Balliol restoration. As the hastily and ill-prepared Scots advanced to meet the rebel army at Dupplin Moor, many of the Bruce nobles deserted his banner, resulting in an overwhelming victory for the usurpers and the death of Donald of Mar. With the defeat at Dupplin Moor support for David II continued to deteriorate as Balliol marched triumphantly to Scone to be anointed sovereign in September. However, the newly crowned Edward's usurpation soon proved to be transitory as the Scottish barons and prelates became aligned with David II's kingship when the new king began to seize their privileges, titles and lands and transfer them to his allies and friends. By the end of the year Edward Balliol and his coalition of dissident Scottish lords had been defeated and compelled to flee to the safety of the Plantagenet court as the rule of David II was reestablished.

With the government of the Bruce king firmly secured in Scotland, Edward Balliol entered into negotiations with the Plantagenet crown for England's armed intervention to buttress his campaign for the seizure of the Scottish realm. On November 23 Balliol recognized Edward III as his overlord and ceded much of southern Scotland to English sovereignty in return for an invasion army. Under the provisions of his treaty with the Pretender, in May 1333 the troops of Edward III advanced to the north to besiege the stronghold of Berwick. To counter the attack the Scottish militia under the command of Archibald Douglas was mobilized, marching to the relief of Berwick. On July 19 the well prepared and ably commanded English force of knights and archers outmaneuvered and destroyed the Scots at Halidon Hill. Following the defeat Edward Balliol, backed by a strong English army of occupation, again seized the monarchy while the Bruce faction could claim only a few areas of support. As the new regime consolidated its authority over Scotland in May 1334, David II and his small household were compelled to flee to the court of the French king, Philip VI, for sanctuary, where he remained for the next seven years.

After being graciously received by the French, David II and his court were given the well-fortified castle of Gaillard in Normandy as a place of residence. At Gaillard the formal education and martial training of the king were resumed under Scottish tutors. The crown's counselors maintained close contacts with the French government, resulting in a steady flow of gold and supplies being sent to Scotland in support of the Bruce allies and friends. As relations between Philip VI and Edward III steadily deteriorated over the issue of liege homage for the duchy of Gascony, the French and Scottish councils began plans for joint military operations against England while the existing 1326 alliance of Robert I was re-affirmed. The Scottish emigrant was an occasional guest at Philip VI's household, where he increasingly came under the influence of French chivalry dogma and traditions, becoming an active participant in the many local jousting tournaments. In 1339, as the Hundred Years War became more bellicose, David II, along with a small company of Scottish knights, joined the French army at the battle of Buirenfosse on the Flemish border to contend the English invasion forces. There was little combat activity, but the Bruce sovereign gained his first experiences with active campaigning.

While David II remained in exile at Gaillard, in Scotland the Bruce faction under the leadership of the king's nephew, Robert Stewart, and the charismatic and dynamic John Randolph was slowly regaining its footing. With Stewart operating in the western fiefdoms and Randolph in the north, by 1335 Edward Balliol's sphere of authority had been reduced to only the Lowland earldoms. The restoration cause of David II was further enhanced as France and the Plantagenet crown moved steadily toward open warfare, resulting in the withdrawal of English troops, military supplies and money from the Balliol occupation. In April 1337 Edward III's focus was solely directed at France as he openly defied the Valois dynasty's legal rights to the monarchy. This served to further weaken Edward Balliol's ability to defend his kingship as the Bruce warlords continued to seize the southern lands. Scottish parliaments were held, a local government was established and taxes were collected in the name of David II. By 1341 Balliol and his English allies had been forced out of Scotland by the relentless attacks of the Bruce magnates. In early June David II crossed the English Channel to his homeland to begin the process of reasserting his personal rule over a dramatically politically altered Scotland devastated by years of war.

Soon after arriving in his realm after an absence of seven years, the seventeen-year-old Bruce ruler toured the base of his support in the south, fully aware that powerful warlords such as Robert Stewart and the Douglas and Randolph families had acquired a large and loyal faction of clergy, nobles and towns. David II energetically assumed his role as king and, by the force of his personality and presence, began to attract a counter–party to contend the formidable magnates. He issued numerous grants of royal lands, honors and privileges while beginning to build a reputation as a successful war leader by leading pillaging raids into northern England. Parliaments were summoned by David II as he was slowly able to establish his government over the kingdom. By late 1346 he had received the oaths of fealty from the Lowland and Highland earldoms to firmly reestablish the Bruce dynasty's rule over Scotland.

After several prolonged truces between the English and French courts, in June 1346 Edward III renewed his military campaign against Philip VI. The Plantagenet throne invaded France through Normandy while its Gascony troops harried the Loire Valley. As the English incursion gained momentum, Philip VI sent an urgent appeal to David II for a diversionary initiative against northern England. In response the Scots initially were able to only mount a series of small raids across the border with David II in personal command as preparations were begun for an invasion in force. By early October the Scottish host had been mobilized and was poised to launch a major punitive foray into the northern counties. As David II marched across the border at a measured pace, his soldiers encountered little opposition. After ravaging the march towns and countryside, he turned south to attack the commercial centzer at Durham. As the Bruce forces delayed their assault to begin negotiations with the city for an amnesty payment, the English barons under the direction of the archbishop of York and Earl Henry Percy quickly assembled their militia advancing against the Scots. On October 17, 1346, the two armies met at Neville's Cross, where the English turned back the repeated infantry charges of David II, completely routing the Scots, taking the wounded king, many of his closest advisors and high magnates as prisoners.

After remaining for several weeks in the north, on orders from Edward III, the Scottish king was taken to London for confinement in the Tower of London. While David II remained in captivity, Robert Stewart, as the heir apparent and a powerful and influential warlord, was elected lieutenant of Scotland at a parliament in May 1347. However, lacking the prestige and authority of an invested monarch, he could not fully assert his control over the recalcitrant nobles and prelates, resulting in only a limited and ineffective central government.

As the crown's lieutenant struggled to enforce his rule, from London David II mounted an aggressive political campaign to gain his release. After prolonged negotiations in 1351 an agreement was reached to secure his freedom for the payment of a large cash ransom, the return of the forfeited Scottish estates to the disinherited English barons and the recognition of a son of Edward III as the successor designate, replacing Robert Stewart. However, when the accord was presented for ratification before the Scottish Parliament in May, under the influence and lobbying efforts of Stewart, the terms were soundly rejected. During the summer months the deliberations were renewed between the king and Plantagenet court, resulting in a revised treaty. To acquire his parliament's approval, David II was granted a parole, traveling to Scotland to personally present the settlement before the nobles, clergy and town delegates. The assembly was summoned to Scone in February 1352 but despite his pleas the proposal was again defeated. By late March David II had re-crossed the border and was once again under English custody. With the king the prisoner of the Plantagenets, Robert Stewart reassumed control of the Bruce regime, continuing to govern in the name of his uncle.

From his London captivity David II again attempted to re-open negotiations for his release, succeeding in July 1354 in forging a new treaty with Edward III. Under the revised settlement his freedom was to be secured by the payment of an indemnity payable in nine yearly installments and the delivery of twenty Scottish hostages. However, the Hundred Years War between the Plantagenet and Valois courts had once again been renewed, presenting the prospects for rich pillaging raids and territorial gains in the northern English lordships and the Lowland warlords had little interest in reaching an accord. David II only gained his liberty in October 1357 after the capture of the French monarch at the battle of Poitiers changed the political outlook decisively in Edward III's favor. The English victory quickly resulted in a prolonged period of peace between the two cross–Channel rivals and, with the loss of opportunity for further plunder in the border counties, along with growing internal disorder, the Scottish magnates increasingly favored the return of their king, permitting deliberations to resume in earnest. By September 1357 a new agreement had been reached and under the terms of the Treaty of Berwick, for a large cash ransom payable over ten years and the transfer of twenty hostages, David II was granted his parole.

On October 6, 1357, the Scottish sovereign crossed the border into his realm for the first time in almost eleven years to begin the task of reasserting his kingship over a faction of powerful and influential magnates, who had governed the kingdom and used his captivity to enhance their lands and autonomy. David II once again employed the strategy that he had utilized in June 1341 after his return from exile in France to secure his reign. The Bruce court used liberal royal patronage as a means to expand its power base among the earldoms as the stature and authority of the Stewart, Moray and Douglas families became increasingly reduced. Slowly he was able to replace key administrative officials with his favorites to steadily increase the acceptance of his sovereignty. David II had developed an appreciation for English institutions and style of government, which he sought to introduce into his regime. He gained favor with the towns and merchants when he negotiated the right for his tradesmen to move freely across the frontier and for Scottish money to be exchanged at parity with English specie. By 1362 David II had largely restored his control over Scotland as his laws and justice were widely acknowledged and respected. However, the relationship with the earls of Moray and Douglas along with the Stewart family, continued to remain strained and potentially hostile.

As the monarchy increasingly reimposed its supremacy over the kingdom's dominant warlords, in March 1363 the earl of Douglas began to conspire to recapture his lost autonomy and lands. The Douglas lord quickly negotiated an alliance with Robert Stewart and Patrick Dunbar of March, who both had similar grievances against the Bruce court, resulting in the brief War of the Three Earls. The revolt was initiated by the Douglas family's seizure of the royal castle at Dirleton. Emboldened by the Douglas success, the Stewart and Dunbar factions mounted similar attacks against the Bruce throne's magnates and allies as the uprising spread across southern Scotland. David II responded to the open insurrection with speed and resolve, mobilizing his loyal vassals and infantry. His army marched out of Edinburgh, launching a determined assault against the earl of Douglas, forcing him to flee from the battlefield. With his overwhelming display of power and military might, the levies of Stewart and Dunbar soon were compelled to submit. By the end of April the three earls had renewed their pledges of fealty to the crown and were graciously reinstated with their estates, as the king exacted no revenge to prevent grounds for future rebellion by their families and supporters.

While the Scottish king was energetically enforcing his supremacy over the warlords, negotiations were begun with the court of Edward III to secure redress to the Treaty of Berwick. In November 1363 David II traveled to London to personally discuss a reduction in the annual ransom in exchange for the recognition of Edward III's third son, John of Gaunt, as the heir designate in lieu of Robert Stewart. The English monarch quickly rejected the terms, offering a counter-proposal to eliminate the payment and indemnify the disinherited English lords for their forfeited Scottish estates if he was acknowledged as the successor. The Bruce ruler was left with no remedy, agreeing to present the English proposal to his parliament for approval. In the interim between David II's return to Scotland in January 1364 and the convening of the Scone Parliament of March, Robert Stewart mounted an aggressive campaign of opposition to the accord, winning the overwhelming approval of the delegates, which served to widen the gulf between the two rivals.

Under the terms of the Treaty of Northhampton negotiated between Robert I and the Plantagenet court, in July 1327 the four-year-old David had been married to Joan, the sister of Edward III. In the political union the king and his queen were ill suited to each other, spending the majority of their marriage in separate households while he took numerous mistresses. In 1359 Joan returned permanently to London where she died in 1362, leaving her husband, who was still without a direct successor, free to marry again. In February 1363 he married his mistress, Margaret of Drummond, in the hope of securing the much-needed heir. However, the second marriage also was unhappy and ended childless. With the kingdom still in need of the stability provided by an established ongoing dynasty, in 1368 divorce proceedings were begun against the new queen. Margaret, who had a strong and energetic personality, refused to accept the separation, appealing directly to the papacy for support, causing the divorce petition to become bogged down in legal disputes.

After the failure of the 1364 Scone Parliament to ratify the modifications to the Treaty of Berwick, David II continued to hold periodic discussions with various English envoys to secure more favorable terms for the payment of his ransom. Both courts suggested several new provisions and finally, in May 1365, Edward III agreed to reduce the yearly installment by nearly half, with both regimes pledging to end their cross-border raids and honor a truce for five years. With a temporary peace secured, additional negotiations were held to find a permanent accord and military alliance.

As David II devoted his energies and crown policy toward negotiating a new treaty with the Plantagenet regime, his relationship with the Scottish parliament grew increasingly hostile. The assembly openly complained about Queen Margaret's abuses of royal prerogatives to enrich her family with gifts of lands, privileges, honors and high offices. The Bruce court's popularity continued to wane in response to its pro–English orientation, excessive taxation and lack of a successor.

While the Bruce throne became increasingly isolated, the Hundred Years War was once again renewed as the French regained their fighting spirit under the leadership of their new king, Charles V. Their battlefield successes caused an escalation of anti–English sentiment among the Scottish nobles and bishops, producing a revival in the level of raiding activities among the Lowland warlords across the border. David II supported the attacks as a means to force better ransom terms from Edward III, since he was again fully engaged and distracted with events on the continent. The March 1369 Parliament authorized him to pursue additional negotiations with the Plantagenet court for a revision to the Berwick Treaty. In April David II personally traveled to London where his rival warmly greeted him. The English needed to assure Scottish neutrality, soon agreeing to a fourteen-year extension of the existing 1370 truce and to again reduce the yearly indemnity payment.

With peace safeguarded on his southern borders, David II pressed the divorce petition from Queen Margaret before the papal courts. Plans had already been arranged for his marriage to Agnes Dunbar, the daughter of the earl of March. The political union would secure and enhance his relationship with the powerful and prominent northern warlord in a region where he needed reliable allies and friends. While continuing negotiations with the papacy, the throne began a series of new initiatives to regain its popularity. To pacify the recalcitrant magnates and bishops in the central earldoms, there were numerous grants of castles and titles to the loyal advisors and knights who had served the crown's cause while the rebellious western Galloway fiefdom was subdued with the appointment of the capable Archibald Douglas as overlord. However, the king's increasing autocratic style and the attempts to control the decisions of parliament through the introduction of royal-appointed commissions with the full authority of the assembly caused a revival of ill will among the nobles and prelates. In October 1369 David II moved against the mutinous lords in the northern earldom of Moray, who had long defied royal supremacy. With an overwhelming show of force, the local warlords were quickly subjugated and compelled to pledge fealty to the Bruce court. By 1370 the diplomatic and military actions resulted in an expansion of the regime's power, regaining a measure of its lost acceptance.

By 1370 Edward III's position on the continent had deteriorated under the weight of the French king's victories. Charles V's successes encouraged the Scots to delay the yearly ransom installment and to reopen alliance contacts with the Valois government. David II openly sanctioned the renewal of plundering raids into the border counties as the Scots attempted to force the Plantagenet court to abandon the indemnity payment and cede lands in the northern earldoms as terms for a permanent peace.

While talks were renewed with the English court, in late 1370 David II's health began to seriously deteriorate. He had long suffered from the head wounds received in 1346 at the battle of Neville's Cross and the embedded arrowhead continued to be the source of an ongoing infection. As his condition worsened he began to prepare for his death by bringing Robert Stewart into his government and the heir apparent increasingly assumed the functions of the monarchy with his own advisors and officials. On February 22, 1371, David II died at Edinburgh Castle at age forty-seven and after a reign of nearly forty-two years to be succeeded by his nephew, Robert II, and the beginning of the Stewart dynasty.

Appendix: Contemporary Gothic Rulers of Europe

I. Kings of France

Hugh I Capet	987–996	Philip III	1270–1285
Robert II	996–1031	Philip IV	1285–1314
Henry I	1031–1060	Louis X	1314–1316
Philip I	1060–1108	Philip V	1316–1322
Louis VI	1108–1137	Charles IV	1322–1328
Louis VII	1137–1180	Philip VI Valois	1328–1350
Philip II	1180–1223	John II	1350–1364
Louis VIII	1223–1226	Charles V	1364–1380
Louis IX	1226–1270		

II. Counts of Flanders

Baldwin IV	988–1037	Margaret I	1191–1194
Baldwin V	1037–1067	Baldwin VIII	1194–1195
Baldwin VI	1067–1070	Baldwin IX	1195–1205
Arnulf III	1070–1071	Ferdinand & Jean I	1205–1244
Robert I	1071–1093	Margaret II	1244–1279
Robert II	1093–1111	Guy I	1279–1305
Baldwin VII	1111–1119	Robert III	1305–1322
Charles I	1119–1127	Louis I	1322–1346
William I Clito	1127–1128	Louis II	1346–1384
Thierry I	1128–1168	Margaret III	1384–1405
Philip I	1168–1191		

III. Dukes of Brittany

Geoffrey I	992–1008	Guy I	1203–1206
Alan III	1008–1040	Alix	1206–1221
Conan II	1140–1066	Arthur II	1305–1316
Hoel II	1066–1084	Peter I	1221–1237
Alan IV	1084–1112	John I	1237–1286
Conan III	1112–1148	John II	1286–1305
Eon I & Hoel I	1148–1156	John III	1316–1341
Conan IV	1156–1168	Charles of Blois	1341–1364
Geoffrey II Plantagenet	1168–1186	John of Montfort	1341–1345
Constance I	1186–1201	John IV	1345–1399
Arthur I Plantagenet	1201–1203		

(Breton War of Succession, 1341–1364, between Charles of Blois and John of Montfort and his son, John IV)

IV. Dukes of Normandy

Rollo	911–927	Henry I	1106–1135
William I	927–942	Stephen	1135–1144
Richard I	942–996	Geoffrey Plantagenet	1144–1150
Richard II	996–1027	Henry II	1150–1189
Richard III	1027–1028	Richard IV	1189–1199
Robert I	1028–1035	(Richard I of England)	
William II	1035–1087	John	1199–1204
(William I of England)		(1204: Normandy lost to France)	
Robert II	1087–1106		

V. Princes of Wales *(Wales was comprised of numerous autonomous fiefdoms, with Gwynedd and Deheubarth the most important. The entire principality was conquered and subjugated by England in 1283.)*

GWYNEDD

Llewelyn ap Seisyll	1005–1023	Owain Gwynedd	1137–1170
Iago ap Idwal	1023–1039	David ap Owain	1170–1194
Gruffydd ap Llewelyn	1039–1063	Llewelyn ab Iorwerth	1194–1240
Bleddyn ap Cynfyn	1063–1075	David ap Llewelyn	1240–1246
Trahaearn ap Caradog	1075–1081	Llewelyn ap Gruffydd	1246–1282
Gruffydd ap Cynan	1081–1137	David ap Gruffydd	1282–1283

DEHEUBARTH

Edwin and Cadell ab Einion	1005–1018	Rhys ab Tewdwr	1078–1093
Llewelyn ap Seisyll	1018–1023	Under Norman occupation	1093–1155
Rhydderch ab Iestyn	1023–1033	Rhys ap Gruffydd	1155–1197
Hywel ab Edwin	1033–1044	Gruffydd ap Rhys	1197–1201
Gruffydd ap Rhydderch	1044–1055	Maelgwyn ap Rhys	1201–1230
Gruffydd ap Llewelyn	1055–1063	Rhys Gryg	1230–1234
Maredudd ab Owain	1063–1072	Under the princes	
Rhys ap Owain	1072–1078	of Gwynedd	1234–1283

VI. Holy Roman Emperors

Henry II	1002–1024	Frederick II	1212–1250
Conrad II	1024–1039	Conrad IV	1250–1254
Henry III	1039–1056	Richard	1257–1272
Henry IV	1056–1105	Rudolf I	1273–1291
Henry V	1106–1125	Adolf	1292–1298
Lothar II	1125–1137	Albert I	1298–1308
Conrad III	1138–1152	Henry VII	1308–1313
Frederick I	1152–1190	Louis IV	1314–1347
Henry VI	1190–1197	Charles IV	1347–1378
Philip I	1197–1208	Wenceslaus	1378–1400
Otto IV	1208–1212		

VII. Popes of Rome

John XVIII	1003–1009	Victor IV	1138–1138, Anti-Pope
Sergius IV	1009–1012	Celestine II	1143–1144
Benedict VIII	1012–1024	Lucius II	1144–1145
John XIX	1024–1032	Eugene III	1145–1153
Benedict IX	1032–1045	Anastasius IV	1153–1154
Sylvester III	1045–1045	Adrian IV	1154–1159
Benedict IX	1045–1045	Alexander III	1159–1181
Gregory VI	1045–1046	Victor IV	1159–1164, Anti-Pope
Clement II	1046–1047		
Benedict IX	1047–1048	Paschal III	1164–1168, Anti-Pope
Damasus II	1048–1048	Lucius III	1181–1185
Leo IX	1049–1054	Urban III	1185–1187
Victor II	1055–1057	Gregory VIII	1187–1187
Stephen X	1057–1058	Clement III	1187–1191
Benedict X	1058–1059, Anti-Pope	Celestine III	1191–1198
		Innocent III	1198–1216
Nicholas II	1058–1061	Honorius III	1216–1227
Alexander II	1061–1073	Gregory IX	1227–1241
Honorius II	1061–1072, Anti-Pope	Celestine IV	1241–1241
		Innocent IV	1241–1254
Gregory VII	1073–1085	Alexander IV	1254–1261
Clement III	1080–1100, Anti-Pope	Urban IV	1261–1264
		Clement IV	1265–1268
Victor III	1086–1087	Gregory X	1271–1276
Urban II	1088–1099	Innocent V	1276–1276
Paschal II	1099–1118	Adrian V	1276–1276
Sylvester IV	1105–1111	John XXI	1276–1277
Gelasius II	1118–1119	Nicholas III	1277–1280
Gregory VIII	1118–1137	Martin IV	1281–1285
Calixtus II	1119–1124	Honorius IV	1285–1287
Honorius II	1124–1130	Nicholas IV	1288–1292
Innocent II	1130–1143	Celestine V	1294–1294, Anti-Pope
Anacletus II	1130–1138		

Appendix

Boniface VIII	1294–1303	Innocent VI	1352–1362
Benedict XI	1303–1304, Anti-Pope	Urban V	1362–1370
		Gregory XI	1370–1378
Clement V	1305–1314	Urban VI	1378–1389
John XXII	1316–1334	Clement VII	1378–1394, Anti-Pope
Nicholas V	1328–1330, Anti-Pope	Boniface IX	1389–1404
Benedict XII	1334–1342	Benedict XIII	1394–1423, Anti-Pope
Clement VI	1342–1352, Anti-Pope		

Bibliography

Appleby, John T. *The Troubled Reign of King Stephen.* New York: Barnes and Noble, 1969.

Ashley, Maurice. *The Life and Times of King John.* London: Weidenfeld and Nicolson, 1972.

Ashley, Mike. *The Mammoth Book of British Kings & Queens: The Complete Biographical Encyclopedia of the Kings and Queens of Britain.* New York: Carroll & Graf Publishers, 1998.

Barber, Richard. *Henry Plantagenet 1133–1189: A Biography.* New York: Roy Publishers, 1964.

_____. *The Devil's Crown: Henry II, Richard I, John.* London: British Broadcasting Corporation, 1978.

Barlow, Frank. *The Life of Edward the Confessor.* Berkeley and Los Angeles: University of California Press, 1970.

Barrell, A. D. M. *Medieval Scotland.* Cambridge: Cambridge University Press, 2000.

Barrow, G. W. S. *Kingship and Unity: Scotland 1000–1306.* London: E. Arnold, 1981.

_____. *Robert Bruce and the Community of the Realm of Scotland.* Berkeley: University of California, 1965.

_____. *William Rufus.* New Haven and London: Methuen, 1983.

Bates, David. *William the Conqueror.* Stroud, Gloucestershire: Tempus Publishing Ltd., 2001.

Bingham, Caroline. *The Crowned Lions: The Early Plantagenet Kings.* London: David and Charles, 1978.

_____. *The Life and Times of Edward II.* London: Weidenfeld and Nicolson, 1973.

Brooke, Christopher. *The Saxon and Norman Kings.* London: Collins/Fontana, 1963.

Brundage, James A. *Richard Lion Heart: A Biography.* New York: Scribner, 1974.

Campbell, Marion. *Alexander III: King of Scots.* Isle of Colonsay, Argyll: House of Lochar, 1999.

Chambers, James. *The Norman Kings.* London: Weidenfeld and Nicolson, 1981.

Chancellor, John. *The Life and Times of Edward I.* London: Weidenfeld and Nicolson, 1981.

Costain, Thomas B. *The Last Plantagenets.* Garden City, NY: Doubleday, 1962.

Crouch, David. *The Reign of King Stephen: 1135–1154.* New York: Longman, 2000.

Davis, R. H. C. *King Stephen: 1135–1154.* Berkeley: University of California Press, 1967.

Donaldson, Gordon. *Scottish Kings.* New York: Wiley, 1967.

Fraser, Antonia. *The Lives of the Kings and Queens of England.* New York: Weidenfeld and Nicolson, 1975.

Gillingham, John. *Richard I.* New Haven and London: Yale University Press, 1999.

Hallam, Elizabeth, ed. *Four Gothic Kings: The Turbulent History of Medieval England and the Plantagenet Kings (1216–1377), Henry III, Edward I, Edward II, Edward III, Seen through the Eyes of Their Contemporaries.* New York: Weidenfeld and Nicolson, 1987.

Harvey, John. *The Plantagenets.* London: Batsford, 1959.

Hollister, C. Warren. *Henry I.* New Haven and London: Yale University Press, 2001.

Hume, David. *The History of England from the Invasion of Julius Caesar to the Revolution of 1688* Chicago: University of Chicago Press, 1975.

Humble, Richard. *The Saxon Kings.* London: Weidenfeld and Nicolson, 1980.

Hutchison, Harold F. *The Hollow Crown: A Life of Richard II.* New York: John Day Co., 1961.

_____. *Edward II.* New York: Stein and Day, 1971.

Johnson, Paul. *The Life and Times of Edward III.* Westerham, Kent: Weidenfeld and Nicolson, 1973.

King, Edmund. *Medieval England: 1066–1485.* Oxford: Phaidon, 1988.

Knight, Charles. *The Popular History of England.* London: James Sangster & Co., 1876.

Lappenberg, J. M. *A History of England under the Anglo-Saxon Kings.* London: J. Murray, 1845.

Lawson, M. K. *Cnut: The Danes in England in the Early Eleventh Century.* London, New York: Longman, 1993).

Lynch, Michael. *Scotland: A New History.* London: Century, 1991.

Mackie, J. D. *A History of Scotland.* New York: Penguin, 1985.

Magnusson, Magnus. *Scotland: The Story of a Nation.* New York: Atlantic Monthly Press, 2000.

Miller, David. *Richard the Lionheart: The Mighty Crusader.* London: Phoenix, 2003.

Oram, Richard. *David I: The King Who Made Scotland.* Stroud, Gloucestershire: Tempus Publishing Ltd., 2004.

_____. *The Canmores: The Kings & Queens of the Scots, 1040–1290.* Stroud, Gloucestershire: Tempus Publishing Ltd., 2002.

_____. *The Kings & Queens of Scotland.* Stroud, Gloucestershire: Tempus Publishing Ltd., 2001.

Ormrod, W. M. *The Reign of Edward III: Crown and Political Society in England, 1327–1377.* Stroud, Gloucestershire: Tempus Publishing Ltd., 2000.

Owen, D. D. R. *William the Lion: Kingship and Culture 1143–1214.* East Linton, Scotland: Tuckwell, 1997.

Packe, Michael. *King Edward III.* London: Routledge & Kegan Paul, 1983.

Palgrave, Sir Francis. *History of the Anglo-Saxons.* London: W. Tegg, 1876.

Penman, Michael. *David II, 1329–71.* Edinburgh: John Donald Publishers, Ltd, 2004.

Prestwich, Michael. *The Three Edwards: War and State in England.* London: Weidenfeld and Nicolson, 1980.

_____. *Edward I.* New Haven and London: Yale University Press, 1997.

Rex, Peter. *Harold II: The Doomed Saxon King.* Stroud, Gloucestershire: Tempus Publishing Ltd., 2005.

Robinson, John Martin. *The Dukes of Norfolk: A Quincentennial History.* Oxford: Oxford University Press, 1983.

Salzman, L. F. *Edward I.* New York: Praeger, 1968.

Saul, Nigel. *The Three Richards: Richard I, Richard II, and Richard III.* London: Hambledon and London, 2005.

Scott, Ronald McNair. *Robert the Bruce.* New York: P. Bedrick Books, 1982.

Smith, Goldwin. *A History of England.* New York: Scribner, 1957.

Slocombe, George. *William the Conqueror.* London: Hutchinson, 1959.

Trow, M. J. *Cnut: Emperor of the North.* Gloucestershire: Sutton Publishing Ltd., 2005.

Turner, Ralph V. *King John.* New York: Longman, 1994.

Walker, Ian W. *Harold: The Last Anglo-Saxon King.* Gloucestershire: Sutton Publishing Ltd., 2000.

Warren, W. L. *Henry II.* Berkeley: University of California Press, 1973.

Whitlock, Ralph. *The Warrior Kings of Saxon England.* New York: Dorset Press, 1991.

Index

Aelgar (Earl of Mercia) 25, 28–30
Al-Adil (brother of Saladin) 73–74
Alexander I (King of Scotland) 121, 130–133, 136
Alexander II (King of Scotland) 85, 148, 150–155
Alexander III (King of Scotland) 1, 154–160, 162–163, 165, 173
Anselm (Archbishop of Canterbury) 45–46, 50–52
Arthur (Duke of Brittany) 75, 77–78

Baldwin V (Count of Flanders) 37–38
Baldwin IX (Count of Flanders) 75
Balliol, Edward (pretender to Scottish throne) 103–104, 162, 175–176
Balliol, John (King of Scotland) 92–93, 103, 161–166
Bannockburn Battle 98, 171–172
Becket, Thomas (Archbishop of Canterbury) 103–104, 162, 175–176
Bolingbroke, Henry (Duke of Lancaster) 111, 113–114
Breton War of Succession 104–105
Bruce, Edward (King of Ireland) 170, 172

Charles IV (King of France) 100, 103
Charles V (King of France) 107, 179
Charles VI (King of France) 110, 112–113
Cnut (King of England) 1, 9–14, 17, 20, 24, 29
Comyn, John (Earl of Badenoch) 163, 167–169

Comyn, Walter (Earl of Menteith) 155–157
Conrad II (Emperor of Germany) 13–14
Crecy Battle 105

David I (King of Scotland) 1, 56–57, 62, 119, 121, 131–142
David II (King of Scotland) 104–107, 161, 165, 174–180
De Montfort, Simon (Earl of Leicester) 86, 88–89
Despenser, Hugh (Earl of Glamorgan) 96, 98, 100
Donald III (King of Scotland) 45, 47, 120, 122, 124–129, 131, 133
Duncan II (King of Scotland) 45, 47, 121, 122, 125–128
Dupplin Moor Battle 175
Durward, Alan (Lord of Scotia) 155–157

Edgar I (King of Scotland) 121, 125–126, 128–131, 133–134, 158
Edgar Atheling (pretender to the English throne) 25–26, 40, 42, 121, 123
Edmund II (King of England) 10–12, 20
Edward I (King of England) 61, 84–96, 103–104, 156, 159–169
Edward II (King of England) 61, 93–101, 160, 168–173
Edward III (King of England) 61, 96, 100–108, 120–121, 174–179
Edward III, the Confessor (King of England) 8, 11, 14–15, 18–32, 39–40, 87, 120–121
Eleanor (Duchess of Aquitaine) 62–63, 65–66, 68–70, 76, 78, 142

Emma (Queen of England) 8, 11, 14–20, 34
Erik II (King of Norway) 159–160
Ethelred II (King of England) 8–10, 11, 14, 17–19, 39
Eustace (Count of Boulogne) 59–60, 63, 65
Evesham Battle 86, 89

Fergus of Galloway 143, 145
First Crusade 46, 48, 50–51

Gaveston, Piers 95–98
Geoffrey (Count of Anjou) 37–38
Geoffrey (Duke of Brittany) 66–69, 76–77
Geoffrey Plantagenet (Count of Anjou) 54, 56–57, 59, 61–62
Gillebrigte (King of Argyll) 137
Godwine (Earl of Wessex) 13, 15–18, 20–23, 27–28
Gruffydd (Prince of Wales) 24–25, 29–30
Guy of Lusigan (King of Jerusalem) 72

Hakon IV (King of Norway) 153, 155, 158
Hakon V (King of Norway) 171
Harold I (King of England) 14–16, 17–18, 20–21
Harold II (King of England) 8, 23–35, 39, 121
Harold III Hardrada (King of Norway) 30–33, 39, 121
Hastings Battle 8, 33, 39–40, 121
Henry (Bishop of Winchester) 56, 58
Henry (Earl of Northumbria) 139–141, 144
Henry I (King of England) 43,

187

45–46, 48–56, 122, 130, 132–134, 136, 138–139
Henry I (King of France) 36–38
Henry II (King of England) 54, 59–71, 76, 140, 142–148
Henry III (King of England) 1, 61, 82–89, 152–157, 159, 162
Henry the Younger (Prince of England) 64–67, 69–70, 76, 146
Holy River Battle 12
Hundred Years War 61, 103, 105, 107, 111, 176, 179

Isabella (Queen of England) 96, 100–102

John (King of England) 61, 67, 70, 75–82, 149–152
John II (King of France) 106–107
John of Gault (Duke of Lancaster) 108–111, 113

Lanfranc (Archbishop of Canterbury) 41, 43, 45
Lewes Battle 86, 88
Llewelyn (Prince of Wales) 79–80, 90–91
Lords Appellant 111–113
Louis (Prince of France) 80, 82–85, 89, 152
Louis VI (King of France) 53–54, 57
Louis VII (King of France) 62, 67, 69, 142, 144–146
Louis IX (King of France) 84–86, 89, 151, 154

Macbeth (King of Scotland) 24, 119–120, 124
MacMurrough, Art (King of Leinster) 112–113
MacWilliam, Guthred (Earl of Ross) 150–151
Magna Carta 81–83, 90, 94, 109, 151
Magnus VI (King of Norway) 158–159

Malcolm (Earl of Moray) 136–137
Malcolm III (King of Scotland) 1, 24, 41, 45, 119–128, 130, 133–134
Malcolm IV (King of Scotland) 64–65, 141–145, 165
Margaret (Queen of Scotland) 121–122, 125, 128, 130, 132–134
Margaret I (Queen of Scotland) 2, 92, 119, 159–162, 165
Matilda (Queen of England) 51, 54–61, 138–140
Mortimer, Roger (Earl of Glamorgan) 99–102

Neville's Cross Battle 105–106, 177, 180

Odo (Bishop of Bayeux) 39–40, 42, 44
Olaf II (King of Norway) 12–13
Ordinance Articles 97–98
Otto IV (Emperor of the Holy Roman Empire) 80–81

Peasants' Revolt 109, 138
Philip I (King of France) 38, 42–43, 46, 52
Philip II (King of France) 67–68, 70–72, 74–75, 77–80, 82, 149
Philip IV (King of France) 91–92, 96–97, 163, 168, 170
Philip V (King of France) 100
Philip VI (King of France) 103, 105, 175–176
Poitiers Battle 106, 177
Pope Urban II 46, 50
Provisions of Oxford 86–89

Randolph, Thomas (Earl of Moray) 171–175
Raymond V (Count of Toulouse) 65, 70, 144
Richard I (King of England) 66–77, 148–149
Richard II (King of England) 2, 108–114

Robert I (Duke of Normandy) 35–36
Robert I, Bruce (King of Scotland) 1, 93–94, 96–99, 102, 160–162, 164–174, 176, 178
Robert II, Curthose (Duke of Normandy) 37, 42–45, 47–52, 123, 134–135

Seventh Crusade 89
Sluys Battle 104
Somerled (King of Argyll) 11, 141–142
Standards Battle 57, 139
Stephen (Count of Blois) 155
Stephen (King of England) 1, 54–63, 138–140
Stewart, Robert (founder of Stewart dynasty) 172, 176–178, 180
Swein I, Folkbeard (King of England) 1, 8–9, 19, 26, 39

Third Crusade 71–74, 77, 148
Thomas (Duke of Gloucester) 111–113
Thomas (Earl of Lancaster) 97–100
Tostig (Earl of Northumbria) 24–26, 28–29, 30–32, 39, 121
Tyler, Wat (leader of Peasants' Revolt) 109

Wallace, William (Guardian of Scotland) 93, 95, 165–167
War of Three Earls 178
William I (King of England) 1, 31–43, 52, 55, 121–123, 126–127, 164
William I (King of Scotland) 65, 67, 74, 79, 143–151, 161, 165
William II, Rufus (King of England) 43–51, 123, 125–131, 133
William Atheling (heir of King Henry I) 51, 53, 55
William Clito (Duke of Normandy) 52–55, 135

www.ingramcontent.com/pod-product-compliance
Ingram Content Group UK Ltd.
Pitfield, Milton Keynes, MK11 3LW, UK
UKHW050524150426
5217IPUK00026B/1784